W9-BLO-233

3 1668 04290 0313

water Damage noted

613.2833 FEDER 2010
Feder, David
The skinny carbs diet

East Regional   09/08/2010

EAST REGIONAL

The Skinny Carbs Diet

{ **Eat Pasta, Potatoes, and More!**
Use the power of *resistant starch*
to make your favorite foods fight fat
and beat cravings!

David Feder, RD, and the Editors of **Prevention.**   Recipes by **David Bonom**

RODALE

This book is intended as a reference volume only, not as a medical manual. The information given here is designed to help you make informed decisions about your health. It is not intended as a substitute for any treatment that may have been prescribed by your doctor. If you suspect that you have a medical problem, we urge you to seek competent medical help.

Mention of specific companies, organizations, or authorities in this book does not imply endorsement by the author or publisher, nor does mention of specific companies, organizations, or authorities imply that they endorse this book, its author, or the publisher.

Hi-maize is a legal trademark of National Starch LLC.

Internet addresses and telephone numbers given in this book were accurate at the time it went to press.

© 2010 by Rodale Inc.

All rights reserved. No part of this publication may be reproduced or transmitted in any form or by any means, electronic or mechanical, including photocopying, recording, or any other information storage and retrieval system, without the written permission of the publisher.

Rodale books may be purchased for business or promotional use or for special sales. For more information, please write to: Special Markets Department, Rodale Inc., 733 Third Avenue, New York, NY 10017

Prevention® is a registered trademark of Rodale Inc.

Printed in the United States of America

Rodale Inc. makes every effort to use acid-free ⊗, recycled paper ♻.

Photographs by John Kernick; food styling by Cyd Raftus McDowell; prop styling by Philippa Brathwaite

Book design by Jessica Sokol

Library of Congress Cataloging-in-Publication Data

Feder, David
    The skinny carbs diet : eat pasta, potatoes, and more! use the power of resistant starch to make your favorite foods fight fat and beat cravings / David Feder, and the editors of Prevention ; recipes by David Bonom.
        p.   cm.
    Includes bibliographical references and index.
    ISBN-13 978–1–60529–567–1 hardcover
    ISBN-10 1–60529–567–1 hardcover
    1. Low-carbohydrate diet.   I. Bonom, David.   II. Prevention (Emmaus, Pa.)   III. Title.
RM237.73.F43   2010
613.2'833—dc22   2010019643

Distributed to the trade by Macmillan

2   4   6   8   10   9   7   5   3   1   hardcover

LIVE YOUR WHOLE LIFE™

We inspire and enable people to improve their lives and the world around them.

To my dad, O"H

Acknowledgments

THERE'S NO "I" IN "BOOK," so first thanks go to anyone I inadvertently left out of this acknowledgment—you know I'll think of you immediately after this goes to print.

My personal support team, Rachel and Yael, deserve the most credit. Mom, your input was invaluable. Other David, always a pleasure working with you; you turned my recipe concepts into delicious reality. And I'd have gone nowhere fast without my wonderful friends (and stereo nutrition PhDs), Mark and Kantha. Or either of the two Andreas—sister and editor—who helped immensely. (The latter earns extra kudos: You truly redefine going above and beyond the call of duty; I thank you greatly.)

Special thanks to all the volunteer test panelists who agreed to follow the RS diet and act as consultants during the beginning stages of this project.

To Audrey and everyone—students and teachers—in the undergraduate and graduate Departments of Nutritional Sciences at the University of Texas at Austin 1991-95, my heartfelt thanks for your patience. Thanks, too, to Dave F., Seta, and Hope, for each of your very different contributions.

But at the end of the day, without you, Rhonda, this book absolutely would not exist—I mean that most sincerely and humbly.

{cont

ents}

Introduction

WELCOME TO A TRULY DIFFERENT APPROACH to weight loss and long-term weight maintenance—one that, thankfully, upends the conventional wisdom about carbohydrates. I say "thankfully" because those of us who love our breads, pastas, and cereals have long been made to feel guilty about our enjoyment of these comforting foods, especially if we were trying to slim down. With this book, we leave behind the fad diets that didn't take into account the foods we like to eat, didn't explain how our favorite foods could work for us, and just plain didn't work.

For generations, the study of diet and nutrition has focused on the three so-called macronutrients: carbohydrates (which include starches, fiber, and sugars), fats, and proteins. Most eating plans for weight loss or weight maintenance make a case for eating more or less of one of the main nutrients. Eat carbs. Don't eat carbs. Eat less fat. Eat more protein. Yet decades of science and hundreds of diets later, we are facing epidemic obesity and a global type 2 diabetes crisis. Clearly, what we've been doing hasn't been working.

The fact is, all three macronutrients have very specific functions in our bodies. Eliminating one or another can set us up for a host of health problems, not to mention weight gain. Fats are a good example: Once the bane of dieters, they've undergone something of an image makeover, thanks to studies showing that certain fats contribute to weight loss and good health. Now similar redemption may await carbohydrates, thanks to a particular type of carb known as *resistant starch*, or RS.

Recent research has opened our understanding of fundamental differences among carbs, especially with regard to how our bodies metabolize and use them. As nutrition science is showing, resistant starch is particularly favored by the body as an optimal source of energy, satiety, and glucose regulation. And it has been right under our noses all along.

As we learn more about resistant starch—including which foods are the best sources and how various cooking methods affect it—we are compelled to rethink the role of carbohydrates in weight loss and weight maintenance. The fact is, carbs are okay. And if eating the right kinds of carbs—namely, those rich in resistant starch—can help us to take off and keep off those extra pounds, that's all the better!

Weight Loss Made Better

Behind any effective weight loss plan—including this one—is a very simple equation: calories in < calories out = weight loss. The question is whether a diet equips you to easily achieve that goal by allowing you to eat in a way that satisfies your taste buds and your appetite while delivering a good mix of essential nutrients. In other words, a diet that works has to be a diet you can live with.

The Skinny Carbs Diet is not just about increasing your resistant starch intake, though that's central to the plan. It's about getting more fiber, eating foods that energize you, and learning to make healthy choices that support your weight-loss efforts. And once you reach your goal, you'll continue eating this way not because you have to, but because you want to.

Because this diet will feel less restrictive, it will require less effort than most weight-loss plans. You'll be less likely to fall into a pattern of yo-yo dieting and instead make real lifestyle changes. Over time, this will become your natural eating style.

The weight loss that comes from adding resistant starch to your diet is different from that of standard calorie-restrictive diets. In a 2004 study led by Janine Higgins, PhD, of the Center for Human Nutrition at the University of Colorado Health Sciences Center in Denver, people who consumed 5.4 percent of their total carbohydrate intake as resistant starch experienced a 20 to 25 percent increase in fat metabolism. This rate held steady throughout the day.

Resistant starch fuels weight loss by burning both body fat and visceral fat (aka "belly fat"), which surrounds your internal organs. This "hidden" fat has been shown in some studies to be a marker of increased disease risk. RS also enhances your body's ability to metabolize nutrients. Because it helps you feel full, you tend to consume

Author's Note

I came to nutrition and dietetics after more than 15 years as a professional chef. My decision to enter the nutrition field stemmed from the discovery that few registered dietitians at the time appeared to possess anything more than a rudimentary knowledge of food from a culinary standpoint. In fact, I was dismayed to learn that far too many RDs actually held an adversarial attitude toward food! This revelation propelled me through the 5 years of university study and clinical practicums required to become a registered dietitian.

It's often been said by my peers who "get it" that "people eat food, not nutrition." Ask someone to recall a favorite food memory from his or her youth and I guarantee that it won't be the time that Grandma visited and spent the whole day in the kitchen making fat-free, vitamin-infused rice cakes spread with tofu cream cheese.

The field of nutrition and dietetics has changed a great deal since I came aboard. Still, there are pockets of resistance among dietitians who put nutrition ahead of flavor, who consider food and cuisine to be separate entities—who just plain don't like food. But the idea that I've promoted during my years as a chef-dietitian remains the same: Food is to be enjoyed and celebrated, not feared and isolated. I hope that comes through in this book, especially in the recipe concepts that David Bonom turned into amazing and delicious, easy-to-make recipes.

As I collected my research for this book, what impressed me most is that nutrition research seems to finally be catching up with our food preferences. We've reached a point where good nutrition can meet both our needs and our wants, with foods we love to eat forming the backbone of a plan to help us lose weight and have more energy, all the while reducing our risk of diabetes, cancer, and heart disease. That is what every dietitian should be striving for, after all.

fewer calories at each meal—and remember, taking in fewer calories than you burn is the key to weight-loss success.

But the benefits of RS don't stop with weight loss. There's compelling evidence that the starch can protect against insulin resistance and cancer, reduce chronic inflammation, improve digestion, and perhaps even relieve depression. So while you may follow the Skinny Carbs Diet for the weight-loss effects, you'll be doing your body good in other ways.

Now, this diet does require you to make changes to your eating and lifestyle habits. Study after study has demonstrated that achieving and maintaining a healthy weight is not a matter of sheer willpower. It's about consciously rethinking your food choices. A diet that emphasizes fresh, plant-based foods—fruits, vegetables, and whole grains— while limiting red meats, sweets, soft drinks, and processed foods can help us to better manage our biochemistry. It makes sense that the Skinny Carbs Diet would be designed around this same nutritional framework.

The beauty of incorporating more resistant starch (and fiber) into your meals is that you won't feel as though you're missing out on your favorite foods. And that alone is worth its weight in willpower.

How the Diet Works

The Skinny Carbs Diet builds on groundbreaking research into the relationship between resistant starch, fiber, weight control, and optimal health. The 6-week plan provides simple guidelines for consuming an optimal amount of resistant starch to promote fat burning and satiety. We'll go into the details of the plan in Chapter 3; the following overview will whet your appetite.

In Phase 1 of the plan, which lasts for 1 week, you'll aim to consume at least 5 grams of resistant starch daily. This is only slightly more than the amount of RS that the typical American already consumes. The goal of this phase is for you to learn to recognize the best food sources of resistant starch, so you can begin working them into your meals. You'll also be paying attention to your fiber intake, increasing to at least 20 grams per day if you aren't at that level already. Like resistant starch, fiber is an excellent natural weight-loss aid and has other impressive health benefits. Remember, RS is a starch that acts like a fiber.

Once you get to Phase 2 of the plan, you'll bump up your RS intake to at least 10 grams daily. This amount is considered optimal for fat burning. Your fiber intake will increase to at least 25 grams per day.

After 4 weeks, you can stay at Phase 2, or you can continue on to Phase 3, which we consider a "booster" week. Your goal here will be to increase RS to at least 20 grams daily and fiber to at least 30 grams daily. At this level of RS, research has identified cancer-preventive effects, among other health benefits.

After you complete the 6-week program, you can use either Phase 2 or 3 for as long as you wish to continue weight loss or maintain the weight at which you've arrived—or simply for general health and energy. And while it's entirely up to you how long to enjoy a healthful, RS-rich diet, we feel the ease and truly enjoyable satisfaction you'll feel from this way of eating will make it something you'll be glad to stick with for years to come.

Before You Begin

Hopefully we've piqued your interest in resistant starch—and tempted your taste buds, too! But before we get into the "meat" of this plan, we do want to mention a couple of important caveats. The first is this: No diet plan is a silver bullet, and not all diets work for all people. Aside from individual variations in metabolism, some people have challenges that may require more intensive intervention to lose weight in a safe, effective, healthful manner.

Which brings us to our second caveat: This plan should not replace any nutritional or medical advice provided by a physician or registered dietitian. Be sure to consult your doctor or a dietitian before making any changes to a prescribed eating plan. This is especially critical if you have a preexisting medical condition such as diabetes, heart or kidney disease, or a digestive ailment.

Keep in mind, too, that the Skinny Carbs Diet isn't just about weight loss. It's about feeling better, having more energy, and achieving your full health potential. To borrow the wise words attributed to President Abraham Lincoln, "In the end, it's not the years in your life that count. It's the life in your years."

Chapter

What Is Resistant Starch?

THERE ARE ENOUGH BARRIERS to weight loss and weight maintenance without throwing the word *resistance* into the mix. But a little resistance can be a good thing, as long as it's in the form of resistant starch, or RS. A type of starch that acts like a fiber, resistant starch is proving to be a major breakthrough in our understanding of how our bodies want to use—and can use—carbohydrates.

RS is not some "made-up" ingredient created in the lab of a food manufacturer; it occurs naturally in certain common foods. While groundbreaking in its value to weight management and general health, the real revelation lies in what it can do for us on a metabolic level. These findings came at a time when nutrition misinformation had reached an apex characterized by a flood of fad diets and unchecked, sensationalist reporting on the relationships between nutrition and health.

It was during this "gold rush" of popular diets from the 1970s through the 1990s that a host of self-styled experts competed to be the next diet guru, taking advantage of an increasingly obese America's desperation to get fit. The last generation of diets demonized carbohydrates, especially starch. These plans all but completely disregarded the fact that carbohydrates are the primary fuel source for the human body and brain.

A core issue in weight management is the type of carbohydrates we eat and the form they take. It's no mystery that a cream-filled doughnut is far less beneficial for weight loss than, say, a bowl of oatmeal. But not all such beneficial food choices are quite so obvious.

Potatoes, condemned during the no-carb craze of the 1990s, are still saddled with an undeserved negative image in the minds of many "experts" and the general populace alike. Yet when cooked slowly and at low heat (by, say, boiling or steaming), potatoes are among the healthiest carbohydrates you can eat. In fact, scientific studies of foods rich in resistant starch found that such "low and slow" cooking techniques significantly increase the amount of RS in the final products, even more so after the foods cool. Potato salad, anyone?

At the core of a great deal of nutrition misconception is the fact that most people—including many health practitioners—think of carbohydrates in rudimentary categories: starch, sugar, and fiber. While scientific advances have long since given us a more nuanced understanding of carbs, too many nutrition resources continue to perpetuate this oversimplified concept. In plain English, a carbohydrate is not a carbohydrate, and a starch is not a starch.

Carbohydrates: A Not-So-Complex History

Without delving too deeply into chemistry (although a little bit is necessary here), carbohydrates are made of simple sugar molecules, which in turn are combinations of carbon, hydrogen, and oxygen. Picture a carbohydrate as a chain, with each link in the chain representing a sugar molecule such as glucose, fructose, lactose, or galactose. These chains are known as saccharides, and they connect via chemical bonds to form carbohydrate chains of various lengths.

Simple carbohydrates contain only one or two sugar molecules—hence their respective names, monosaccharides and disaccharides. Complex carbs are formed by linking together many sugar molecules. These longer chains are known as polysaccharides, which means "many sugars." Both fibers and starches are polysaccharides. (You might also see the term *oligosaccharide,* which refers specifically to small- and medium-chain polysaccharides.)

Which sugar units are strung together, how, and in which order determine the nature of the carbohydrate. For example, a glucose molecule joined to a fructose molecule forms the disaccharide sucrose, or table sugar. A starch is a bit more complex, consisting of long strings of glucose units attached by chemical bonds. Some of these bonds can be broken by protein compounds called *enzymes.* (Enzymes are proteins that trigger and enhance chemical processes throughout the body, such as breaking down foods into their component molecules.)

Many different digestive enzymes are necessary to digest all the food we eat. Only one enzyme, alpha-amylase, allows humans to break down complex carbohydrates, specifically starch. Although we typically refer to starches as "chains" of sugar molecules, the most common food starch, amylopectin, is actually more like a tree, with many different "branches" of molecules. The amylase enzymes begin breaking bonds from the end of each branch, so the more branches a starch has, the more starting points the

Factoid

No Sugar in Your Beans

Sugar can inhibit some resistant starch formation, due to interference with the crystallization process of the starch chains. This can result in a lower total amount of resistant starch in the final product, although this appears to happen only when sugars are added in high concentration.

enzymes have. Therefore, the more branches a starch has, the faster your body will digest it. The faster your body breaks down a starch, the more sugar it releases into your body at a time. If this sugar isn't used immediately, it may be converted to glycogen or fat.

When the body does not make the type of enzyme necessary to break the chemical bonds between sugar units, we call the resulting carbohydrate a fiber. Here's an example of the difference between a starch and a fiber: Both the carbohydrates amylose and cellulose contain strings of glucose units held together by a chemical bond. But while the body makes an enzyme that can break apart the bonds connecting the sugar molecules in amylose (that is, digest it), it does not make one for cellulose. Therefore, cellulose is a fiber. (Incidentally, some mammals, especially ruminants such as cows, do make the enzyme that digests cellulose. If cows could talk, they might make the argument that cellulose is a starch. Silly, yes, but it's a way of illustrating the point that whether a carbohydrate is a fiber or a starch boils down to the breakability of its chemical bonds.)

How Our Bodies Use Carbs

Amylase, the enzyme that breaks down starch, is produced in the mouth, so the digestion of starches begins as soon as you take your first bite. (Before, actually. Your mouth starts amylase production as soon as you anticipate that first bite of food.) This is why you will notice a hint of sweetness when you're chewing a starchy food; it comes from the individual sugar molecules. As the food continues along the digestive path, it won't encounter amylase again until it reaches the small intestine.

Typically, the sugars and starches for which the body produces digestive enzymes, and therefore those it can metabolize, are broken down and absorbed in the upper gastrointestinal (GI) tract. This pathway runs from the mouth through the esophagus and into the stomach before reaching the small intestine. We tend to think of the stomach as the center of digestion. In fact, the primary function of the stomach is to convert large chunks of food into smaller, more manageable pieces.

"Real" digestion occurs in the small intestine, which also happens to be where amylase re-enters the picture, being secreted into the GI tract from the pancreas. Therefore, the small intestine is the chief point of absorption for carbohydrates. This is where sugars and starches are either converted to energy for immediate use or moved into the body's fat stores.

When you cook a starch, a process called *gelatinization* occurs. This is when broken-off pieces, or granules, of the starch molecule bind to water molecules. A single granule of starch molecules can attach to so many water molecules that it swells to up to five times its original size, with no organized overall structure.

You can easily visualize this. Think of what happens when you mix flour and water for baking. You end up with a sticky blob to which you add more starch, more liquid, or other ingredients. This allows you to pour, shape, or otherwise turn the blob into bread, cookies, pie crust, or other treats. In the presence of heat, such as in cooking, gelatinized starches swell before breaking down again, in the process releasing the liquid and changing the starches into other forms. If the heat of cooking is low and slow, the starches remain complex and thus harder to digest. If the heat is high and fast, the starches can be broken down further into shorter—and sweeter—structures.

Carbohydrates undergo similar transformations inside our bodies via the digestive system. Less complex forms, such as sugars, are easily metabolized in the upper GI tract, then absorbed into the bloodstream. Gelatinized starches—that is, those which have already been partially broken down by the heat of cooking—are similarly easily digested and release more sugar molecules into the system, faster. More complex carbohydrates, including non- or partially gelatinized starches, are less readily broken down. Moreover, some escape digestion in the small intestine and reach the colon as potentially fermentable carbohydrates, a beneficial effect we'll describe later.

Complex carbs in the form of fiber or resistant starch are even more stubborn to digest.

Cut the Yo-Yo String

According to Mark Anthony, PhD, of St. Edwards University, the human body sees any extreme diet as a state of stress. When our carbohydrate intake is drastically reduced, we start to metabolize fat and muscle, releasing byproducts called *ketones*, which the brain uses for fuel. However, ketones can be toxic, and the brain can't use them for a prolonged period. "We need carbohydrates," says Dr. Anthony. "There's a reason most people find it difficult to adhere to low-carbohydrate diets without eventually craving them and bingeing. When we satisfy hunger effectively, we gain more energy from food; when we gain more energy from food, we match hunger with what the body actually needs. And that's the ticket to freedom from the cycle of yo-yo dieting."

They may be partially broken down or fermented in the lower GI tract—specifically, the large intestine. Or, they may hold a lot of water and primarily provide bulking, eventually exiting the body in the usual fashion.

Fiber: Carbs with Benefits

Dietary fibers are classified as either soluble (that is, dispersible in water) or insoluble (able to absorb water). These simple definitions focus on general actions in the gastrointestinal tract.

By being dispersible in water, soluble fibers—found in nuts, grains, oat bran, fruits, and root vegetables such as carrots, parsnips and beets, among other foods—end up staying in the stomach longer. This increases their digestion time, which allows nutrients to be released more slowly and metabolized more completely and efficiently. Moreover, soluble fibers bind to substances such as fatty acids and cholesterol, helping to clear them from the bloodstream. By reducing the amounts of these compounds that are stored, soluble fibers help protect against diseases associated with the buildup of fats in the heart and arteries. This is why soluble fibers are recognized as helping to lower the risk of heart disease and other cardiovascular diseases.

Because of their extended digestive times and the resulting slowed absorption of their component sugars, some soluble fibers also are effective at balancing blood sugar levels. This quality not only helps keep energy levels on an even keel throughout the day, it also helps lower the risk of type 2 diabetes. Some soluble fibers may also ferment in the large intestine and support immune function, increase mineral absorption, and promote bone health.

Insoluble fibers absorb water like a sponge, which binds to the food passing through your system and bulks up the remnants so everything moves along more quickly. In this way, insoluble fibers help keep you "regular," preventing constipation and expediting the removal of waste materials and toxins. Insoluble fibers also help balance acid levels in the GI tract. Both of these attributes are

Factoid

Drink Tea

Polyphenols, tannin, and catechins—chemical compounds found in tea—have been shown in lab studies to slow the breakdown of starch, inhibit the action of the digestive enzyme amylase in the digestive tract, and lower the glycemic response, all of which help RS work better to regulate blood sugar and burn fat.

Glycogen to the Rescue

A portion of the glucose that you consume gets stored in your muscles and liver as a molecular complex called *glycogen*. While the glycogen in your muscles serves as their fuel source, the liver releases its glycogen into the bloodstream when your blood sugar drops. The brain also keeps a small supply of glycogen for its needs.

"Glycogen is like a stored tank of fuel at the ready when we need it," explains Mark Anthony, PhD. "By efficiently filling this tank with the best fuel sources—that is, the right foods—we can avoid using other forms of storage such as fat, which gets stashed in those other, less desirable places like spare tires, love handles, and saddlebags."

In a healthy person, the body carefully regulates the amount of glucose in the bloodstream. When your glucose gets too low because you haven't eaten (or, at least, haven't eaten enough carbohydrates), your liver taps its glycogen stores to make up for the shortfall. Once these stores are used up, your body will begin metabolizing protein from muscles and other tissues.

Obviously, you want to keep a good supply of glycogen on hand. The best place to get this storage form of glucose is from gradually introduced, slowly metabolized starches that are stowed in your muscles and liver instead of being converted to body fat.

important, as the harmful effects of toxins on the cells lining the lower intestinal tract are believed to be a factor in the development of colon cancer. Reining in these toxins, as well as maintaining a healthy acid balance, helps keep the damage in check. You'll find insoluble fibers in dark leafy greens, string beans, fruits (especially the peels), whole wheat, whole oats, corn, seeds, and nuts.

Bear in mind that these are just basic descriptions of the two main classes of dietary fiber. In fact, "dietary fiber" encompasses a wide variety of complex carbohydrates with a diverse array of structures and functions. Moreover, all plant foods contain several different types of fiber. The foods featured in this book have been singled out because they have a particular balance of specific starches and fibers.

We Americans have a fiber problem. In fact, all modernized industrial cultures do. As we made the shift from an agricultural society to an industrial one, we began processing an ever-greater proportion of our food supply. Unfortunately, this processing means that we've been removing fiber from food, and a lot of important nutrients along with it. As Mark Anthony, PhD, a nutrition researcher and instructor at St. Edwards University in Austin, Texas, explains, it's as though every meal became dessert, in the form of simple sugars and bleached flours. Likewise, beverages shifted from water and natural fruit juices to sugary liquids and sugar-caffeine infusions.

When the Western diet consisted primarily of unprocessed plant foods, we ate plenty of fiber. The average daily intake then was much higher than it is today. Obesity, diabetes, heart disease, and even cancer were not nearly as prevalent.

Resistant Starch: A "Third Kind of Fiber"

Much of what scientists have learned about resistant starch and its health effects has come from their efforts to understand why fiber and whole grains are so beneficial. Some researchers believed whole grains were little packages of discrete compounds that collectively provided protection from the diseases associated with diets low in whole grains. Others argued that some overarching quality of whole grains was at work. For example, since whole grains are harder to digest, they naturally reduce caloric absorption (by bulking, binding, and increasing transit time through the GI tract) and lower glycemic response. In fact, the benefits of whole grains and fiber are likely the product of the synergy of the properties described by these two ideas.

Here's where resistant starch comes into the picture. From a chemistry point of view, fiber is fiber and starch is starch. But about 25 years ago, scientists studying cereal grains discovered a starch that didn't act like a starch as much as it behaved like a fiber. Specifically, it was resistant to digestion and didn't break down until it reached the lower intestinal tract. The structure of these so-called resistant starch molecules, not their bonds, is the key to their ability to resist digestion.

Resistant starch takes three forms in nature. The first, RS1, is prevalent in seeds, legumes (beans, lentils, and chickpeas), and unprocessed or partially processed whole grains. With RS1, the starch molecules are packed into dense granules and have more of the cell walls intact, creating a physical barrier that leaves few ends for the enzyme amylase to access.

RS2 contains a lot of the carbohydrate amylose. It is packed into dense granules, like RS1, but it is not gelatinized—that is, the starch has not begun to break down and absorb water. For this reason, it yields very slowly to the digestive process, remaining relatively intact until it reaches the lower GI tract. In addition, because amylose is a relatively linear starch, it has fewer branches subject to attack by amylase, so it digests more slowly. You'll find RS2 in potatoes, corn (especially varieties bred by starch manufacturers to have high levels of amylose), underripe bananas, and flour.

The third form of resistant starch, RS3, becomes resistant when portions of the starch chain expand and then contract during food preparation. RS3 is another high-amylose starch, but the amylose forms during cooking. As described earlier, during

Glycemic Index

You might have read or heard a lot about something called the *glycemic index*. (It is not to be confused with *glycemic response*, the term for how the body responds metabolically to an influx of glucose.) The glycemic index rates and ranks foods according to how much they raise or lower blood glucose (blood sugar). White bread is the center point for extrapolating the glycemic index of all other foods. It is said to have a glycemic index value of 100.

This scale was developed primarily for use by people with diabetes. But some marketers have glommed on to the science and are attempting to pitch the glycemic index as a weight-loss tool. Don't allow yourself to be fooled by such marketing ploys. While it *is* an effective tool for assessing the influx of blood sugar (which can help keep you from feeling ravenously hungry and overeating), the glycemic index does not take into account the relative nutritional value of a food. For example, potato chips, which are high in unhealthy fats and offer little in the way of nutrients, have a more positive glycemic index rating than a boiled potato, which is among the best sources of complex carbohydrates—including resistant starch and fiber—as well as other nutrients such as vitamin C.

cooking, the starch gelatinizes, the amylose making a double-coil crystalline form that is highly branched and therefore easily digested. However, as the starch cools, the amylose structure condenses so that it no longer has as many branch points that are vulnerable to attack by amylase. And, as mentioned above, since amylose has fewer branch points (i.e., than amylopectin) to begin with, this reduces breakdown. Thus, RS3 is not susceptible to being broken down by amylase and so is completely resistant. Among the common food sources of RS3 are potatoes, breads, and cereals (like cornflakes).

There is a fourth type of resistant starch (called RS4, of course). Unlike the other resistant starches, which occur naturally, RS4 is a chemically modified starch created by treating starch compounds with heat and/or chemicals so that they take on structures that withstand digestion. RS4 has both soluble and insoluble properties, but it may or may not behave like a fiber, depending on the conditions and processing to which it is subjected.

Where to Get Resistant Starch

Once resistant starch was discovered in such foods as grains—specifically corn, wheat, and barley—the hunt was on to see just how prevalent it was in the plant kingdom. That research is still ongoing. In determining which foods naturally contain resistant starch, analysis so far has turned up a few surprises. Certain foods rich in fiber—which you might expect to contain goodly amounts of resistant starch—have come up short. Apples, an excellent source of pectin fiber, apparently have no resistant starch, while bananas and mangoes do. Corn and potatoes are among the best sources of natural resistant starch; root vegetables such as carrots contain modest, if any, amounts.

What has made calculating resistant starch values especially difficult is that, even among specific groups of plant foods, the RS values can range from a trace to an abundance. Legumes are a good example: Whereas peas and red beans contain exceptional amounts of resistant starch, soybeans have only trace amounts. What is known is that, as with fiber, there are incredible health benefits to including a lot more resistant starch–carrying foods in our diets. According to the Commonwealth Scientific and Industrial Research Organisation (CSIRO) in Adelaide, Australia, one of the leading centers for RS research, "intakes in the order of 20 grams per day" may be necessary to reap the most significant health benefits. Scientists examining data collected from around the world have determined that in most developed countries, the average person consumes only 3 to 7 grams of resistant starch per day.

Part of the reason we aren't getting enough RS—even if we eat a lot of carbs—is that a number of conditions can alter the amount of resistant starch in any given food. In the case of fruits and vegetables, for example, ripeness is an indicator that the starches have already broken down to their simpler forms—that is, sugars. Even within general categories of fruits and vegetables, the amount of RS and other nutrients can vary widely. Two bunches of broccoli, when analyzed under laboratory conditions, will contain different amounts of the same vitamins and minerals, so gauging the levels of resistant starch would show similar variation depending on their growing seasons, soil, weather conditions, and any number of other factors.

Cooking methods also affect levels of resistant starch. Potatoes, peas, corn, and barley experience declines in RS as heat breaks down amylose and amylopectin, two common types of carbohydrates. But then as the starch products cool, amylopectin breaks down into shorter pieces, thus raising the level of resistant starch. This is why cooked potatoes are fluffy when first cooked but become dense when left at room temperature or colder. This process happens with greater efficiency when a food containing amylose and/or amylopectin is subjected to low, slow cooking.

As you can imagine, all these factors make determining the exact amount of resistant starch in any one food a major challenge. Scientists are hard at work developing and refining methods of measuring RS. (Some good news is that, as we get better at the task, we're finding more foods with RS.) In the meantime, the charts in this book listing RS values (pages 35 and 36) have been compiled from multiple sources, which in turn are based on averages observed and measured under various laboratory conditions. Be aware, too, that there are some foods for which a "standard" resistant starch value has yet to be determined. We know it's there; we're just not sure how much is average for that food.

Grains have garnered the most attention as RS sources, perhaps because scientific awareness of RS grew from studies of the health effects of fiber and whole grains. The more amylose that whole grains contain, the more resistant

Factoid

Green Peas

In addition to being high in resistant starch, peas, beans, lentils, and chickpeas also contain highly bioavailable proteins, vitamins, and minerals. But wait, there's more: Peas and beans are also a naturally sustainable crop that fixes nitrogen into soil and requires less water than most grain crops. As one of the cheapest, greenest, and easiest-to-attain protein sources on the planet, peas and beans hold promise for economically stressed regions to provide sufficient high-quality nutrition to their populations.

they are to digestion. Standard grains vary in their amylose content, but within the past few years, scientists have begun developing crossbred grains that provide up to three times as much amylose. For example, flour made from a standard strain of corn delivers about 25 percent of its starch as amylose. That number jumps to 70 percent for flour made from a special hybrid strain. Legumes—beans, peas, lentils, and chickpeas—also have naturally high levels of amylose.

Resistant Starch and the Mediterranean Diet

As you read the list of resistant starch foods, it may occur to you that these foods have something else in common. Whole grains, beans and other legumes, rice, and nuts are central to the Mediterranean Diet, a plant-based diet that emphasizes enjoyment of naturally healthy foods, not restrictions and denial.

"Most good sources of resistant starch are what we might call 'peasant food'—the everyday dishes of traditional cultures," says Cynthia Harriman, director of food and nutrition strategies for the Whole Grains Council. But don't peasants by definition typically live in a state of bare-bones subsistence?

"Actually, the problem was always in the quantity of food available rather than the quality," Harriman notes. "In southern Italy, for instance, many simple peasant meals consist of beans and greens—wild leaves from the fields, with legumes, flavored with herbs and olive oil. This is a great balanced diet.

"As new scientific techniques evolve for delving into the components of foods, we find over and over the reasoning behind why things turn out to be good for us," Harriman adds. "Whole grains and legumes are such a good example of this. We've known they're good for us for a long time. At first, we thought it was just because of the fiber. Then we discovered that they had more protein, and two to three times more vitamins and minerals. Then we found out they have off-the-charts antioxidant activity. And now we've learned that they offer resistant starch, too."

In Chapter 3, we'll show you how you can increase the proportion of RS in your daily diet. The simplest solution, of course, is to eat more foods rich in RS. Potatoes, pastas, bananas, and beans are excellent sources, as are green beans, peas, corn, and even mangoes. (You'll find a longer list on pages 35 to 36.) Ideally, you're eating these foods in their fresh, whole state—but we realize that isn't always possible. Certain processed foods, such as partially milled grains, contribute to your daily quota. Those would include barley (an especially good source), oats, kamut, quinoa, rye, wheat, and even flax—also known for its high levels of omega-3 fatty acids, a beneficial fat.

There is another way to get more resistant starch into your diet. You can add it yourself. Some companies that distribute grains to food companies have been supplying RS to manufacturers of breads, cereals, snacks, and other baked products. At least two of these companies, National Starch Food Innovation and MGP Ingredients, are manufacturing RS-rich corn and wheat flour products for retail sale.

You'll notice that a number of recipes beginning in Chapter 4 call for Hi-maize resistant starch, a flour made with 70 percent resistant starch. A number of supermarkets carry this product; it's also available online. Stirring a tablespoon of this RS-rich flour into smoothies, soups, sauces, batters, or any dish of your choice adds a 6.5-gram burst of resistant starch. Hi-maize resistant starch is also available from Celiac Specialties Inc. (www.celiacspecialties.com), which also certifies it as gluten-free.

Finally, as you'll see, the RS content in food actually increases after it has been heated and cooled. So most of the 150 recipes in this book include instructions to cool before serving. This is a change that may take some getting used to. But the recipes make it easy, because they're so delicious and satisfying.

Resistant Starch vs. Sugar

In most discussions of nutrition, sugar is vilified as the culprit behind obesity, diabetes, and cancer. But for all of the controversy, sugar's contribution to the diet is pretty basic. It's a simple carbohydrate consisting of glucose and fructose and providing 4 calories per gram.

Often these calories are described as "empty" calories, alluding to the fact that sugar is devoid of vitamins and minerals. When too many calories come from sugar, other necessary nutrients get shortchanged.

Resistant starch tames sugar cravings by helping the body to better utilize its glucose load. As a bonus, resistant starch delivers just 2 to 3 calories per gram, compared to the 4 calories per gram of sugar (and 9 calories per gram from fat).

ARTIFICIAL SWEETENERS

While RS's calorie count is higher than that of zero- and low-calorie sweeteners, there are other reasons to consider choosing resistant starch foods and ingredients over their no-cal and low-cal counterparts.

For example, a 2005 study from researchers at the University of Texas Health Science Center at San Antonio showed that rather than promoting weight loss, diet drinks could be a factor in increasing weight gain and obesity. Study participants who drank diet sodas appeared more likely to gain weight than those who drank calorie-laden, naturally sweetened sodas.

Sharon Fowler, MPH, who conducted the study, suggests that the diet drinks themselves may not be to blame. Rather, she proposes, these beverages are simply a symptom of weight gain, not a cause. That is, the person who is overweight or obese may turn to diet drinks as a component of their weight-loss efforts.

Fowler further speculates that "giving the body the 'taste' of energy-rich foods triggers a search for the real thing." Or, as nutrition expert Leslie Bonci, MPH, RD, describes it, "People think they can just fool the body. But maybe the body isn't fooled. If you are not giving your body the food energy you promised it, maybe your body will retaliate by wanting more energy."

While much more research remains to be done before any definitive conclusion can be drawn, the fact that resistant starch can both increase satiety while providing low-calorie carbohydrate satisfaction points to at least some benefits over totally calorie-free products.

NATURAL SWEETENERS

A number of natural compounds and sugar derivatives are used in place of sugar to sweeten foods. These include syrups and honeys, as well as short-chain starches such as maltodextrin, which add texture and water solubility to foods and beverages while imparting a slightly sweet flavor.

One natural sweetener that is becoming widely popular is agave syrup, the sticky-sweet syrup from the same cactus that gives us tequila. It's mostly fructose, so it is slightly sweeter than table sugar and therefore can be used in more modest amounts.

HIGH-FRUCTOSE CORN SYRUP

The idea of a popular sweetener with high levels of fructose brings us to the one sugar substitute that merits special attention, if only because it is so ubiquitous and so controversial: high-fructose corn syrup. Although rarely used at the table, it appears in thousands of processed food and beverage products across every category—including soft drinks, fruit juices, salad dressings, soups, sauces, snacks, and dairy products such as yogurt and ice cream.

A lot has been written about high-fructose corn syrup in the past 20 years, most of it unreservedly negative. Yet most anti-corn syrup condemnations hinge on a shockingly simple misunderstanding of just what high-fructose corn syrup is. The main ingredient is corn starch that has been chemically converted—via enzymes, just as in the human body—into a syrup that consists primarily of glucose. Where does the fructose come in? Another series of chemical reactions turns 42 to 55 percent of the glucose into fructose, also known as fruit sugar.

So all the misdirection surrounding high-fructose corn syrup appears to hinge on the word "high," which in this case means in comparison to pure glucose syrup, not in comparison to table sugar. Hundreds of studies have been unable to definitively prove or disprove that high-fructose corn syrup is more of a culprit in our epidemic of obesity than any other refined sugar, although some recent research does suggest that both possible differences in how we metabolize fructose compared to other sugars and the pervasiveness of fructose in processed products might be associated with higher risks of obesity and disease than are other sweeteners.

Ultimately, a gram of fructose delivers the same 4 calories as a gram of glucose. In weight loss, it's all about burning up the calories we absorb.

Chapter

{2}

What Resistant Starch Can Do for You

A S MENTIONED IN CHAPTER 1, scientists have been aware of resistant starch for about 25 years. But it remained just another blip on the nutritional science radar until 2006, when a comprehensive review of more than 140 studies delineated its overwhelmingly positive health effects. That's when experts and the media alike began to take notice.

In this chapter, we'll explore the trail of RS research to date and reveal some of the more significant findings, particularly with regard to weight loss and disease risk reduction. The beauty of RS is that we can gain all of these benefits just by eating foods we love. What could be better?

Resisting the Pounds with RS

The past quarter-century of research shows natural resistant starch can assist in weight loss and weight management in a few different ways.

First, RS lowers the caloric density of foods, delivering between 2 and 3 calories per gram versus 4 calories per gram for regular carbohydrates. Secondly, RS encourages your body to burning fat instead of carbohydrates as its energy source. In fact, in a 2004 study, Janine Higgins, PhD, of the University of Colorado Health Sciences Center found that eating one daily meal containing 5 grams of resistant starch increased the ability to burn fat by 23 percent.

The third way RS helps you lose weight is that it boosts your body's production of satiety hormones, those hormones that say to your brain, "I'm full!" This effect has been shown to be long-lasting, too—in some studies for as long as the whole day.

And, RS helps decrease deposits of body fat in several ways. As with fiber, it helps move fat molecules through your digestive tract faster, keeping the fat from being absorbed. But it also enhances the digestive tract's ability to better metabolize the fat that does get digested. Multiple studies show these effects, and a 2007 study of persons with diabetes found that eating foods made with 30 grams of resistant starch per day decreased total Body Mass Index. In addition, an animal study earlier this year demonstrated that resistant starch can have a direct effect on the hypothalamus gland (the metabolism and mood center in the brain) as well as hunger/fullness hormones. Importantly, the subjects showed weight loss and reduced visceral fat independent of the digestive tract's reaction to "feeling full."

The ability of RS to rev up overall energy metabolism while boosting satiety and fat-burning adds up to lasting weight loss.

What's in a Name?

When you're reading food labels, take notice of any ingredient with the suffix "-ose." It means that the ingredient is a type of sugar. Most natural sugars have 4 calories per gram, while some manufactured sugars and sugar alcohols (which use the suffix "-ol") have calorie counts 25 to 80 percent lower than that.

The suffix "-glyceride," on the other hand, indicates a fat or a component of fat. A fat molecule consists of a glycerol (sugar alcohol) "backbone" that supports three glyceride branches for holding on to fatty acids. If there's just one fatty acid taking advantage of the opportunity to attach to the glycerol, you have a monoglyceride; two make a diglyceride; and if all three positions fill up, it's a triglyceride—a complete fat molecule. Fats, in whole or part, supply around 9 calories per gram.

So how does resistant starch stack up? It provides only 2 to 3 calories per gram.

Staying Satisfied with RS

A number of studies have examined how including resistant starch in the diet influences hunger. In the best of these studies, participants were given meals identical in composition and calorie content, except that one group received a food item containing RS. The other group (the control) got the same food, only made with a rapidly digesting starch. Both groups could eat any foods they wanted, in any amount they wanted, following their meal and before their next meal.

The results of these types of studies have been remarkably consistent: The people given the meal containing resistant starch ate less between meals. So something about resistant starch increases the level of satiety—that is, the feeling of fullness and satisfaction a person has after eating. When tracked across an entire 24-hour period, the inclusion of resistant starch in a meal reduced feelings of hunger. In some studies, calorie intake declined by as much as 10 percent over the course of a day.

Resistant starch exerts its antihunger effects in a number of ways. While its resistance to digestion promotes a sensation of fullness (similar in many ways to fiber with fewer calories), as well as slowing the absorption of glucose, research suggests RS triggers a number of different biochemical pathways that can help people eat less and still feel satisfied.

Along one of these pathways, resistant starch leads to a significantly lower insulin response. Insulin, known for its role in breaking down and metabolizing glucose, also is considered one of three major hunger hormones (ghrelin and leptin are the other two). Hormones are the body's chemists, initiating and regulating a variety of chemical reactions. If the amount of glucose entering the bloodstream stays on a relatively even keel, the body doesn't need as much insulin to control it. This reins in peaks and valleys in insulin levels, which are known to fuel cravings for carbohydrates, especially sugars. And this, in turn, improves insulin sensitivity.

Reduced insulin sensitivity is characteristic of insulin resistance, in which the liver (as well as muscle and adipose tissue) is getting insulin but is not responding well to it. As a result, the body begins to break down fat and release it into the bloodstream as an energy source. In muscle tissue, insulin resistance impairs the capacity to store glucose as glycogen. To compensate, the liver pumps more glucose into the bloodstream.

The dual increases in blood glucose and blood insulin cascades into the medical condition known as *metabolic syndrome,* which raises a person's risk not only of type 2 diabetes but also of high blood pressure, as well as heart, vascular, and kidney disease. But there is good news: Research has shown that a diet providing 25 to 30 grams of resistant starch a day can effectively reverse insulin resistance, even in people with active type 2 diabetes.

A pair of 2008 studies, one from the University of Kuopio in Finland and the other from Pennington Biomedical Research Center in Baton Rouge, Louisiana, went a step further. They concluded that better regulation of insulin in response to certain grain products is "determined by the form of food and botanical structure rather than by the amount of fiber." The researchers were referring to resistant starch.

These studies also point to the effects of resistant starch on neuropeptides—hormones that allow nerve cells in the brain to communicate with each other—specifically glucagon-like peptide and peptide YY (PYY). These hormones exert a number of positive effects on satiety, insulin uptake, and digestion. For example, they increase intestinal growth (allowing for more efficient digestion and nutrient metabolism), enhance intestinal function, impede bone breakdown, and protect the GI tract's neurological structure. Increasing the amount of resistant starch in the diet appears to boost levels of both of these hormones, the presence of which reduced both caloric intake and total body weight in animal and human study subjects.

Burning Fat with RS

Fat burning, the familiar term for fat metabolism or oxidation, is a common claim among marketers of diet pills and potions. But with resistant starch, we have scientific evidence of a fat-burning effect. In animal studies using resistant starch from high-amylose corn, individual fat cells around internal organs—the visceral fat that's considered a major marker for increased disease risk—actually got smaller, as did normal areas of fat deposit. Researchers attributed these changes to the inhibition of enzymes associated with fat production (known as lipid synthesis). RS also inhibited the drawing of glucose into fat cells for storage.

Subsequent studies involving humans showed similar changes; specifically, fat oxidation rose by 20 percent or more, and the effect lasted throughout the day. This fat-burning capacity also affects satiety: If our bodies are using energy more efficiently, hunger signals are more likely to be suppressed.

Staying Healthy with RS

As the research into resistant starch continues to gain momentum, it isn't far-fetched to imagine the health effects of this "super-starch" rivaling those of omega-3 fatty acids and soy. Of course, this research is far from conclusive, and, as with any nutrition discovery, much more investigation is necessary to confirm the health effects of resistant starch. By all accounts, scientists have just scratched the surface in their understanding of what RS can do for us in terms of not just our waistlines but our energy level, mood, and general health. That these benefits come from a component of so many foods we already enjoy is an unexpected boon to anyone seeking to improve the way they look and the way they feel. Here are some of the benefits discovered so far.

Fighting Inflammation with RS

In the past few years, the focus of some obesity research has centered on inflammation. This is the theory that inflammation sets the stage for metabolic disorders such as insulin resistance and type 2 diabetes. While many of these studies are attempting to determine cause and effect (i.e., does obesity trigger an inflammatory response that leads to metabolic dysfunction, or does metabolic dysfunction brought on by obesity cause inflammation?), they are pointing to a valuable role for resistant starch in reducing inflammation and its associated health risks.

In a joint study conducted by researchers at Lund University in Sweden and the University of Copenhagen in Denmark, and published in the April 2008 issue of the *Journal of Nutrition*, the inclusion of resistant starch at dinner led to shorter gastric emptying time, improved glucose tolerance, and a reduced glucose response (by as much as 28 percent). The collective effect was "lower blood glucose peak increments" that lasted into the next day. The study participants also reported a greater sense of satiety after the following day's breakfast, a finding that was confirmed by positive changes in associated chemical markers. Most important for our discussion here, adding resistant starch to the evening meal reduced specific markers of inflammation called *interleukins*.

Deterring Diabetes with RS

With diabetes emerging as a major public health issue, it's no surprise that the disease became an early focal point for studying the therapeutic effects of resistant starch. Reduced weight and balanced blood sugar levels help to lower the risk of type 2 diabetes and the terrible complications associated with it, such as arterial disease, kidney failure, and vision loss.

Building on preliminary research from the late 1980s and early 1990s, researchers such as Janine Higgins, PhD, of the University of Colorado Health Sciences Center began investigating the effects of RS on insulin sensitivity and insulin resistance. Insulin resistance is a common precursor to type 2 diabetes, as well as diabetes complications such as cardiovascular and kidney disease. Dr. Higgins theorized that nonpharmaceutical intervention with resistant starch could reduce or even prevent insulin resistance.

In presenting her research findings at a 2007 international symposium on natural resistant starch, Dr. Higgins described the basic mechanism of RS this way:

During the day, people experience swings in blood sugar levels and energy depending on what they eat. For example, immediately following a meal, rapidly rising blood sugar levels give more energy. An hour or two later, when blood sugar levels fall, energy levels may decline as well. This drop in blood sugar can lead to drowsiness, lack of concentration, and increased appetite—which may result in low productivity and food cravings.

Foods rich in resistant starch can help modulate these swings, especially if they replace foods high in simple carbohydrates. This can result in a feeling of more balanced energy throughout the day.

Resistant starch owes this moderating effect to its ability to not only lower glycemic and insulin response but to also

Factoid

Spicy Science

Cinnamon has demonstrated surprising effectiveness at helping the body regulate blood sugar levels. Stirring some cinnamon into resistant starch recipes could very well increase the health benefits for people with diabetes or prediabetes.

sustain energy release. As Dr. Higgins explained, "[Resistant starch] releases part of its energy in the small intestine as glucose and part of its energy in the large intestine many hours later as fermentation by-products, such as acetate and butyrate. While glucose is the exclusive energy source for the brain, acetate is used as an energy source in muscle and fat tissue."

Meanwhile, across the globe in Adelaide, Australia, chief scientist David Topping, PhD, FTSE, and his colleagues at the Commonwealth Scientific and Industrial Research Organisation were exploring how resistant starch can cause fundamental changes in the chemistry of our digestive system. By generating a series of interconnected environmental conditions, Dr. Topping and his team proposed that RS could protect against colon cancer by enhancing immune response and antioxidant activity and countering damage to the DNA of cells in the GI tract.

The work of scientists such as Dr. Higgins, Dr. Topping, and the Pennington Biomedical Research Center greatly enhanced scientific understanding of how resistant starch influences both insulin regulation and satiety. This property certainly has something to do with RS's fiberlike qualities, but it also involves RS's ability to influence the body's hormone responses that regulate hunger as well as carbohydrate and fat metabolism. All of these benefits work not in place of but in tandem with those fiberlike effects in order to give resistant starch a distinct nutritional profile—especially with regard to its fermentation in the lower GI tract. This fermentation factor demonstrates that the antihunger, anticancer, and other positive health effects of resistant starch occur at a biochemical level rather than simply mimicking fiber by increasing bulking and transit time through the digestive tract.

Improving Digestion with RS

Certain food components, or by-products of the digestion of those components, can cause damage on a genetic level to the cells lining the GI tract. Among these harmful particles are oxygen by-products, the effects of which can be offset by antioxidants or compounds with antioxidant properties. Although the mucosal layer of the GI tract affords some protection, it isn't foolproof. Plus, the lower section of the GI tract is teeming with one-celled critters that can be helpful or hurtful. In a healthy digestive system, the former outnumber the latter—but that isn't always the case.

As with fiber, resistant starch "waits" until it reaches the colon to break down, which it does through fermentation. Some recent research suggests that starches that don't get digested in the small intestine—like RS—are important to the healthy function of the lower GI tract. At first researchers believed this had something to do with the fiberlike action of resistant starch in helping to clear the GI tract of toxins through bulking and binding. But more recent studies point to another mechanism at work.

Both resistant starch and fiber undergo fermentation in the lower section of the GI tract. But fiber can vary widely in how it's fermented and what the by-products of this process are. The fermentation of resistant starch favors production of a short-chain fatty acid called *butyrate*.

Butyrate performs several functions, and some distinctly important ones at that. As an energy source for the friendly bacteria that inhabit the colon, butyrate is a prebiotic that aids digestion, prevents overgrowth of harmful bacteria, boosts metabolism, and assists in maintaining electrolyte balance in the gut. Butyrate and other short-chain fatty acids also promote the absorption of beneficial minerals while inhibiting the uptake of compounds that possess toxic or carcinogenic potential.

Butyrate stimulates colonic blood flow, increases intestinal tone, and facilitates nutrient flow. This in turn promotes growth of new cells in the colon and reverses atrophy associated with low-fiber diets. This means RS helps protect against colitis, inflammatory bowel syndrome, and other diseases of the lower digestive system.

Resistant starch also prevents colonic damage from high-protein diets. Animal studies from Dr. Topping's group in Australia showed that the more protein animals ate, the more damage was done to their DNA. This makes sense because protein fermentation produces ammonia and phenols, which are known to be harmful compounds within the colon. However, when RS was added to the diet, the DNA damage did not happen—the damage was completely prevented by the resistant starch.

Factoid

Adults Only?

A recent animal study investigating the ability of resistant starch to affect appetite hormones uncovered an RS-triggered increase in a natural compound called proopiomelanocortin. The natural opiate-like hormone, by itself or through other compounds derived from it, not only helps the body regulate appetite and manage caloric energy but also control pain, modulate the immune response, and even affect sexual arousal.

Preventing Cancer with RS

A flurry of recent scientific analyses has connected the fermentation of resistant starch, and the resulting increased production of butyrate, to a lowered incidence (and therefore decreased risk) of colorectal cancers. The prebiotic action of butyrate described above and the subsequent increased colonic blood flow indirectly help protect against colorectal cancer.

If recent research is any indication, butyrate—and resistant starch—may work in another, more direct way to lower our colorectal cancer risk. "In the colon, the RS2 and RS3 starches ferment; the products of their fermentation trigger the expression of cancer-related genes,"

The Perks of Fiber without the "Feedback"

Remember our discussion in Chapter 1 about the polysaccharide structure of certain carbohydrates? Well, the difficulty of breaking down polysaccharide chains may be what's to blame for the infamous aftereffects of beans and other high-fiber foods.

Interestingly, normal dietary amounts of resistant starch do not appear to cause symptoms of digestive distress, even though it is made of polysaccharide chains and passes through the small intestine largely intact, much like fiber. In studies, some people who consumed what would be considered very high daily doses of resistant starch—on the order of 40 grams per day—experienced some digestive "rumbling" but few other negative consequences.

Since digestive enzymes can't break down resistant starch, the polysaccharide chains in RS maintain their natural starch granule shape. The bacteria in the large intestine cannot easily consume these starch granules, so the fermentation occurs very slowly. For this reason, resistant starch is very well tolerated and does not typically cause digestive distress.

A potential drawback of a high-fiber diet is that not only by decreasing the transit time of food—especially while the body is adjusting to the extra fiber—but by binding to certain minerals, fiber can essentially decrease the body's uptake of them. The structure of RS prevents this from occurring.

This may be less of an issue if you're building your diet around plant-based foods, which are loaded with vitamins, minerals, antioxidants, phytochemicals, and other key nutrients. On a diet like this, even if your body isn't absorbing all of the available nutrients, it's getting enough to cover your needs. Furthermore, your body eventually will adjust its ability to absorb needed compounds like these more efficiently.

By Phase 3 of the Skinny Carbs Diet, you'll be aiming for at least 20 grams of resistant starch and 30 grams of fiber daily. Neither amount is enough to have a negative nutritional impact.

explains Kantha Shelke, PhD, director of Corvus Blue, a Chicago-based nutrition science consultancy. "In studies, this process prevented normal tissue from becoming cancerous. Butyrate stimulates normal colon cell growth and maturation and helps to break the pattern of abnormal cell growth."

This was supported a few years later by Dutch researchers Fred Brouns and Bernd Kettlitz of the Cerestar Vilvoorde Research & Development Centre in Havenstraat, Vilvoorde, Belgium, and Eva Arrigoni of the Institute of Food Technology and Food Science in Zurich, Switzerland. They concluded that butyrate, together with another short-chain fatty acid, propionate, "have the potential to support the maintenance of a healthy gut and to reduce risk factors that are involved in the development of gut inflammation" and cancer, emphasizing the role of butyrate in the "regeneration of the diseased lining of the gut." The researchers noted how butyrate actually inhibited growth of precancerous cells at specific points of potential tumor development.

Sodium Shocker

Sodium has been so much in the news lately that it may come as a shock to learn that the connection between dietary sodium and high blood pressure (hypertension) in healthy people has failed to be established definitively. So why do so many health experts still warn us about the dangers of consuming too much salt?

About one in five Americans have a predisposition for high blood pressure—or already have it. And of those one in five, another one in four or five have what is termed *salt-sensitive hypertension*. For this group, restricting sodium intake will be helpful in controlling their blood pressure. And, although not all overweight persons will develop salt-sensitive hypertension, excess weight already puts them at higher risk than the average population, so it's still a good idea in such cases to avoid excessive amounts of sodium.

Enhancing Immunity with RS

A series of animal studies has raised the possibility that RS could enhance immune function. While these findings require corroboration through other studies, the implications are exciting. As Stig Bengmark, MD, PhD, wrote in 2002 in the journal *Current Opinion in Critical Care*, "Approximately 70 percent of the immune system is localized in the gastrointestinal tract: its glands, mucosa, and mucosa-associated lymphoid system." As we've seen, RS plays a big role in the healthy functioning of the GI tract, which in turn supports immune function.

Reducing Osteoporosis Risk with RS

Preliminary research, mostly involving animals in controlled laboratory settings, has piqued scientific interest in the possibility that resistant starch might enhance the bioavailability of certain minerals, especially calcium. This ties in to an observed ability of RS to not only preserve bone mineral density but also increase mineral density in bones already experiencing loss. Researchers believe this may be because repeating cycles of weight loss and gain negatively affect bone mineral density; RS, as we've seen, can halt this frustrating cycle by promoting steady and lasting weight loss.

In addition, RS increases production of the short-chain fatty acids butyrate and acetate. These fatty acids lower the pH in the colon, making the environment more acidic. Calcium needs an acidic environment for optimal absorption, so increasing RS can aid calcium absorption, thus reducing osteoporosis risk. Both animal and human studies show enhanced calcium absorption and a more efficient interplay between calcium and vitamin D when fermentable carbohydrates are on board.

The human studies were especially encouraging. Increased calcium uptake and a speculated increase in bone mineral density were seen in adolescent girls taking calcium supplements and enjoying a diet of different fermentable starches as well as in postmenopausal women. There's more: With fermentable starches showing a capacity to increase the surface area of the GI tract, research suggests this affords many more opportunities for calcium and other minerals to be taken up by the body.

Halting Hypertension and Heart Disease with RS

In addition to reducing the risk of osteoporosis, RS's promotion of calcium absorption can help stop hypertension, or high blood pressure. Because blood pressure is regulated by the kidneys and intimately involves a balance of sodium, chloride, calcium, and other minerals in the blood system, with improved calcium balance, kidney function is enhanced and blood pressure better regulated.

But another way in which RS can help reduce hypertension has to do with its ability to contribute to the mitigation of diabetes and metabolic syndrome. As pointed out above, RS helps reduce both the risk of developing type 2 diabetes and the symptoms associated with the disease. Diabetes, hypertension, and heart disease go hand in hand for many individuals because of decreased flow to the finer blood vessels called capillaries.

In addition, many studies show that increased RS and fiber lower blood lipids, which curtails atherosclerosis—the hardening of arteries—which leads to blockages that raise blood pressure and can lead to heart attacks.

Easing Depression with RS

The link between resistant starch and depression isn't clear-cut. But that may change with studies like one from the University of California Extension, Sonoma, which found a higher incidence of anxiety and depression among people with diabetes. In the study, which appeared in the February 2009 issue of *Diabetic Medicine*, the authors cited a number of possible influencing factors, including glycemic control. As we now know, resistant starch can play an important role in effective glycemic control and, therefore, may help ease depressive symptoms. Results of another study, by Ferdinand Van der Does, Nico de Neeling, and Frank Snoek of the Research in Extramural Medicine, Vrije Universiteit, Amsterdam, The Netherlands, and published in *Diabetes Care*, noted the resultant data "suggest that better glycemic control in type 2 diabetes is associated with fewer physical symptoms, better mood, and better well-being." Interestingly, the positive correlation between symptoms of depression and glycemic control was shown to be higher in women in a study by Power and Snoek, published in the same journal 8 years earlier.

Depression also interferes with the body's basic metabolic processes and negatively affects insulin, leptin, and ghrelin, the hunger hormones that we talked

Factoid

Feeling Good

Research into resistant starch has uncovered its ability to regulate hunger and satiety hormones such as insulin, leptin, and ghrelin, as well as the vital neurotransmitter serotonin, which in turn can lead to better moods. But there's another way resistant starch could help us feel better. One of the best natural sources of resistant starch is beans, which also happen to contain omega-3 fatty acids. In studies, an increase in omega-3 intake has been shown to help relieve some symptoms of depression.

about earlier. This may help explain why people who have depression are between 20 and 50 percent more likely to be obese than people who aren't depressed. Resistant starch helps to regulate the uptake and balance of these key hormones. Plus, losing weight and maintaining a healthy weight with RS goes further to reduce this increased risk of depression.

There is another more fundamental way in which resistant starch could make you feel better. By helping to regulate the amount of glucose released into your bloodstream, RS could alter your brain chemistry. Serotonin, for example, is directly influenced by carbohydrate intake and metabolism. It also should be recalled that some RS-containing foods contain omega-3 fatty acids. These have shown an ability to help ease symptoms of depression while enhancing cognitive function. Other resistant starch foods—specifically rice, potatoes, oats, and bananas—are good sources of tryptophan. This amino acid not only helps regulate sleep (and better sleep equals better mood), but it's also a precursor of serotonin. Many of the pharmaceuticals with which depression is treated are designed to mimic, redistribute, or alter serotonin, among other neurotransmitters. What if resistant starch could do the same thing but without the side effects?

Active Endeavors

Many weight-loss plans make the mistake of focusing solely on diet. Little if any mention is made of activity or the whole-lifestyle change that is the key to real and lasting weight-loss success.

If you are reading this book with the idea of dropping some pounds, lowering your disease risk, and increasing your energy, then there's no way around it: You gotta get moving. But you needn't "be like Ahnuld" and pump iron for 4 hours a day or copy "Lance in France" and bike 100 miles at a time. In fact, it's surprising how little exercise you need to have a huge impact on your waistline and your health. A brisk 30-minute walk, 3 or 4 days per week, will burn between 400 and 600 calories. Make it a daily walk, and you can lose 20 pounds or more per year.

But just as with eating healthfully, exercising regularly can be a major lifestyle change, especially if you tend toward the couch potato end of the activity scale. Your best strategy is to ease into it and then keep at it, with help from tips like these. Bonus: Multiple studies show regular exercise increases mood and makes you feel better about yourself overall.

1 **SEEK OUT OPPORTUNITIES FOR "MINI" EXERCISE SESSIONS.** Some old tricks work wonders. Parking on the far side of the parking lot when you go to the store or a restaurant can give you a few minutes of extra activity that add up to long-term losses. Taking the stairs requires little expenditure of time but can quickly add up to calories burned. Taking a 5-minute break to do a quick round of jumping jacks will burn a cookie's worth of calories plus energize you in the middle of a lackluster day. All these tricks help you lose weight the way you gain it: a few dozen calories at a time.

2 **DRINK A GLASS OF WATER BEFORE A MEAL.** Research proves drinking $1\frac{1}{2}$ to 2 cups of water or broth 30 minutes before a meal cuts down on the amount you eat at that meal by up to several hundred or more.

3 **FIND A CANINE COMPANION.** The nurturing and companionship that come from hanging out with a dog can leave you feeling good about whatever activity you choose to do—whether you're going for a walk or playing chase. Don't have a dog of your own? Contact a local shelter and offer your services as a volunteer dog walker.

4 **SWAP TV FOR ACTIVITY.** It's time to forsake the evening show that you've become "iffy" about—you know, the one that "jumped the shark" and you now watch strictly out of habit. Just like that, you've found 30 minutes—if not an hour—for your workout.

5 **FOR THE SHOWS YOU DO LIKE, BREAK OUT THE WEIGHTS.** You might as well make your TV time work for you! Although some folks have gone to the extreme of hooking up their TVs to a bicycle generator, simply doing some arm curls and lifts can turn a weight-gaining activity into a fat-burning one. Don't have hand weights? A 1-gallon water jug weighs 8 pounds and can be used in a pinch. Or just do crunches and push-ups instead.

6 **MARK TIME.** For a few bucks, you can pick up a stopwatch or pedometer to help you not only keep track of your activity but also set proactive goals—adding an extra 10 minutes of walking or biking or inching up by a thousand steps a day every week.

7 **EXERCISE AS AN APPETIZER.** A funny thing happens when you work out: Instead of making you hungrier, for some it can actually depress appetite. Recent studies show that the hunger-inducing hormone ghrelin decreases following exercise, leading some people to eat less following moderate physical activity. Scheduling your exercise before your main meal of the day can help reduce your overall calorie intake while enhancing the calorie-burning effects. It's a two-for-one deal that can't be beat.

Chapter

{3}

Get More Resistant Starch

THE SKINNY CARBS DIET ISN'T SO MUCH a diet as a way of life. By this we mean that you're going to develop a pattern of eating that ultimately delivers an optimal amount of resistant starch on a daily basis.

As you learn which foods are good sources of resistant starch and adapt cooking techniques that preserve a food's RS content, your "new" dietary style will quickly become second nature to you. And because you'll never feel hungry—remember, satiety is a key RS benefit—you'll have no problem making these dietary changes stick.

Your Daily Dose

At the very least, all of us should be getting 10 grams of resistant starch a day. That's the amount associated with weight management and a measure of glucose control. For even better glucose control plus optimal colon cancer protection, the ideal intake is 20 grams of RS daily. That's a pretty sizable increase from the 5 grams or less per day most Americans are getting. By comparison, the people of India average 10 grams a day, while those in China are close to the recommended 20 grams a day.

Collected data show little difference between men and women in their resistant starch consumption, while socioeconomic, racial, and ethnic factors play more significant roles. For example, those who live in poorer, nonurban communities with ethnic populations appear to have higher levels of resistant starch intake, perhaps because they eat more RS-rich foods like potatoes, corn, and beans.

Bear in mind that calculating RS intake, as well as the RS content of foods, is not an exact science. As noted in Chapter 1, while resistant starch and fiber are frequently found in the same foods, they do not always go hand in hand. So determining which foods naturally contain RS—and how much—has

Factoid

Resistant Starch Labels

Although resistant starch is technically a starch that acts like a fiber, in processed foods it sometimes can be included in the amount of total fiber listed on the nutrition panel. It typically appears on ingredient labels as *resistant corn starch (dietary fiber)*.

been an ongoing process. The values in the tables here, for example, are estimates based on averages drawn from a variety of resources. As scientists develop more accurate methods of analyzing RS values, you may have even more options for increasing your RS intake.

RESISTANT STARCH FOODS

A simple way to get more resistant starch into your diet is to find ways to incorporate these top-notch food sources into your meals and snacks. To better help you match resistant starch–rich ingredients to your recipes and the daily amounts recommended for each phase, we've divided them into 5-gram and 1-gram categories and indicated the serving size of each food that will give you that amount of RS.

FOODS WITH 5 GRAMS RS PER SERVING

Food	Serving Size	Calories
Banana	1 large (100 g)	120
Barley, pearl (cooked and cooled)	about ½ cup (56 g)	100
Beans, fava (cooked and cooled)	about ½ cup (90 g)	75
Beans, kidney (cooked and cooled)	about ½ cup (90 g)	75
Beans, navy (cooked and cooled)	about ½ cup (90 g)	75
Chickpeas (cooked and cooled)	about ½ cup (90 g)	75
Haricot verts (cooked and cooled)	about ½ cup (30 g)	115
Lima beans (cooked and cooled)	about ⅔ cup (100 g)	100
Lentils (cooked and slightly cooled)	about ½ cup (60 g)	115
Pasta (cooked and cooled)	about 1 cup (100 g)	200
Peas, frozen (cooked and cooled)	about 1 cup (100 g)	125
Plantain (cooked and slightly cooled)	about ¾ cup (125 g)	135
Potato (boiled and cooled)	about ½ small (50 g)	60
Rice, long-grain white	about ⅔ cup (80 g)	100
Yam (boiled or steamed and cooled)	about ⅔ cup (100 g)	110

FOODS WITH 1 GRAM RS PER SERVING

Food	Serving Size	Calories
Bread, whole grain	about 2 slices (100 g)	140
Corn	about ½ cup (50 g)	72
Cornflakes	about 1¼ cups (35 g)	125
Muesli	about ⅔ cup (50 g)	190
Oatmeal (cooled slightly)	about 1 cup (50 g)	160
Oats, rolled (cooked)	about ⅓ cup (30 g)	102
Pasta (cooked, still hot)	about 1 cup (100 g)	200
Tortilla, corn	one 8" (50 g)	75

6 Weeks with Resistant Starch

Although the Skinny Carbs Diet is appropriate for men and women, the calorie levels (about 1,400 a day for the first week and 1,600 a day for the rest of the plan) are calculated for women of average height and activity level. Men should aim for 1,800 calories per day for the first week and 2,000 calories per day for the rest of the plan. To keep tabs on your calorie intake, read food labels and pay attention to the suggested serving sizes. (You might want to check out *Prevention*'s free HealthTracker program, available online at www.prevention.com/healthtracker. It allows you to keep tabs on the number of calories—and RS or anything else you want to track—that you consume each day.)

Once you decide on an appropriate calorie level, how you get your resistant starch is entirely up to you. We've developed a collection of 150 recipes, which you can mix and match to create daily menus. If you'd rather, you can start more simply by incorporating foods from the

Factoid

Wave Good-Bye

Microwaving actually decreases the amount of resistant starch, especially in potatoes and legumes. That's all the more reason to opt for "low and slow" cooking methods for maximum resistant starch composition.

lists just shown into your meals and snacks. Just remember to keep your total calories—as well as your total daily resistant starch and dietary fiber—within range of your daily requirements. For best results, try to stay within 100 calories of your daily intake goal, but don't obsess. If you happen to eat 1,650 calories on a 1,600-calorie day, don't sweat it.

In the 6-Week Skinny Carbs Diet Menus, we've included a sample menu for you, but feel free to create your own according to your tastes.

The Plan

■ **Phase 1:** For this phase, which lasts just 1 week, your goal is to consume at least 5 grams of resistant starch per day. As you now know, this is only slightly more than the average American normally consumes on a daily basis. The similarity is intentional; right now we just want you to become mindful of choosing RS-rich foods and maintaining what is likely your current RS intake. You'll also aim for at least 20 grams of dietary fiber per day.

The calorie marks for Phase 1 are 1,400 a day for women and 1,800 a day for men. Spread your calories as evenly as possible throughout the day.

■ **Phase 2:** Over the 4 weeks of this phase, you'll be bumping up your RS intake to at least 10 grams per day. This is believed to be the minimum level necessary to experience resistant starch's most impressive health effects: satiety, fat burning, blood glucose control, and weight loss. Your dietary fiber intake will increase as well, to at least 25 grams per day total. This is toward the high end of the range of fiber intake that experts usually recommend.

As for total calories, aim for about 1,600 per day if you're a woman, 2,000 per day if you're a man. Again, try to spread them throughout the day.

■ **Phase 3 (optional):** If you would like to optimize not just the weight loss but also the health benefits from RS, for the final week of the program you'll be raising your RS intake to at least 20 grams per day, the amount perceived as optimal for cancer prevention. Your dietary fiber intake will increase to 30 grams total. The calorie guidelines match those of Phase 2 as well (1,600 per day for women, 2,000 per day for men). If you choose not to move on to Phase 3, stick with Phase 2 for your sixth and final week of the program.

■ **Beyond Phase 3:** Once you've reached your weight and health goals, you'll surely want to maintain them. And the best way to do that is to keep up the healthy habits you've learned on this plan. Aim to eat at least 25 to 35 grams of fiber and 10 to 20 grams of RS daily for life.

After all, what could be easier or more enjoyable than a diet that includes potatoes, bananas, pasta, beans, and plenty of fresh fruits and vegetables?

Cooking with Resistant Starch

From a practical standpoint, the success of any weight-loss or weight-maintenance plan can be enhanced by doing as much advance preparation as possible—creating menus, shopping for ingredients, making recipes (or parts of recipes) ahead of time. These strategies are especially helpful where RS-containing foods are concerned, as cooking and cooling certain foods before serving can increase their RS values. Planning ahead is a great time saver as well.

A few things to keep in mind as you embark on this plan:

■ Some of the recipes call for Hi-maize resistant starch. For every cup of regular flour, you can substitute up to ¼ cup of that 1 cup with Hi-maize. So, if a recipe calls for 1 cup of regular flour, use ¾ cup regular flour and ¼ cup Hi-maize.

■ As mentioned above, the amount of resistant starch in a dish changes with temperature; foods that are cooked and then allowed to cool generally have the highest RS levels. This is one reason that many of the recipes instruct you to cool before serving.

■ Staying hydrated not only helps you lose weight, it allows RS to do its work under optimal conditions. Try to drink plenty of fluids throughout the day, especially water (either unflavored or naturally flavored with slices of lemon, lime, or cucumber). Sparkling water and unsweetened tea are other good options.

Ready to get started? Consider the next 6 weeks to be your kick-off to a slimmer, healthier you. Ultimately, your goal is to change your eating habits to make resistant starch the smart, nutritious centerpiece of your diet.

Eating Out with Resistant Starch

In restaurants, try to choose at least one RS-rich food per meal. For example, you might order oatmeal or a banana at breakfast or a boiled potato or steamed corn for lunch or dinner. Just be sure to keep an eye on serving sizes, since restaurant portions tend to have little resemblance to the amounts we eat at home. Here are some general guidelines to help you gauge portion size:

■ Your fist = a medium-size fruit or 1 cup of rice or pasta

■ Your thumb = 1 ounce of cheese

■ The tip of your thumb = 1 teaspoon of butter or oil

■ The palm of your hand (not counting fingers or thumb) = 4 ounces of meat, poultry, or fish

■ Cupped handful = 1 serving of cereal, pretzels, or chips

Calculate Your Ideal Weight

Over the past 130 years or so, a number of formulas have been developed to determine the optimal weight for a given height. All of them differ, though usually only slightly.

The most convenient formula isn't as precise as other calculations, nor does it work well for either side of the 5' to 6' height range. But it can be done without a calculator. For women, the formula is this: Start with 100 pounds for the first 5' of height, then add 5 pounds for each additional inch. Allow a 10 percent cushion on either side of this value to accommodate variations in body type. Men start with 110 pounds for the first 5' and add 6 pounds per inch above that, allowing the same 10 percent flexibility. Using this formula, the ideal weight for a woman who is 5'2" is 110 pounds, give or take 11 pounds. For a man who is 5'9", his ideal weight is 164 pounds, with 16½-pound margins.

In part to better account for the wide variety of body types, body sizes, plus other factors such as race and gender, the formulas have largely been replaced by body mass index (BMI), which is a nominal measure of body fat percentage. To calculate BMI, divide your weight (in kilograms) by the square of your height (in meters). Or, visit www.prevention.com and search "BMI calculator." A BMI between 25 and 29 is considered overweight; a BMI of 30 or higher means you're technically obese. However, keep in mind that even the BMI is not perfect. Because it doesn't take body composition into account (and because muscle weighs more than fat), sometimes athletes or other very fit people will fall into the overweight category.

Top 10 Excuses for Not Losing Weight

Psychologists have known for decades that the hardest thing for us humans to do is to challenge a routine in which we are entrenched. The top four life stressors—death of a loved one, divorce, job loss, and moving—are all about major change. But guess what? You can make a major change in how you live your life because you likely have done it many times before. By the time we reach middle age, most of us will have experienced one of the above stressors—perhaps more than one at a time and more than once each.

Here are some common pitfalls and excuses that can sabotage weight-loss efforts, and some simple and sensible tips on how to counter them.

1 **"I DON'T HAVE ANY WILLPOWER."** This is a good excuse. No, really. As mentioned above, making a major change is the hardest thing you can do. But the good news is that, as with any other life-altering event, finding and relying on a support network of family and friends can be highly effective. A landmark, 120-day study of more than 150 subjects at the Western Psychiatric Institute and Clinic of the University of Pittsburgh School of Medicine found that when people hooked up with relatives or good buddies to exercise, they lost more weight at the end of the 4-month period of investigation. Better, their attitude boost lasted for nearly a year after the study's term. Think of them as your confidants and cheerleaders, there to help you when you need motivation, intervention, or a pat on the back for a job well done. .

2 **"I'M TOO BUSY TO GO ON A DIET."** Whether you're running a family or working a high-stress job—or both—time is a rare commodity. Combat this excuse in black and white: Make a calendar, wall-size if possible, and incorporate your diet and exercise program right into your daily schedule.

3 **"I CAN'T AFFORD TO GO ON A DIET."** You're in luck: The best sources of resistant starch happen to be foods that are not only affordable but also widely available. The Skinny Carbs Diet makes ample use of beans, peas, and lentils, which are among the least expensive sources of protein around. And many of our recipes feature pasta and potatoes—both tasty, low-cost comfort foods. You'll save while you lose!

4 **"DIETS MAKE ME HUNGRY."** The filling nature of resistant starch is one of the things that makes the Skinny Carbs Diet so amazingly successful at controlling hunger, satiety, and weight.

5 **"I DON'T HAVE TIME TO COOK."** The 150 recipes in this cookbook were created by expert professional chefs especially for busy people who can't spend hours in the kitchen. All of the recipes are easy to prepare, with plenty of make-ahead dishes to keep this diet simple and doable.

6 **"I DON'T WANT TO COOK SEPARATE MEALS FOR MYSELF AND MY FAMILY."** Most of the recipes serve four and can be adapted to serve more. Trust us: Your family will love them! Come to think of it, you could go on the Skinny Carbs Diet without telling your spouse or kids, and they'd likely never know the difference. The foods are healthful and wholesome for everyone, not just those who want to drop some pounds. They boost energy, too, which means your whole family could have more get-up-and-go for their busy days.

7 **"I'M TOO OLD TO GO ON A DIET."** This plan is suitable for anyone who wants to lose weight and get healthy. It is a good idea, though, to talk with your doctor before embarking on any diet, just to make sure that it's appropriate for you and your nutritional needs.

8 **"EXERCISE IS BORING/INTIMIDATING/TIRING."** Though the focus of this book is food, exercise is an important component of the weight-loss equation. And most of us have a million reasons not to do it. First, banish the word *exercise* if it's discouraging you. Next, choose activities that are fun or associated with something (or someone) you enjoy.

9 **"I WEIGH TOO MUCH."** Some physicians and weight-loss experts believe that once a person is 200 pounds overweight, he or she is probably beyond what a conventional weight-loss program can accomplish. It simply isn't true. While some people in this category may benefit from surgical interventions, anyone can lose weight through a program of consistent diet and exercise. The more you want to lose, the longer it will take, but it can be done. Set specific, staged goals, and employ these other tips to make them happen. And be patient: The safest, healthiest, and most effective weight loss is that which comes gradually.

10 **"I ALWAYS FAIL."** Most people who set out to lose weight "fail" multiple times. This is because they haven't found the right program for them. The Skinny Carbs Diet gives you your best shot at success by emphasizing great food that fits any budget and lifestyle.

Chapter

{4}

Breakfasts

Sweet Breakfast Porridge

RS: 4 g

prep time
10 minutes

total time
2 hours +
5 minutes
to stand

makes
4 servings

6 cups water
¾ cup long-grain
   white rice
¼ teaspoon salt
½ cup golden raisins
⅓ cup honey
1 teaspoon vanilla
   extract

1 Bring the water to a boil in a large saucepan over medium-high heat. Stir in the rice and salt and cover. Reduce the heat to medium-low and simmer for 1½ hours.

2 Stir in the raisins, honey, and vanilla extract. Increase the heat to medium and return to a simmer. Cook for 10 minutes, or until starting to thicken. Remove from the heat and let stand for 5 minutes before serving.

per serving 267 calories, 3 g protein, 65 g carbohydrates, 1 g fiber, 0 g fat, 152 mg sodium

Savory Breakfast Porridge

RS: 4 g

prep time
10 minutes

total time
2 hours
10 minutes

makes
4 servings

7 cups water

¾ cup long-grain white rice

2 teaspoons sesame oil, divided

2 large eggs, lightly beaten

4 ounces deli-sliced ham, cut into ½" pieces

1 tablespoon grated fresh ginger

½ cup frozen peas

4 scallions, chopped

7 teaspoons reduced-sodium soy sauce

1 Bring the water to a boil in a large saucepan over medium-high heat. Stir in the rice and cover. Reduce the heat to medium-low and simmer for 1½ hours. Increase the heat to medium, uncover, and simmer for 20 minutes, or until starting to thicken.

2 Meanwhile, heat 1 teaspoon of the oil in a large nonstick skillet over medium-high heat. Add the eggs and cook, stirring, for 1 to 2 minutes, or until firm and scrambled. Transfer to a bowl and reserve.

3 Heat the remaining 1 teaspoon oil in the skillet and add the ham and ginger. Cook, stirring often, for 2 to 3 minutes, or until the ham is lightly browned. Stir in the peas and cook for 1 minute, or until bright green. Add the eggs and scallions and cook for 30 seconds. Stir the egg mixture and soy sauce into the rice and serve.

per serving 235 calories, 12 g protein, 33 g carbohydrates, 1 g fiber, 5.8 g fat (1.4 g saturated fat), 609 mg sodium*

*Limit sodium intake to 2,300 milligrams per day.

Dried Cherry and Honey Oats

RS: 1 g

prep time
5 minutes,
including
standing time

total time
13-15 minutes

makes
2 servings

2 cups water
⅛ teaspoon salt
¼ cup dried tart cherries
2 tablespoons honey
⅔ cup quick-cooking steel-cut oats (such as McCann's)

Combine the water and salt in a medium saucepan over medium-high heat. Bring to a boil and add the cherries and honey. Return to a boil. Add the oats, cover, and reduce the heat to medium-low. Simmer, stirring often, for 5 to 7 minutes, or until the oats are tender and most of the liquid has been absorbed. Remove from the heat and let stand for 2 to 3 minutes, or until thickened.

per serving 317 calories, 6 g protein, 64 g carbohydrates, 10 g fiber, 2.7 g fat (0 g saturated fat), 146 mg sodium

Creamy Cheddar and Corn-Studded Grits

RS: 1 g

prep time
5 minutes

total time
21 minutes

makes
6 servings

2 cups 1% milk

2 cups water

½ teaspoon salt

1 cup quick-cooking grits

1½ cups frozen corn kernels

4 ounces shredded low-fat sharp Cheddar cheese (such as Cabot 50% Less Fat Cheddar Cheese)

Combine the milk, water, and salt in a medium saucepan over medium-high heat. Bring to a boil and whisk in the grits in a slow, steady stream. Cook, stirring often, for 10 minutes, or until thickened. Mix in the corn and cook, stirring often, for 4 to 5 minutes, or until thick and creamy. Stir in the cheese and cook for 1 minute, or until melted. Serve immediately.

per serving 214 calories, 12 g protein, 33 g carbohydrates, 1 g fiber, 4.4 g fat (2.6 g saturated fat), 346 mg sodium

Hot Barley with Apples, Raisins, Milk, and Honey

RS: 8 g

prep time
10 minutes

total time
25-30
minutes +
5 minutes
to cool

makes
4 servings

1 cup quick-cooking barley

¼ teaspoon salt

2 medium Golden Delicious apples, peeled, cored, and chopped

⅓ cup fat-free milk

⅓ cup raisins

¼ cup honey

⅛ teaspoon ground cinnamon

Cook the barley with the salt per the package directions. Stir in the apples, milk, raisins, honey, and cinnamon and cook for 2 minutes longer. Remove from the heat and let stand for 5 minutes before serving.

per serving 271 calories, 5 g protein, 58 g carbohydrates, 6 g fiber, 0.5 g fat (0 g saturated fat), 158 mg sodium

Scrambled Eggs with Two-Potato Hash

RS: 6 g

prep time
10 minutes

total time
50 minutes +
10 minutes
to cool

makes
4 servings

8 ounces sweet potato

8 ounces baking potato

1 tablespoon unsalted butter

1 small onion, chopped

1 small green bell pepper, chopped

½ teaspoon paprika

½ teaspoon salt

¼ teaspoon freshly ground black pepper

4 large eggs

4 large egg whites

3 tablespoons fat-free milk

1 Combine the sweet and baking potatoes in a large saucepan with enough water to cover by 2". Bring to a boil over medium-high heat and cook until a knife inserted into the center comes out fairly easily—20 to 22 minutes for the sweet potato and 22 to 24 minutes for the baking potato. Transfer to a work surface and cool for 10 minutes. Peel the potatoes and cut into ½"-thick slices.

2 Melt the butter in a large nonstick skillet over medium-high heat. Add the onion and bell pepper and cook for 2 to 3 minutes, or until starting to soften. Add the baking potato and cook, stirring occasionally, for 2 to 3 minutes, or until lightly browned. Reduce the heat to medium and add the sweet potato, paprika, ¼ teaspoon of the salt, and ⅛ teaspoon of the pepper. Cook, stirring occasionally, for 4 to 5 minutes, or until the potatoes are browned and tender. Keep warm.

3 Whisk together the eggs, egg whites, milk, and remaining ¼ teaspoon salt and ⅛ teaspoon pepper in a bowl. Coat a medium nonstick skillet with cooking spray and heat over medium-high heat. Add the egg mixture and cook, stirring occasionally, for 3 to 4 minutes, or until the eggs are set. Divide the eggs among 4 plates and serve with the potatoes.

per serving 213 calories, 12 g protein, 24 g carbohydrates, 3 g fiber, 8 g fat (3.4 g saturated fat), 451 mg sodium

Potato, Red Pepper, and Parmesan Frittata

RS: 4 g

prep time
15 minutes

total time
28 minutes +
20 minutes
to cool

makes
4 servings

1 baking potato (12 ounces), peeled and cut into ½" cubes

4 large eggs, lightly beaten

4 large egg whites, lightly beaten

⅓ cup grated Parmesan cheese

¼ cup water

½ teaspoon salt

¼ teaspoon freshly ground black pepper

1 teaspoon olive oil

1 medium onion, chopped

1 medium red bell pepper, chopped

½ teaspoon dried marjoram

1 Preheat the oven to 475°F.

2 Combine the potato in a small saucepan with enough water to cover by 2". Bring to a boil over medium-high heat and cook for 8 to 9 minutes, or until the potato is tender but holds its shape. Drain and cool for 3 minutes.

3 Combine the eggs, egg whites, cheese, water, salt, and pepper. Stir in the slightly cooled potato and reserve.

4 Heat the oil in a 10" ovenproof nonstick skillet over medium-high heat. Add the onion, bell pepper, and marjoram and cook, stirring occasionally, for 5 to 6 minutes, or until the onion starts to brown. Reduce the heat to medium, pour in the egg mixture, and stir until well distributed, 30 seconds. Cook for 4 to 5 minutes, or until partially set.

5 Reduce the oven temperature to 400°F. Transfer the skillet to the oven and bake for 10 to 12 minutes, or until the eggs are completely set. Cool for 20 minutes. Slide the frittata onto a cutting board and cut into 4 wedges to serve.

per serving 214 calories, 15 g protein, 21 g carbohydrates, 2 g fiber, 8 g fat (2.9 g saturated fat), 524 mg sodium

Bacon and Red Pepper Strata

RS: 1 g

prep time
15 minutes

total time
1 hour
20 minutes +
2 hours
to chill and
10 minutes
to stand

makes
6 servings

4 slices low-fat bacon (such as Oscar Mayer Center Cut, 30% Less Fat), chopped

1 medium onion, chopped

1 large red bell pepper, chopped

2 cloves garlic, minced

1 teaspoon dried basil

8 slices multigrain bread, halved diagonally

4 ounces shredded low-fat sharp Cheddar cheese (such as Cabot 50% Less Fat Cheddar Cheese)

1½ cups egg substitute

2 cups 1% milk

¼ teaspoon salt

¼ teaspoon freshly ground black pepper

1 Heat a medium nonstick skillet over medium-high heat. Add the bacon and cook for 4 to 5 minutes, or until crisp. Transfer to a paper towel–lined plate and reserve. Add the onion, bell pepper, garlic, and basil to the skillet and cook, stirring occasionally, for 5 to 6 minutes, or until the vegetables just start to brown. Remove from the heat.

2 Coat an 11" × 7" baking dish with cooking spray. Arrange half of the bread in the bottom with all the triangles facing the same direction. Spread the onion mixture over the bread in a single layer. Top with the bacon and cheese. Arrange the remaining bread over the filling with the triangles facing the opposite direction of the bottom layer. Combine the egg substitute, milk, salt, and pepper in a bowl. Pour the mixture over the bread. Press on the bread to help absorb the milk mixture. Cover with plastic wrap and chill for 2 hours or overnight.

3 Preheat the oven to 350°F.

4 Remove the plastic wrap and bake the strata for 50 to 55 minutes, or until puffed, golden, and a knife inserted into the center comes out clean. Let stand for 10 minutes before serving.

per serving 244 calories, 21 g protein, 27 g carbohydrates, 6 g fiber, 6.4 g fat (3 g saturated fat), 636 mg sodium*

*Limit sodium intake to 2,300 milligrams per day.

Egg and Bacon Breakfast Sandwich

RS: 1 g

prep time
5 minutes

total time
10 minutes

makes
1 serving

1 light multigrain 100-calorie English muffin, split

¼ cup egg substitute

1 slice Canadian bacon

1 tomato slice

½ ounce low-fat sharp Cheddar cheese

1 Toast the English muffin and place cut side up on a serving plate.

2 Meanwhile, coat a small nonstick skillet with cooking spray and heat over medium-high heat. Add the egg substitute and cook for 45 seconds, or until starting to set. Turn over and cook for 1 minute longer, or until set. Place on a muffin half.

3 Return the skillet to the heat and add the bacon and tomato slice. Cook for 30 seconds, turn over, and top the bacon with the cheese. Cover the skillet and cook for 1 to 1½ minutes longer, or until the tomato and bacon are hot and the cheese is melted. Place the bacon and tomato on top of the egg substitute. Top with the remaining muffin half. Serve immediately.

per serving 214 calories, 22 g protein, 27 g carbohydrates, 8.2 g fiber, 5.8 g fat (2.1 g saturated fat), 784 mg sodium*

*Limit sodium intake to 2,300 milligrams per day.

Corn Tortilla Huevos Rancheros

RS: 3 g

prep time
15 minutes

total time
21 minutes

makes
2 servings

2 teaspoons olive oil
⅓ cup chopped red bell pepper
¼ cup chopped white onion
⅛ teaspoon dried oregano
¼ cup frozen corn kernels, thawed
1 clove garlic, minced
1 cup egg substitute
1 tablespoon chopped fresh cilantro
¼ teaspoon salt
⅛ teaspoon freshly ground black pepper
4 corn tortillas
4 tablespoons prepared fat-free black bean and corn salsa (such as Newman's Own)

1 Heat the oil in a medium nonstick skillet over medium-high heat. Add the bell pepper, onion, and oregano and cook, stirring occasionally, for 2 to 3 minutes, or until starting to soften. Mix in the corn and garlic and cook, stirring occasionally, for about 1 minute, or until the corn is bright yellow. Pour in the egg substitute, cilantro, salt, and pepper and cook, stirring occasionally, for 1 to 1½ minutes, or until the eggs are set. Remove from the heat.

2 Heat the tortillas per the package directions. Overlap 2 tortillas on each of 2 serving plates. Top each with half of the egg substitute mixture and dollop with 2 tablespoons salsa.

per serving 256 calories, 17 g protein, 36 g carbohydrates, 4.5 g fiber, 1 g fat (0.1 g saturated fat), 670 mg sodium*

* Limit sodium intake to 2,300 milligrams per day.

Potato Pancakes with Eggs

RS: 5 g

prep time
10 minutes

total time
40 minutes +
15 minutes
to cool

makes
4 servings

1 pound baking
potatoes

¼ cup fat-free milk

¼ cup (2 ounces) fat-
free cream cheese

2 large egg whites

½ teaspoon salt

⅛ teaspoon freshly
ground black
pepper

½ cup plain dry bread
crumbs

2 teaspoons unsalted
butter

4 large eggs

1 Prick the potatoes with a fork in several places. Microwave on high power for 8 to 9 minutes, or until tender. Let cool for 5 minutes. Peel the potatoes, transfer to a bowl, and mash with the milk and cheese. Cool for 10 minutes. Stir in the egg whites, salt, pepper, and ¼ cup of the bread crumbs.

2 Preheat the oven to 350°F. Coat a baking sheet with cooking spray.

3 Divide the potato mixture into 4 equal portions, about ⅔ cup each, and form into 3½"-diameter patties. Spread the remaining ¼ cup bread crumbs on a plate. Dredge the patties in the crumbs to coat.

4 Melt the butter in a large nonstick skillet over medium-high heat. Add the patties and cook for about 4 minutes per side, or until lightly browned. Transfer the patties to the prepared baking sheet. Bake for 10 minutes, or until hot and cooked through. Keep warm.

5 Coat the skillet with cooking spray and heat over medium heat. Add the eggs and cook for 3 minutes, or until the whites are almost set. Gently flip the eggs, being careful not to break the yolks, and cook for 1 minute longer. Place a pancake on each of 4 plates and top each with an egg. Serve immediately.

per serving 240 calories, 14 g protein, 28 g carbohydrates, 2 g fiber, 7.9 g fat (3 g saturated fat), 575 mg sodium

Note: If you have time, boil the potato in Step 1 instead of microwaving it. This will preserve even more RS.

Whole Grain Blueberry Buttermilk Pancakes

RS: 5 g

prep time
10 minutes

total time
26 minutes

makes
4 servings
(4 pancakes
each)

1 cup all-purpose flour

¼ cup Hi-maize resistant starch

¼ cup old-fashioned rolled oats

2 tablespoons sugar

1 teaspoon baking powder

¼ teaspoon baking soda

⅛ teaspoon salt

1 cup low-fat buttermilk

½ cup water

1 large egg, lightly beaten

1 tablespoon walnut oil

¾ cup fresh or thawed frozen blueberries

¼ cup maple syrup

1 Combine the flour, resistant starch, oats, sugar, baking powder, baking soda, and salt in a large bowl. Combine the buttermilk, water, egg, and oil in a separate bowl. Add to the flour mixture, stirring until smooth. Gently fold in the blueberries.

2 Coat a large nonstick skillet with cooking spray and heat over medium heat. Pour 4 scant ¼-cups of the batter into the skillet and cook for about 2 minutes, or until the tops are covered with bubbles and the edges look cooked. Turn the pancakes and cook for 2 minutes longer. Transfer to a plate and keep warm. Repeat with the remaining batter.

3 Divide the pancakes among 4 plates and drizzle each with 1 tablespoon maple syrup.

per serving 309 calories, 8 g protein, 60 g carbohydrates, 6 g fiber, 5.9 g fat (1.1 g saturated fat), 336 mg sodium

Lemon-Barley Silver Dollar Pancakes

RS: 7 g

prep time
15 minutes

total time
33 minutes +
20 minutes
to cool

makes
4 servings
(9 pancakes
each)

½ cup quick-cooking barley

1 cup all-purpose flour

¼ cup sugar

3 tablespoons Hi-maize resistant starch

2½ teaspoons baking powder

⅛ teaspoon salt

1 cup fat-free milk

1 large egg, lightly beaten

¼ cup fresh lemon juice

1 tablespoon walnut oil

½ teaspoon lemon extract

2 tablespoons confectioners' sugar

1 Cook the barley per the package directions. Transfer to a bowl and let cool for 20 minutes.

2 Combine the flour, sugar, resistant starch, baking powder, and salt in a medium bowl. Combine the milk, egg, lemon juice, oil, and lemon extract in a separate bowl. Add to the flour mixture, stirring until smooth. Fold in the barley.

3 Coat a large nonstick skillet with cooking spray and heat over medium heat. Add the batter by slightly rounded tablespoons. Cook for 2 to 3 minutes, or until the tops of the pancakes have small bubbles and the edges look dry. Turn the pancakes and cook for 2 to 3 minutes longer. Transfer to a plate and keep warm. Repeat with remaining batter.

4 Divide the pancakes among 4 plates and sprinkle with the confectioners' sugar before serving.

per serving 318 calories, 9 g protein, 63 g carbohydrates, 6 g fiber, 5 g fat (0.75 g saturated fat), 373 mg sodium

Apple Dutch-Baby Pancake

RS: 4 g

prep time
10 minutes

total time
38 minutes

makes
4 servings

2 tablespoons
unsalted butter

2 medium Golden
Delicious apples,
peeled, cored, and
cut into ¼"-thick
wedges

4 tablespoons sugar

¾ cup all-purpose flour

¼ cup Hi-maize
resistant starch

¼ teaspoon ground
cinnamon

¼ teaspoon salt

2 large eggs, lightly
beaten

1 cup 1% milk

1 teaspoon vanilla
extract

1 tablespoon
confectioners' sugar

1 Preheat the oven to 400°F.

2 Melt the butter in a heavy ovenproof 10" nonstick skillet over medium-high heat. Add the apples and cook, stirring occasionally, for 4 to 5 minutes, or until lightly browned and softened. Stir in 2 tablespoons of the sugar and cook for 1 minute longer. Remove from the heat.

3 Meanwhile, combine the remaining 2 tablespoons sugar, the flour, resistant starch, cinnamon, and salt in a bowl. Stir in the eggs, milk, and vanilla extract until smooth.

4 Pour the batter over the apples and transfer the skillet to the oven. Bake for 22 to 24 minutes, or until puffed and golden. Slide onto a serving platter, sprinkle with the confectioners' sugar, and cut into 4 wedges. Serve immediately.

per serving 306 calories, 8 g protein, 52 g carbohydrates, 6 g fiber, 9 g fat (4.9 g saturated fat), 209 mg sodium

Spiced Yam Waffles with Maple Syrup

RS: 8 g

prep time
15 minutes

total time
1 hour
(4-5 minutes
to cook
each waffle)

makes
6 servings
(2 waffles
each)

12 ounces yam
1 large egg, lightly beaten
1 large egg white, lightly beaten
1 cup 1% milk
1 cup water
2 tablespoons walnut oil
3 tablespoons sugar
1¾ cups all-purpose flour
½ cup Hi-maize resistant starch
2 teaspoons baking powder
1 teaspoon pumpkin pie spice
⅛ teaspoon salt
6 tablespoons maple syrup

1 Prick the potato with a fork in several places. Microwave on high for 8 to 9 minutes, or until tender. Cool for 5 minutes. Peel, transfer to a bowl, and mash.

2 Add the egg, egg white, milk, water, oil, and sugar to the yam and mix well. Combine the flour, resistant starch, baking powder, pumpkin pie spice, and salt in a bowl. Add into the egg mixture, stirring until combined.

3 Preheat the oven to 200°F. Heat a waffle maker per the manufacturer's directions.

4 Using the manufacturer's recommendations for batter, spoon in the batter and spread quickly. Close the top and cook for 4 to 5 minutes, or until puffed and golden or according to manufacturer's directions. Transfer to a baking sheet and keep warm in the oven.

5 Repeat with the remaining batter to make 12 waffles. Serve with the maple syrup.

per serving 336 calories, 8 g protein, 67 g carbohydrates, 8 g fiber, 6.3 g fat (1 g saturated fat), 239 mg sodium

Note: If you have time, boil the potato in Step 1 instead of microwaving it. This will preserve even more RS.

Sautéed Banana–Filled Crepes

RS: 5 g

prep time
15 minutes

total time
23 minutes +
1 hour
to chill

makes
4 servings
(2 crepes
each)

Crepes

6 tablespoons all-
purpose flour

3 tablespoons Hi-
maize resistant
starch

1 tablespoon sugar

⅛ teaspoon ground
nutmeg

⅛ teaspoon salt

2 large eggs, lightly
beaten

1 cup fat-free milk

Filling

1 tablespoon
unsalted butter

3 large bananas, cut
into ¼"-thick slices

2 tablespoons sugar

⅛ teaspoon ground
cinnamon

1 To make the crepes: Combine the flour, resistant starch, sugar, nutmeg, and salt in a bowl. Whisk together the eggs and milk in a separate bowl. Add to the flour mixture, whisking until well combined. Cover and let rest in the refrigerator for at least 1 hour or overnight.

2 Coat a nonstick crepe pan or 8" skillet with cooking spray and heat over medium heat. Pour 3 tablespoons of the crepe batter into the pan, tipping to coat the bottom evenly, and cook for 1 to 1½ minutes per side, or until lightly browned. Repeat with the remaining batter. Keep the crepes warm.

3 To make the filling: Melt the butter in a medium nonstick skillet over medium-high heat. Add the bananas, sugar, and cinnamon and cook, stirring occasionally, for 2 to 3 minutes, or until the bananas are softened.

4 Arrange 2 crepes on a work surface. Spoon 2 tablespoons of the banana mixture across half of each, then roll up jelly roll-style. Repeat with the remaining filling and crepes. Serve warm.

per serving 249 calories, 8 g protein, 47 g carbohydrates, 6 g fiber, 5.8 g fat (2.8 g saturated fat), 142 mg sodium

Blueberry Corn Muffins

RS: 2 g

prep time
10 minutes

total time
25 minutes +
15 minutes
to cool

makes
12 servings

¾ cup all-purpose flour

¾ cup stone-ground yellow cornmeal

¼ cup Hi-maize resistant starch

1½ teaspoons baking powder

½ teaspoon salt

2 large eggs, lightly beaten

½ cup agave nectar

⅓ cup fat-free milk

¼ cup corn or walnut oil

1 cup fresh or thawed frozen blueberries

1 Preheat the oven to 400°F. Line 12 standard muffin cups with liners.

2 Combine the flour, cornmeal, resistant starch, baking powder, and salt in a bowl. Combine the eggs, agave nectar, milk, and oil in a separate bowl. Add to the flour mixture, stirring until just moistened. Gently fold in the blueberries. Spoon the batter evenly into the prepared muffin cups.

3 Bake for 12 to 15 minutes, or until the muffins are lightly golden and a wooden pick inserted into the centers comes out clean. Transfer the muffins to a rack and cool for at least 15 minutes before serving.

per serving 156 calories, 3 g protein, 26 g carbohydrates, 2.4 g fiber, 5.7 g fat (0.9 g saturated fat), 162 mg sodium

Banana-Pecan Oat Muffins

RS: 4 g

prep time
15 minutes

total time
33 minutes +
15 minutes
to cool

makes
12 muffins

1¼ cups all-purpose flour

1 cup rolled oats

½ cup Hi-maize resistant starch

1½ teaspoons baking powder

¼ teaspoon baking soda

½ teaspoon salt

1 cup mashed ripe banana (about 2 medium)

⅔ cup low-fat buttermilk

1 large egg, lightly beaten

⅓ cup honey

¼ cup walnut oil

¼ cup pecan halves, chopped

1 Preheat the oven to 375°F. Line 12 standard muffin cups with liners.

2 Combine the flour, oats, resistant starch, baking powder, baking soda, and salt in a large bowl. Combine the banana, buttermilk, egg, honey, and oil in a separate bowl. Add to the flour mixture, stirring until just combined. Gently fold in the pecans. Divide the batter among the muffin cups.

3 Bake for 17 to 18 minutes, or until the muffins are lightly golden and a wooden pick inserted into the centers comes out clean. Transfer the muffins to a rack and cool for at least 15 minutes before serving.

per serving 194 calories, 4 g protein, 32 g carbohydrates, 4.4 g fiber, 7.3 g fat (0.8 g sat fat), 194 mg sodium

Multigrain French Toast with Honeyed Strawberries and Bananas

RS: 4 g

prep time
5 minutes

total time
25 minutes +
20 minutes
to stand

makes
4 servings

3 medium bananas, sliced

1 cup strawberries, sliced

1 tablespoon honey

3 large eggs

1 large egg white

¼ cup fat-free milk

½ teaspoon vanilla extract

⅛ teaspoon ground cinnamon

4 slices multigrain bread

1 Combine the bananas, strawberries, and honey in a bowl and let stand at room temperature for 20 minutes.

2 Beat together the eggs, egg white, milk, vanilla extract, and cinnamon in a large bowl.

3 Coat a large nonstick skillet with cooking spray and heat over medium-high heat. Working 1 slice at a time, dip both sides of the bread into the egg mixture to coat. Add to the hot skillet and cook for about 3 minutes per side, or until lightly browned. Place 1 slice on each of 4 plates, spoon ½ cup of the fruit mixture over, and serve.

per serving 285 calories, 14 g protein, 48 g carbohydrates, 9 g fiber, 5.7 g fat (1.3 g saturated fat), 285 mg sodium

Maple, Oat, Raisin, and Walnut Granola

RS: 1 g

prep time
5 minutes

total time
52 minutes +
time to cool

makes
12 servings
(½ cup each)

4 cups old-fashioned rolled oats

½ cup walnut halves, coarsely chopped

1 teaspoon ground cinnamon

⅛ teaspoon ground allspice

¼ teaspoon salt

½ cup maple syrup

¼ cup agave nectar

1½ tablespoons walnut oil

1 teaspoon vanilla extract

1 cup golden raisins

1 Preheat the oven to 300°F. Coat a baking sheet with cooking spray.

2 Combine the oats, walnuts, cinnamon, allspice, and salt in a medium bowl. Combine the maple syrup, agave nectar, oil, and vanilla extract in a separate bowl. Pour over the oat mixture and stir well to coat. Spread evenly on the prepared baking sheet.

3 Bake, stirring every 10 minutes, for 45 to 55 minutes, or until lightly toasted. Stir in the raisins and cool completely. Store in an airtight container.

per serving 249 calories, 6 g protein, 43 g carbohydrates, 4 g fiber, 6 g fat (0.5 g saturated fat), 53 mg sodium

Yogurt, Granola, and Banana-Strawberry Parfait

RS: 5 g

prep time
5 minutes

total time
5 minutes

makes
1 serving

½ cup Greek-style plain fat-free yogurt

½ cup Maple, Oat, Raisin, and Walnut Granola (page 64)

1 small banana, sliced

2 tablespoons seedless strawberry fruit spread, warmed

Spoon ¼ cup of the yogurt into the bottom of a parfait glass. Sprinkle with ¼ cup of the granola, then top with half of the banana slices and 1 tablespoon of the fruit spread. Repeat the layering and serve.

per serving 385 calories, 14 g protein, 75 g carbohydrates, 5 g fiber, 4 g fat (0.4 g saturated fat), 75 mg sodium

Chapter

{5}

Soups

Beef and Mushroom-Barley Soup

RS: 4 g

prep time
25 minutes

total time
1 hour
25 minutes

makes
4 servings
(1½ cups
each)

½ ounce dried porcini mushrooms

2 teaspoons olive oil

8 ounces lean top round beef, trimmed and cut into ¾" cubes

2 leeks, white and light green parts, chopped, washed, and drained

2 medium carrots, chopped

8 ounces sliced mushrooms

4 cloves garlic, minced

4 cups reduced-sodium beef broth

½ cup quick-cooking barley

¼ teaspoon salt

¼ cup grated Parmesan cheese

1 Combine the porcini mushrooms and 2 cups boiling water in a bowl and let stand for 20 minutes, or until softened. Drain.

2 Heat 1 teaspoon of the oil in a Dutch oven over medium-high heat. Add the beef and cook, turning occasionally, for about 4 minutes, or until browned. Transfer to a plate and reserve.

3 Heat the remaining 1 teaspoon oil in the Dutch oven and add the porcini mushrooms, leeks, carrots, sliced mushrooms, and garlic. Cook, stirring occasionally, for 7 to 8 minutes, or until softened. Stir in the reserved beef and the broth, scraping up any browned bits from the bottom of the pan. Bring to a boil and reduce the heat to medium-low. Cover and simmer for 20 minutes.

4 Stir in the barley, return to a simmer, and cook for 22 to 25 minutes, or until the barley is cooked and the beef is tender.

5 Stir in the salt. Divide the soup among 4 bowls. Top each serving with 1 tablespoon cheese and serve.

per serving 262 calories, 24 g protein, 28 g carbohydrates, 5 g fiber, 7.8 g fat (2 g saturated fat), 596 mg sodium

Pasta Fagioli

RS: 6 g

prep time
20 minutes

total time
43 minutes

makes
4 servings
(1½ cups
each)

3 slices low-fat bacon (such as Oscar Mayer Center Cut, 30% Less Fat), chopped

1 cup chopped onion

¾ cup chopped carrot

½ cup chopped fennel

3 cloves garlic, minced

1 teaspoon dried oregano

3 cups reduced-sodium chicken broth

1 can (14.5 ounces) no-salt-added, fire-roasted diced tomatoes

1 can (15 ounces) no-salt-added navy beans, rinsed and drained

4 ounces mini penne

¼ cup grated Parmesan cheese

¼ teaspoon freshly ground black pepper

Cook the bacon in a Dutch oven over medium-high heat, stirring occasionally, for 3 to 4 minutes, or until just starting to brown. Stir in the onion, carrot, fennel, garlic, and oregano and cook for 2 to 3 minutes, or until starting to soften. Pour in the broth, tomatoes, beans, and penne and bring to a boil. Cook, uncovered, for 9 to 10 minutes, or until the penne is tender. Remove from the heat, stir in the cheese and pepper, and serve.

per serving 257 calories, 13 g protein, 43 g carbohydrates, 7 g fiber, 3.7 g fat (1.8 g saturated fat), 586 mg sodium

Chicken and Whole Grain Noodle Soup

RS: 3 g

prep time
25 minutes

total time
1 hour
25 minutes

makes
6 servings
(1⅓ cups
each)

1 tablespoon olive oil

1 large onion, chopped

2 medium carrots, chopped

2 parsnips, chopped

2 ribs celery, chopped

½ teaspoon dried thyme

5 cups reduced-sodium chicken broth

1½ pounds bone-in, skinless split chicken breasts

1 tablespoon chopped fresh parsley + sprigs for garnish

5 ounces medium eggless whole grain noodle-style pasta

¼ teaspoon salt

¼ teaspoon freshly ground black pepper

1 Heat the oil in a Dutch oven over medium heat. Add the onion, carrots, parsnips, celery, and thyme and cook, stirring occasionally, for 9 to 10 minutes, or until the vegetables are softened. Increase the heat to medium-high and stir in the broth, chicken, and parsley. Bring to a boil and reduce the heat to medium-low. Cover and simmer for 30 minutes, or until the chicken is no longer pink inside. Remove the chicken and transfer to a cutting board. Let cool for 10 minutes.

2 Meanwhile, add the pasta to the Dutch oven, cover, and return to a simmer. Cook for about 10 minutes, or until the pasta is tender.

3 With two forks, remove the chicken from the bones and shred. Discard the bones. Stir the chicken, salt, and pepper into the soup and cook for about 1 minute, or until heated through.

per serving 278 calories, 29 g protein, 29 g carbohydrates, 3.6 g fiber, 5.4 g fat (1 g saturated fat), 251 mg sodium

Chicken Tortilla Soup with Avocado

RS: 1 g

prep time
15 minutes

total time
1 hour
15 minutes

makes
4 servings
(1¾ cups
each)

1 tablespoon olive oil

4 corn tortillas, cut into thin strips

1 can (14.5 ounces) no-salt-added, fire-roasted diced tomatoes

3 cloves garlic, minced

1 teaspoon dried oregano

1 teaspoon ground cumin

4 cups reduced-sodium chicken broth

1 pound bone-in, skinless split chicken breasts

1 cup frozen corn kernels

3 tablespoons chopped fresh cilantro

2 tablespoons fresh lime juice

½ teaspoon salt

½ Hass avocado, peeled, pitted, and chopped

1 Heat the oil in a Dutch oven over medium-high heat until hot. Add the tortilla strips and cook, stirring occasionally, for 5 to 7 minutes, or until crisp. Transfer to a paper towel-lined plate to drain and set aside.

2 Return the Dutch oven to the heat and add the tomatoes, garlic, oregano, and cumin. Cook for 3 to 4 minutes, or until starting to thicken. Stir in the broth and chicken and bring to a boil. Reduce the heat to medium-low, cover, and simmer for 30 minutes, or until the chicken is no longer pink inside. Remove the chicken and let cool for 5 minutes.

3 Remove the chicken meat from the bones and cut into bite-size cubes. Discard the bones. Return the chicken to the Dutch oven along with the corn. Increase the heat to medium-high and cook for 2 to 3 minutes, or until heated through.

4 Remove from the heat and stir in the cilantro, lime juice, and salt. Ladle the soup into 4 bowls. Divide the avocado among the bowls, top with the reserved tortilla strips, and serve.

per serving 294 calories, 27 g protein, 28 g carbohydrates, 4.8 g fiber, 8.3 g fat (1.3 g saturated fat), 664 mg sodium*

*Limit sodium intake to 2,300 milligrams per day.

Potato, Corn, and Clam Chowder

RS: 4 g

prep time
15 minutes

total time
45 minutes

makes
6 servings
(1 cup each)

5 slices low-fat bacon (such as Oscar Mayer Center Cut, 30% Less Fat), chopped

1 medium onion, chopped

2 ribs celery, chopped

½ teaspoon dried thyme

½ pound red bliss potatoes, cut into ½" cubes

1 bottle (8 ounces) clam juice

2 cans (6½ ounces each) minced clams, drained, juice reserved

½ cup water

1½ cups fresh or frozen corn kernels

2 cups 1% milk

3 tablespoons all-purpose flour

1 Cook the bacon in a Dutch oven over medium heat, stirring occasionally, for 3 to 4 minutes, or until softened. Add the onion, celery, and thyme and cook for 3 to 4 minutes, or until slightly softened.

2 Stir in the potatoes and cook for 2 minutes. Increase the heat to medium-high and add the bottled clam juice, the clam juice from the minced clams, and the water. Bring to a boil and reduce the heat to medium-low. Cover and simmer for 10 to 11 minutes, or until the potato cubes are tender.

3 Add the corn, cover, and cook for 2 minutes. Combine the milk and flour in a bowl and then stir into the Dutch oven along with the minced clams. Increase the heat to medium and cook, stirring, for 6 to 7 minutes, or until slightly thickened.

per serving 162 calories, 12 g protein, 24 g carbohydrates, 32 g fiber, 3 g fat (1.5 g saturated fat), 651 mg sodium*

*Limit sodium intake to 2,300 milligrams per day.

Roasted Vegetable and Barley Soup

RS: 4 g

prep time
20 minutes

total time
1 hour
15 minutes

makes
4 servings
(1¼ cups
each)

1 medium onion, chopped

2 medium carrots, chopped

2 ribs celery, chopped

1 fennel bulb, chopped

1 large (12-ounce) zucchini, trimmed and diced

1 tablespoon olive oil

4 cups reduced-sodium vegetable broth

1 can (14.5 ounces) no-salt-added, fire-roasted diced tomatoes

1 teaspoon dried basil

½ cup quick-cooking barley

¼ teaspoon salt

¼ teaspoon freshly ground black pepper

1 Preheat the oven to 450°F. Coat a rimmed baking sheet with cooking spray.

2 Combine the onion, carrots, celery, fennel, and zucchini in a large bowl. Add the oil and toss to coat. Spread the vegetables on the prepared baking sheet. Roast, stirring occasionally, for 35 to 40 minutes, or until lightly browned and tender.

3 Transfer the vegetables to a Dutch oven. Pour ½ cup of the broth onto the baking sheet and scrape up any browned bits. Pour into the Dutch oven.

4 Add the remaining broth, the tomatoes, and basil to the Dutch oven and bring to a boil over medium-high heat. Cover, reduce the heat to medium-low, and simmer for 10 minutes. Stir in the barley, cover, and return to a simmer. Cook for 18 to 20 minutes, or until the barley is tender. Stir in the salt and pepper and serve.

per serving 193 calories, 5 g protein, 35 g carbohydrates, 8 g fiber, 4 g fat (0.5 g saturated fat), 592 mg sodium

Navy Bean Gumbo over Rice

RS: 10 g

prep time
15 minutes

total time
1 hour

makes
4 servings

½ cup long-grain white rice

5 tablespoons all-purpose flour

7 teaspoons walnut oil

2 medium onions, chopped

1 large green bell pepper, chopped

2 ribs celery, chopped

3 cloves garlic, minced

1½ teaspoons dried oregano

3 cups reduced-sodium chicken broth

2 cans (15 ounces each) no-salt-added navy beans, rinsed and drained

½ teaspoon hot pepper sauce

¼ teaspoon salt

1 Cook the rice per the package directions.

2 Meanwhile, combine the flour and oil in a Dutch oven over medium-high heat. Cook, stirring constantly with a wooden spoon, for 7 to 8 minutes, or until the flour turns a deep rust color.

3 Stir in the onions, bell pepper, and celery. Cook, stirring often, for about 5 minutes, or until the vegetables begin to soften. Add the garlic and oregano and cook for 2 minutes. Stir in the broth and bring to a boil. Reduce the heat to medium and simmer, uncovered, for 15 minutes.

4 Stir in the beans and cook for 15 minutes longer, or until the flavors are blended. Remove from the heat and stir in the hot pepper sauce and salt. Serve over the rice.

per serving 349 calories, 13 g protein, 56 g carbohydrates, 10 g fiber, 8.8 g fat (0.8 g saturated fat), 536 mg sodium

Tuscan Bread and White Bean Soup

RS: 4 g

prep time
15 minutes

total time
40 minutes

makes
4 servings
(2 cups each)

1 tablespoon walnut oil

1 medium onion, chopped

4 cloves garlic, minced

4 cups reduced-sodium chicken broth

1 can (14.5 ounces) no-salt-added diced tomatoes

1 can (15 ounces) no-salt-added cannellini beans, rinsed and drained

½ pound Swiss chard, woody stems removed, coarsely chopped

4 ounces peasant-style multigrain bread, toasted and cubed

⅓ cup grated Parmesan cheese

¼ cup chopped fresh basil

½ teaspoon salt

¼ teaspoon freshly ground black pepper

1 Heat the oil in a large saucepan over medium heat. Add the onion and garlic and cook, stirring occasionally, for 6 to 7 minutes, or until slightly softened. Stir in the broth, tomatoes, beans, and chard. Increase the heat to medium-high and bring to a boil. Reduce the heat to medium and simmer, stirring occasionally, for 4 to 5 minutes, or until the chard wilts.

2 Add the bread to the soup, return to a simmer, and cook for about 15 minutes, or until the soup thickens. Remove from the heat and stir in the cheese, basil, salt, and pepper.

per serving 292 calories, 18 g protein, 39 g carbohydrates, 8.4 g fiber, 7.8 g fat (1.9 g saturated fat), 659 mg sodium*

*Limit sodium intake to 2,300 mg per day.

Smoky Lentil Soup

RS: 11 g

prep time
20 minutes

total time
1 hour
5 minutes

makes
4 servings
(1½ cups
each)

5 slices low-fat bacon
(such as Oscar
Mayer Center Cut,
30% Less Fat),
chopped

1 cup chopped onion

¾ cup chopped
celery

½ cup chopped
carrot

4 cloves garlic,
minced

1 teaspoon dried
basil

1 cup brown lentils,
picked over and
rinsed

2 cups reduced-
sodium chicken
broth

1 can (14.5 ounces)
no-salt-added, fire-
roasted diced
tomatoes

2 cups water

1 tablespoon lemon
juice

¼ teaspoon salt

¼ teaspoon freshly
ground black
pepper

1 Cook the bacon in a Dutch oven over medium-high heat, stirring occasionally, for 3 to 4 minutes, or until just starting to brown. Stir in the onion, celery, carrot, garlic, and basil. Reduce the heat to medium and cook, stirring occasionally, for 8 to 9 minutes, or until softened.

2 Stir in the lentils and cook for 1 minute. Add the broth, tomatoes, and water. Increase the heat to medium-high and bring to boil. Reduce the heat to medium-low, cover, and simmer for 30 to 32 minutes, or until the lentils are tender. Remove from the heat and stir in the lemon juice, salt, and pepper.

per serving 202 calories, 14 g protein, 30 g carbohydrates, 11 g fiber, 2.6 g fat (1.3 g saturated fat), 662 mg sodium*

*Limit sodium intake to 2,300 mg per day.

Navy Bean Minestrone

RS: 6 g

prep time
25 minutes

total time
1 hour
5 minutes

makes
4 servings
(1¾ cups
each)

1 tablespoon extra
virgin olive oil

1 medium onion,
chopped

1 large (12-ounce)
zucchini, cut into
½" cubes

3 medium carrots,
chopped

½ medium fennel
bulb, chopped

3 cloves garlic,
minced

1 teaspoon dried
basil

3 cups chopped kale

4 cups reduced-
sodium chicken
broth

3 tablespoons
tomato paste

4 ounces ditalini
pasta

1 can (15 ounces)
no-salt-added navy
beans, rinsed and
drained

½ teaspoon salt

¼ teaspoon freshly
ground black
pepper

1 Heat the oil in a large saucepan over medium-high heat. Add the onion, zucchini, carrots, fennel, garlic, and basil and cook, stirring occasionally, for 4 to 5 minutes, or until starting to soften. Stir in the kale and cook for 2 to 3 minutes, or until slightly wilted. Add the broth and tomato paste and bring to a boil. Reduce the heat to medium-low, cover, and simmer for 15 minutes.

2 Stir in the ditalini and return to a simmer. Cover and cook, stirring occasionally, for 10 to 11 minutes, or until the pasta is tender. Stir in the beans, salt, and pepper and cook for 1 to 2 minutes, or until the beans are heated through.

per serving 311 calories, 15 g protein, 55 g carbohydrates, 11 g fiber, 4.9 g fat (0.7 g saturated fat), 459 mg sodium

Green Pea Soup with Whole Grain Croutons

RS: 5 g

prep time
15 minutes

total time
45 minutes +
5 minutes
to cool

makes
4 servings
(1½ cups
each)

3 slices multigrain bread, cut into ½" cubes

1 tablespoon walnut oil

1 medium onion, chopped

2 medium carrots, chopped

2 ribs celery, chopped

1 teaspoon dried tarragon

4 cups reduced-sodium vegetable broth

2 packages (10 ounces each) frozen peas

¼ teaspoon salt

⅛ teaspoon freshly ground black pepper

1 Preheat the oven to 425°F. Coat a baking sheet with cooking spray.

2 Spread the bread cubes on the prepared baking sheet in a single layer. Bake, turning once, for 6 to 8 minutes, or until crisp and lightly browned. Remove from the oven and cool on the baking sheet.

3 Meanwhile, heat the oil in a large saucepan over medium heat. Add the onion, carrots, celery, and tarragon and cook, stirring occasionally, for about 10 minutes, or until the vegetables are soft. Stir in the broth and peas and increase the heat to medium-high. Bring to a boil and reduce the heat to medium-low. Cover and simmer for 10 minutes.

4 Uncover, increase the heat to medium, and simmer for 5 minutes longer, or until the peas are very tender and the soup has thickened very slightly. Remove from the heat and stir in the salt and pepper. Let cool for 5 minutes.

5 Transfer the soup in batches to a blender and puree. Serve warm with the croutons.

per serving 247 calories, 11 g protein, 39 g carbohydrates, 11 g fiber, 4.8 g fat (0.4 g saturated fat), 584 mg sodium

Curried Sweet Potato Soup with Peanut Gremolata

RS: 5 g

prep time
25 minutes

total time
52 minutes +
10 minutes
to cool

makes
6 servings
(1 cup each)

2 teaspoons walnut oil

1 medium onion, chopped

1 tablespoon grated fresh ginger

1 tablespoon curry powder

1½ pounds sweet potatoes, peeled and cut into 1" chunks

3½ cups reduced-sodium chicken broth

2 tablespoons agave nectar

¼ cup light cream

2 tablespoons fresh lemon juice

½ teaspoon salt

¼ cup lightly salted dry roasted peanuts, chopped

3 tablespoons chopped fresh cilantro

2 teaspoons grated fresh lemon zest

1 Heat the oil in a large pot over medium heat. Add the onion and ginger and cook, stirring occasionally, for 3 to 4 minutes, or until starting to soften. Stir in the curry powder and cook for 15 seconds, or until fragrant. Add the sweet potatoes, broth, and agave nectar and increase the heat to medium-high. Cover and bring to a boil. Reduce the heat to medium-low and simmer for 18 to 20 minutes, or until the potatoes are tender. Remove from the heat, stir in the cream, and let cool for 10 minutes.

2 Transfer the soup in batches to a blender and puree. Return to the pot and stir in the lemon juice and salt. The soup should be fairly thick. Keep warm.

3 Combine the peanuts, cilantro, and lemon zest in a small bowl. Divide the soup among 6 bowls, top each with some of the peanut mixture, and serve.

per serving 186 calories, 4 g protein, 29 g carbohydrates, 4 g fiber, 6.7 g fat (1.8 g saturated fat), 514 mg sodium

Caramelized Leek and Potato Soup

RS: 6 g

prep time
20 minutes

total time
55 minutes +
10 minutes
to cool

makes
4 servings
(1¼ cups
each)

1 tablespoon walnut oil

4 large leeks, white and pale green parts, chopped, washed, and drained

1 medium onion, chopped

1 teaspoon sugar

3 tablespoons dry vermouth

1 pound baking potatoes, peeled and cut into chunks

3 cups reduced-sodium chicken broth

⅓ cup light cream

¼ cup chopped fresh parsley

½ teaspoon salt

¼ teaspoon freshly ground black pepper

1 Heat the oil in a Dutch oven over medium heat. Add the leeks, onion, and sugar and cook, stirring occasionally, for 18 to 20 minutes, or until lightly golden and soft.

2 Stir in the vermouth and cook for about 1 minute, or until evaporated. Increase the heat to medium-high, add the potatoes and broth, and bring to a boil. Reduce the heat to medium-low and simmer for about 20 minutes, or until the potatoes are tender. Cool for 10 minutes.

3 Transfer the soup in batches to a blender and puree. Return to the pot and stir in the cream, parsley, salt, and pepper. Cook until heated through and serve.

per serving 272 calories, 8 g protein, 41 g carbohydrates, 4 g fiber, 8.8 g fat (3 g saturated fat), 380 mg sodium

Chapter

{6}

Sandwiches

No-Hassle BBQ Pulled Chicken on Whole Grain Rolls

RS: 1 g

prep time
10 minutes

total time
12 minutes

makes
2 servings

4 ounces cooked chicken breast

2½ tablespoons prepared barbecue sauce

2 tablespoons finely chopped red onion

½ small jalapeño chile pepper, finely chopped

2 whole grain hoagie rolls (about 2½ ounces each)

2 ounces shredded low-fat Cheddar cheese (such as Cabot 50% Less Fat Cheddar Cheese)

4 bread and butter pickle chips

1 Preheat the broiler.

2 With two forks or your fingers, shred the chicken and transfer to a bowl. Stir in the barbecue sauce, onion, and chile pepper.

3 Open the rolls and set cut side up on a baking sheet. Sprinkle the rolls with the cheese. Broil the rolls 5" from the heat for 1 to 1½ minutes, or until the cheese melts. Top with the chicken mixture and pickle chips.

per serving 380 calories, 32 g protein, 44 g carbo-hydrates, 5.5 g fiber, 9.74 g fat (4.1 g saturated fat), 857 mg sodium*

*Limit sodium intake to 2,300 mg per day.

Chicken and Potato Panini with Basil-Lemon Mayonnaise

RS: 3 g

prep time
20 minutes

total time
32 minutes

makes
4 servings

12 ounces boneless, skinless chicken breast halves

½ teaspoon salt

¼ teaspoon freshly ground black pepper

4 ounces red bliss potatoes, cut into ½" cubes

⅓ cup reduced-fat mayonnaise

¼ cup finely chopped red onion

¼ cup finely chopped celery

2 tablespoons chopped fresh basil

1 teaspoon grated fresh lemon zest

1 tablespoon fresh lemon juice

8 slices whole grain bread

1 Coat a grill pan with cooking spray and heat over medium-high heat. Sprinkle the chicken with ¼ teaspoon of the salt and ⅛ teaspoon of the pepper. Add the chicken to the grill pan and cook for 5 to 6 minutes per side, or until a thermometer inserted into the thickest portion registers 165°F. Transfer to a cutting board and cool for 10 minutes. Cut into ½" cubes.

2 Meanwhile, combine the potatoes in a small saucepan with enough cold water to cover by 2". Bring to a boil over medium-high heat and cook for 7 to 8 minutes, or until tender. Drain and cool for 10 minutes.

3 Combine the chicken, potatoes, mayonnaise, onion, celery, basil, lemon zest, lemon juice, and the remaining ¼ teaspoon salt and ⅛ teaspoon pepper in a bowl.

4 Arrange 4 slices of the bread on a work surface. Top each with one-fourth of the chicken mixture. Cover with the remaining slices of bread. Cut each in half diagonally and serve.

per serving 325 calories, 27 g protein, 30 g carbohydrates, 4.7 g fiber, 9.9 g fat (1.7 g saturated fat), 731 mg sodium*

*Limit sodium intake to 2,300 mg per day.

Chicken Soft Tacos with Fast Bean Salsa

RS: 4 g

prep time
15 minutes

total time
28 minutes

makes
4 servings
(2 tacos
each)

12 ounces boneless, skinless chicken thighs, trimmed

½ teaspoon garlic powder

¼ teaspoon ground coriander

⅛ teaspoon freshly ground black pepper

½ teaspoon salt

1 cup rinsed and drained no-salt-added pinto beans

½ cup chopped mango

¼ cup finely chopped white onion

2 tablespoons chopped fresh cilantro

1 tablespoon fresh lime juice

8 corn tortillas (6" each)

1 Coat a grill pan with cooking spray and heat to medium-high. Sprinkle the chicken with the garlic powder, coriander, pepper, and ¼ teaspoon of the salt. Add the chicken to the grill pan and cook for 7 to 8 minutes per side, or until a thermometer inserted into the thickest part of the thigh registers 175°F. Transfer to a cutting board and cut into thin strips.

2 Meanwhile, combine the beans, mango, onion, cilantro, lime juice, and the remaining ¼ teaspoon salt in a bowl.

3 Heat the tortillas per the package directions. Place 2 tortillas on each of 4 serving plates. Top with the chicken and salsa and serve immediately.

per serving 257 calories, 20 g protein, 36 g carbohydrates, 6.7 g fiber, 4.1 g fat (0.9 g saturated fat), 380 mg sodium

Shrimp Salad Rolls

RS: 5 g

prep time
15 minutes

total time
25 minutes

makes
2 servings

4 ounces red potatoes, cut into ¼" pieces

6 ounces cooked, peeled, and deveined shrimp, coarsely chopped

3 tablespoons finely chopped celery

2 tablespoons finely chopped sweet onion

2 tablespoons light mayonnaise

⅛ teaspoon freshly ground black pepper

2 whole grain hot dog buns

1 Combine the potatoes in a small saucepan with enough water to cover by 2". Bring to a boil over medium-high heat, reduce the heat to medium-low, and simmer for 6 to 7 minutes, or until tender. Drain, rinse under cold water, and drain again.

2 Combine the potatoes, shrimp, celery, onion, mayonnaise, and pepper in a bowl and mix well.

3 Toast the hot dog buns. Divide the shrimp mixture between buns and serve.

per serving 294 calories, 23 g protein, 33 g carbohydrates, 4 g fiber, 8 g fat (1.4 g saturated fat), 527 mg sodium

Smoked Salmon on Multigrain Bread with Lemon-Dill Cream Cheese

RS: 1 g

prep time
10 minutes

total time
11 minutes

makes
1 serving

2 tablespoons Neufchâtel cheese, softened

1 teaspoon chopped fresh dill

½ teaspoon grated lemon zest

2 slices multigrain bread

1½ ounces smoked salmon

1 tablespoon minced red onion

4 thin cucumber slices

2 thin tomato slices

1 Combine the cheese, dill, and lemon zest in a small bowl and mix well.

2 Toast the bread. Spread 1 slice with the cheese mixture. Top with the salmon, onion, cucumber, tomato, and then the second slice of bread. Cut in half diagonally and serve.

per serving 445 calories, 40 g protein, 42 g carbohydrates, 11 g fiber, 14 g fat (5 g saturated fat), 508 mg sodium

Teriyaki Tofu Wraps with Brown Rice

RS: 3 g

prep time
20 minutes

total time
30 minutes

makes
4 servings

2 teaspoons toasted sesame oil

1 package (14 ounces) light firm tofu, drained, pressed, and cut into ½" cubes

1 tablespoon grated fresh ginger

2 tablespoons + 1 teaspoon reduced-sodium soy sauce

2 tablespoons honey

1 cup cooked brown rice

½ cup grated carrots

4 scallions, chopped

½ medium cucumber, seeded and chopped

4 multigrain tortillas (7" each)

1 Heat the oil in a large nonstick skillet over medium-high heat. Add the tofu and cook, stirring occasionally, for 4 to 5 minutes, or until starting to become a golden brown. Add the ginger and cook for 1 to 2 minutes longer, or until the tofu is browned. Add 2 tablespoons of the soy sauce and the honey and heat for another 20 seconds. Stir in the rice and cook for 1 minute longer, or until heated through. Remove from the heat and stir in the carrots, scallions, cucumber, and the remaining 1 teaspoon soy sauce.

2 Warm the tortillas per the package directions. Place one-fourth of the tofu mixture down the center of 1 tortilla, leaving a 1½" border at the bottom. Fold the bottom of the tortilla up to slightly cover the filling, then roll up. Repeat with the remaining tortillas.

per serving 313 calories, 14 g protein, 48 g carbohydrates, 4 g fiber, 8.3 g fat (1.3 g saturated fat), 864 mg sodium*

*Limit sodium intake to 2,300 mg per day.

California Wrap

RS: 1 g

prep time
10 minutes

total time
13 minutes

makes
1 serving

4 ounces haricot verts

1 tablespoon fat-free mayonnaise

½ teaspoon balsamic vinegar

½ teaspoon Dijon mustard

1 whole grain tortilla (9" or 10" each)

⅕ medium Hass avocado, peeled, pitted, and sliced

¼ cup thinly sliced cucumber

2 tomato slices (¼" thick)

4 fresh basil leaves

1 Bring a small saucepan of lightly salted water to a boil. Add the haricot verts, return to a boil, and cook for 3 minutes. Drain, rinse under cold water, and drain again.

2 Combine the mayonnaise, vinegar, and mustard in small bowl. Spread over 1 side of the tortilla, leaving a 1" border around the edge. Now leaving a 1" border on both ends, place the avocado in a line down the center of the tortilla. Top with the haricot verts, cucumber, tomato, and basil leaves. Tucking the left and right sides over the filling, roll up jelly roll–style. Slice in half and serve.

per serving 290 calories, 7 g protein, 41 g carbohydrates, 8 g fiber, 8 g fat (0.7 g saturated fat), 392 mg sodium

Black Bean and Cheddar Burritos

RS: 6 g

prep time
15 minutes

total time
35 minutes

makes
4 servings

1 teaspoon olive oil

1 medium onion, chopped

3 cloves garlic, minced

1 teaspoon ground cumin

12 ounces plum tomatoes, chopped

¼ teaspoon salt

1 can (15 ounces) no-salt-added black beans, drained (not rinsed)

½ cup cooked brown rice

4 multigrain tortillas (7" each)

¾ cup shredded low-fat sharp Cheddar cheese (such as Cabot 50% Less Fat Cheddar Cheese)

½ cup prepared fat-free black bean and corn salsa (such as Newman's Own)

1 Heat the oil in a large nonstick skillet over medium-high heat. Add the onion and garlic and cook, stirring occasionally, for 1 to 2 minutes, or until starting to soften. Add the cumin and cook for 15 seconds, or until fragrant. Stir in the tomatoes and salt and cook for 1 to 2 minutes, or until the tomatoes start to wilt. Add the beans and cook for 2 to 3 minutes, or until hot. Stir in the rice and cook for 1 minute.

2 Warm the tortillas per the package directions. Place one-fourth of the bean mixture down the center of 1 tortilla, leaving a 1½" border at the bottom. Top with 3 tablespoons of the cheese and 2 tablespoons of the salsa. Fold the bottom up to slightly cover the filling then roll up. Repeat with the remaining tortillas.

per serving 329 calories, 17 g protein, 54 g carbohydrates, 9 g fiber, 6.5 g fat (2.5 g saturated fat), 580 mg sodium

Grilled Vegetable and Hummus Pitas

RS: 4 g

prep time
15 minutes

total time
25 minutes

makes
4 servings

1 can (15 ounces) no-salt-added chickpeas, rinsed and drained

1 tablespoon fresh lemon juice

4 teaspoons extra virgin olive oil

2 teaspoons tahini

1 clove garlic

½ teaspoon salt

¼ teaspoon freshly ground black pepper

1 medium (8-ounce) zucchini, cut into 12 slices

1 medium red onion, cut into 4 slices (¼" thick each)

4 whole wheat pitas (6" each)

1 large tomato, cut into 8 slices

1 To make the hummus: Combine the chickpeas, lemon juice, oil, tahini, garlic, ¼ teaspoon of the salt, and ⅛ teaspoon of the pepper in the bowl of a food processor. Process until smooth, adding a little water or broth if needed.

2 Coat a nonstick grill pan with cooking spray and heat to medium-high. Lightly coat the zucchini and onion with cooking spray and sprinkle with the remaining ¼ teaspoon of the salt and ⅛ teaspoon of the pepper. Add the zucchini and onion to the grill pan, in batches if necessary, and grill for 3 to 4 minutes per side, or until tender and well-marked.

3 Cut the top ½" off each pita. Open the pockets and fill each with ⅓ cup hummus, 3 zucchini slices, 1 onion slice (separated into rings), and 2 tomato slices.

per serving 314 calories, 12 g protein, 52 g carbohydrates, 9 g fiber, 8.3 g fat (1.1 g saturated fat), 621 mg sodium*

*Limit sodium intake to 2,300 mg per day.

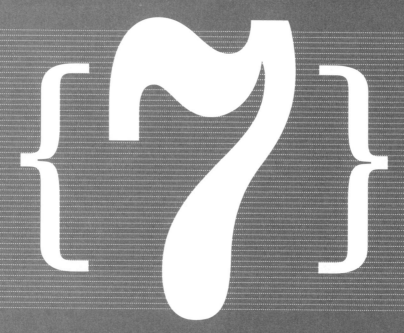

Chapter

{7}

Salads

Warm Succotash Salad with Bacon

RS: 6 g

prep time
10 minutes

total time
30 minutes +
5 minutes
to cool

makes
4 servings

½ cup long-grain white rice

1 cup frozen lima beans

1 cup fresh or frozen peas

1 cup fresh or frozen corn kernels

4 slices low-fat bacon (such as Oscar Mayer, Center Cut Bacon, 30% Less Fat)

1 medium onion, chopped

2 cloves garlic, minced

½ teaspoon salt

⅛ teaspoon freshly ground black pepper

1 tablespoon cider vinegar

¼ cup chopped fresh basil

1 Cook the rice per the package directions, omitting any salt or fat.

2 Meanwhile, bring a medium saucepan of lightly salted water to a boil over medium-high heat. Add the lima beans, return to a boil, and cook for 5 minutes. Stir in the peas and corn, cook for 1 minute, and drain.

3 Cook the bacon in a large nonstick skillet over medium-high heat, turning occasionally, for 5 to 6 minutes, or until crisp. Drain on a paper towel-lined plate and crumble.

4 Return the skillet to the heat and add the onion and garlic to the bacon drippings. Cook, stirring occasionally, for 1 to 2 minutes, or until starting to soften. Add the lima bean mixture and cook for 1 to 2 minutes, or until hot. Stir in the rice, bacon, salt, and pepper and cook for 1 minute. Remove from the heat, stir in the vinegar, and let cool for 5 minutes. Stir in the basil.

per serving 241 calories, 10 g protein, 45 g carbohydrates, 6.2 g fiber, 3 g fat (1.2 g saturated fat), 457 mg sodium

Farfalle Salad with Chicken, Almonds, and Grapes

RS: 4 g

prep time
10 minutes

total time
25 minutes

makes
4 servings

6 ounces farfalle

¼ cup sliced almonds

8 ounces cooked skinless chicken breast, cut into ½" cubes

1 cup seedless red grapes, halved

¼ cup chopped fresh parsley

2 tablespoons red-wine vinegar

1 tablespoon extra virgin olive oil

½ teaspoon salt

¼ teaspoon freshly ground black pepper

1 Bring a large pot of lightly salted water to a boil over medium-high heat. Add the pasta and cook per the package directions. Drain.

2 Meanwhile, heat a small skillet over medium heat. Add the almonds and cook for about 5 to 6 minutes, shaking the pan often, until lightly browned. Transfer to a bowl.

3 Combine the pasta, toasted almonds, chicken, grapes, and parsley in a large bowl. Combine the vinegar, oil, salt, and pepper in a separate bowl. Pour over the pasta mixture and toss well. Serve warm or at room temperature.

per serving 338 calories, 25 g protein, 39 g carbohydrates, 3 g fiber, 9.4 g fat (1.5 g saturated fat), 338 mg sodium

Chicken, Corn, and Black Bean Salad with Lime and Cilantro

RS: 5 g

prep time
20 minutes

total time
21 minutes

makes
4 servings

1½ cups fresh or frozen corn kernels

2 cups cubed cooked chicken breast

1 can (15 ounces) no-salt-added black beans, rinsed and drained

1 cup chopped red bell pepper

1 cup chopped mango

½ cup chopped white onion

2 tablespoons lime juice

2 tablespoons chopped fresh cilantro

1 tablespoon walnut oil

1 teaspoon ground cumin

1 Bring a small saucepan of lightly salted water to a boil. Add the corn and cook for 1 minute. Drain and let cool for 5 minutes.

2 Combine the cooled corn, chicken, beans, bell pepper, mango, and onion in a large bowl. Combine the lime juice, cilantro, oil, and cumin in a separate bowl. Pour over the corn mixture and toss to coat.

per serving 311 calories, 29 g protein, 35 g carbohydrates, 8 g fiber, 7 g fat (1.3 g saturated fat), 75 mg sodium

Salade Niçoise

RS: 8 g

prep time
15 minutes

total time
30 minutes

makes
4 servings

12 ounces red bliss potatoes, cut into ½" cubes

8 ounces haricot verts

4 tuna steaks (4 ounces each), about ¾" thick

½ teaspoon salt

¼ teaspoon freshly ground black pepper

2 tablespoons balsamic vinegar

1 teaspoon Dijon mustard

5 teaspoons extra virgin olive oil

2 tablespoons chopped fresh basil

4 large romaine lettuce leaves

2 cups grape tomatoes

12 niçoise olives

1 Combine the potatoes with enough cold water to cover by 2" in a medium saucepan. Bring to a boil over medium-high heat. Reduce the heat to medium-low and simmer for about 10 minutes, or until tender.

2 Meanwhile, bring a medium saucepan of lightly salted water to a boil. Add the haricot verts, return to a boil, and cook for 3 minutes. Drain, rinse under cold water, and drain again.

3 Coat a nonstick grill pan with cooking spray and heat to medium-high. Sprinkle the tuna with ¼ teaspoon of the salt and ⅛ teaspoon of the pepper. Add to the grill pan and cook for 3 to 4 minutes per side, or until the fish is opaque.

4 Combine the vinegar, mustard, and the remaining ¼ teaspoon salt and ⅛ teaspoon pepper in a bowl. Whisk in the oil until combined, then add the basil.

5 Arrange the lettuce leaves on a serving platter and place the tuna in the center. Toss the still-warm potatoes with 4 teaspoons of the dressing, then mound on the lettuce. Toss the haricot verts with 1 tablespoon of the dressing and mound on the lettuce. Toss the tomatoes with 1 tablespoon of the dressing and mound on the lettuce.

6 Drizzle the tuna steaks with the remaining dressing and top with the olives. Serve immediately.

per serving 319 calories, 30 g protein, 24 g carbohydrates, 4 g fiber, 10 g fat (1.6 g saturated fat), 758 mg sodium*

*Limit sodium intake to 2,300 mg per day.

White Bean Panzanella

RS: 4 g

prep time
15 minutes +
15 minutes
to stand

makes
4 servings

6 ounces peasant-style multigrain bread, toasted and cut into ½" cubes

1 can (15 ounces) no-salt-added cannellini beans, rinsed and drained

1 large cucumber, peeled and sliced

1 pint grape tomatoes, halved

½ cup thinly sliced red onion

⅓ cup fresh basil, julienned

3 tablespoons red-wine vinegar

2 tablespoons extra virgin olive oil

¼ teaspoon salt

¼ teaspoon freshly ground black pepper

Combine the bread, beans, cucumber, tomatoes, onion, and basil in a large bowl. Combine the vinegar, oil, salt, and pepper in a separate bowl. Pour over the bread mixture and toss well. Let stand for at least 15 minutes before serving.

per serving 273 calories, 9 g protein, 39 g carbohydrates, 7 g fiber, 9 g fat (1 g saturated fat), 326 mg sodium

French Lentil Salad

RS: 6 g

prep time
15 minutes

total time
35 minutes

makes
4 servings

1 cup French lentils, picked over and rinsed

4 cloves garlic

½ teaspoon salt

2 ribs celery, chopped

2 medium carrots, chopped

1 cup grape tomatoes, halved

½ cup finely chopped red onion

1 teaspoon grated fresh lemon zest

2 tablespoons fresh lemon juice

2 tablespoons extra virgin olive oil

¼ teaspoon freshly ground black pepper

1 Combine the lentils and garlic in a large saucepan with enough cold water to cover by 3". Bring to a boil over medium-high heat and cook for 19 to 20 minutes, or until the lentils are tender but still hold their shape. Stir in ¼ teaspoon of the salt and cook for 1 minute. Drain, rinse under cold water, and drain again. Discard the garlic cloves.

2 Transfer the lentils to a large bowl. Add the celery, carrots, tomatoes, onion, lemon zest, lemon juice, oil, pepper, and the remaining ¼ teaspoon salt, and toss well.

per serving 250 calories, 12 g protein, 36 g carbohydrates, 9 g fiber, 7.2 g fat (1 g saturated fat), 346 mg sodium

Wheat Berry and Barley Salad with Dried Fruit and Goat Cheese

RS: 5 g

prep time
20 minutes

total time
1 hour
20 minutes–
1 hour
30 minutes +
time to cool

makes
6 servings

½ cup wheat berries

1 cup quick-cooking barley

3 ounces semisoft goat cheese, crumbled

3 scallions, chopped

½ cup dried apricots, chopped

⅓ cup dried tart cherries

¼ cup golden raisins

3 tablespoons chopped fresh chives

3 tablespoons balsamic vinegar

1 tablespoon extra virgin olive oil

½ teaspoon salt

¼ teaspoon freshly ground black pepper

1 Cook the wheat berries per the package directions, 1 hour to 1½ hours. While the wheat berries are cooking, prepare the barley per the package directions. Drain, transfer to a bowl, and cool for 20 minutes. When the wheat berries are tender, drain, transfer to a bowl, and cool for 30 minutes.

2 Combine the wheat berries and barley in a large serving bowl. Add the goat cheese, scallions, apricots, cherries, raisins, chives, vinegar, oil, salt, and pepper and toss until well combined. Serve at room temperature.

per serving 262 calories, 8 g protein, 43 g carbohydrates, 7 g fiber, 7 g fat (3.2 g saturated fat), 272 mg sodium

Israeli Couscous, Chickpea, and Zucchini Salad with Lemon-Agave Dressing

RS: 7 g

prep time
10 minutes

total time
30 minutes +
time to cool

makes
4 servings

¾ cup Israeli couscous

1 can (15 ounces) no-salt-added chickpeas, rinsed and drained

1 large (12-ounce) zucchini, trimmed and cut into ½" cubes

1 large red bell pepper, chopped

¼ cup finely chopped red onion

3 tablespoons fresh lemon juice

2 tablespoons chopped fresh cilantro

1 tablespoon agave nectar

1 tablespoon olive oil

½ teaspoon salt

¼ teaspoon freshly ground black pepper

1 Cook the couscous per the package directions. Transfer to a large bowl and let cool for 20 minutes.

2 Add the chickpeas, zucchini, bell pepper, and onion to the couscous. Combine the lemon juice, cilantro, agave nectar, oil, salt, and pepper in a bowl. Stir into the couscous mixture. Serve at room temperature or chill until ready to serve. Stir before serving.

per serving 249 calories, 8 g protein, 45 g carbohydrates, 6 g fiber, 4.2 g fat (0.5 g saturated fat), 318 mg sodium

Barley, Feta, and Cranberry Salad with Lemon and Mint

RS: 8 g

prep time
20 minutes

total time
32 minutes +
time to cool

makes
4 servings

1 cup quick-cooking barley

2 ribs celery, finely chopped

⅓ cup crumbled reduced-fat feta cheese

¼ cup finely chopped red onion

¼ cup dried cranberries

2 tablespoons fresh lemon juice

2 tablespoons chopped fresh mint

1 tablespoon walnut oil

⅛ teaspoon salt

⅛ teaspoon freshly ground black pepper

1 Cook the barley per the package directions. Drain, transfer to a bowl, and let cool for 20 minutes.

2 Stir in the celery, cheese, onion, cranberries, lemon juice, mint, oil, salt, and pepper and toss well. Serve immediately or refrigerate until ready to serve. If refrigerating, stir well before serving.

per serving 206 calories, 6 g protein, 37 g carbohydrates, 4.8 g fiber, 5.3 g fat (1.3 g saturated fat), 246 mg sodium

Orzo Salad with Grape Tomatoes, Mozzarella, and Basil

RS: 6 g

prep time
15 minutes

total time
25 minutes

makes
4 servings

6 ounces orzo

1 pint grape tomatoes, halved

¼ cup finely chopped fennel bulb

¼ cup finely chopped red onion

¼ cup chopped fresh basil

3 ounces fresh mozzarella cheese, diced

3 tablespoons grated Romano cheese

2 tablespoons balsamic vinegar

1 tablespoon extra virgin olive oil

½ teaspoon salt

⅛ teaspoon freshly ground black pepper

1 Bring a large pot of lightly salted water to a boil over medium-high heat. Add the orzo and cook per the package directions. Drain, rinse under cold water, and drain again. Transfer to a large bowl.

2 Add the tomatoes, fennel, onion, basil, mozzarella cheese, Romano cheese, vinegar, oil, salt, and pepper and toss well.

per serving 293 calories, 12 g protein, 37 g carbohydrates, 3 g fiber, 10.1 g fat (4.7 g saturated fat), 197 mg sodium

Peanut Noodle Salad

RS: 4 g

prep time
10 minutes

total time
20 minutes

makes
4 servings

6 ounces spaghetti

8 ounces sugar snap peas

½ cup halved thinly sliced cucumber

¼ cup chopped scallions

¼ cup natural peanut butter

2 tablespoons cold water

1 tablespoon seasoned rice vinegar

1 tablespoon hoisin sauce

1 tablespoon honey

1 teaspoon sesame oil

1 Bring a large pot of lightly salted water to a boil. Add the spaghetti and cook per the package directions. Add the snap peas during the last 3 to 4 minutes of cooking. Drain, rinse under cold water, and drain again. Transfer to a large bowl and add the cucumber and scallions.

2 Combine the peanut butter, water, vinegar, hoisin sauce, honey, and oil in a small bowl and stir until smooth. Pour over the spaghetti mixture and toss well to coat.

per serving 329 calories, 10 g protein, 49 g carbohydrates, 4 g fiber, 9.8 g fat (1.3 g saturated fat), 236 mg sodium

Chapter

{8}

Side Dishes

Corn-Studded Jalapeño Cornbread

RS: 3 g

prep time
10 minutes

total time
35 minutes +
time to cool

makes
12 servings

1 cup all-purpose flour

1 cup stone-ground cornmeal

½ cup Hi-maize resistant starch

2 teaspoons baking powder

1 teaspoon salt

2 large eggs, lightly beaten

1 cup fat-free milk

1 cup fresh or thawed frozen corn kernels

¼ cup corn oil

2 tablespoons honey

2 jalapeño chile peppers, finely chopped

1 Preheat the oven to 425°F. Coat an 8" × 8" baking pan with cooking spray.

2 Combine the flour, cornmeal, resistant starch, baking powder, and salt in a bowl. Combine the eggs, milk, corn, oil, honey, and chile peppers in a separate bowl. Stir into the flour mixture until just moistened. Pour the batter into the prepared baking pan.

3 Bake for 24 to 25 minutes, or until lightly golden and a wooden pick inserted into the center comes out clean. Transfer to a rack and cool before cutting.

per serving 158 calories, 4 g protein, 25 g carbohydrates, 5 g fiber, 5.9 g fat (0.9 g saturated fat), 283 mg sodium

Grilled Parmesan-Corn Polenta

RS: 4 g

prep time
5 minutes

total time
20 minutes +
30 minutes
to cool

makes
4 servings

3 slices low-fat bacon (such as Oscar Mayer Center Cut Bacon, 30% Less Fat)

2 cups water

1 cup 1% milk

¼ teaspoon salt

¼ teaspoon freshly ground black pepper

½ cup instant polenta

3 tablespoons Hi-maize resistant starch

1 cup fresh or thawed frozen corn kernels

½ cup grated Parmesan cheese, preferably Parmigiano-Reggiano

1 Line an 8" × 8" baking dish with plastic wrap.

2 Cook the bacon in a medium nonstick skillet over medium-high heat, turning occasionally, for 5 to 6 minutes, or until crisp. Drain on a paper towel-lined plate and crumble.

3 Combine the water, milk, salt, and pepper in a medium saucepan over medium-high heat and bring to a boil. Combine the polenta and resistant starch, then slowly whisk into the milk mixture and cook, stirring often, for 3 to 4 minutes, or until thick. Mix in the corn and cook for 1 minute. Remove from the heat and stir in the bacon and cheese.

4 Pour the polenta into the prepared baking dish and spread into an even layer with a spatula. Cool completely for 30 to 35 minutes, or until firm.

5 Turn out the polenta onto a cutting board. With a sharp knife cut into 4 squares, then cut each square in half diagonally to make 8 triangles.

6 Coat a grill pan or a large nonstick skillet with cooking spray and heat over medium-high heat. Add the polenta triangles and cook for about 3 minutes per side, or until well marked, golden in color, and heated through.

per serving 228 calories, 11 g protein, 39 g carbohydrates, 5 g fiber, 5.4 g fat (3 g saturated fat), 432 mg sodium

Corn Flake–Crusted Noodle Kugel

RS: 3 g

prep time
10 minutes

total time
43 minutes +
5 minutes
to stand

makes
8 servings

8 ounces wide
eggless noodles

3 large eggs, lightly
beaten

1½ cups 1% cottage
cheese

½ cup golden raisins

½ cup 1% milk

5 tablespoons sugar

¾ teaspoon vanilla
extract

⅛ teaspoon ground
cinnamon

1½ cups corn flakes,
lightly crushed

1 tablespoon
unsalted butter,
melted

1 Preheat the oven to 350°F. Coat an 11" × 7" baking dish with cooking spray.

2 Bring a large pot of lightly salted water to a boil. Add the noodles and cook per the package directions. Drain and transfer to a large bowl.

3 Combine the eggs, cottage cheese, raisins, milk, 4 tablespoons of the sugar, the vanilla extract, and cinnamon in a bowl. Add to the noodles and toss well. Transfer to the prepared baking dish. Combine the remaining 1 tablespoon sugar with the corn flakes and melted butter in a bowl and mix well. Sprinkle over the top of the noodle mixture.

4 Bake for 35 to 40 minutes, or until the edges are lightly browned and the casserole has set. Let stand for 5 minutes before cutting. Serve hot, warm, or at room temperature.

per serving 272 calories, 14 g protein, 43 g carbohydrates, 2 g fiber, 4.6 g fat (1.8 g saturated fat), 315 mg sodium

Three-Mushroom and Barley Pilaf

RS: 8 g

prep time
10 minutes

total time
35 minutes

makes
4 servings

1 cup quick-cooking barley

5 teaspoons extra virgin olive oil

1 medium onion, chopped

¼ teaspoon dried thyme

6 ounces shiitake mushrooms, stemmed and sliced

4 ounces oyster mushrooms, sliced

4 ounces cremini mushrooms, sliced

3 cloves garlic, minced

⅓ cup dry sherry wine

½ teaspoon salt

¼ teaspoon freshly ground black pepper

1 Cook the barley per the package directions.

2 Meanwhile, heat the oil in a large nonstick skillet over medium-high heat. Add the onion and thyme and cook, stirring occasionally, for 1 to 2 minutes, or until starting to soften. Add the shiitake, oyster, and cremini mushrooms and cook for 6 to 7 minutes, or until softened and starting to brown. Stir in the garlic and cook for 2 to 3 minutes, or until the mushrooms are browned. Add the sherry and cook for 1 minute, or until evaporated.

3 Stir the barley, salt, and pepper into the mushroom mixture and cook for 1 minute. Serve hot.

per serving 226 calories, 7 g protein, 36 g carbohydrates, 6 g fiber, 6.4 g fat (0.8 g saturated fat), 303 mg sodium

Wild Mushroom Barley "Risotto"

RS: 5 g

prep time
10 minutes

total time
35 minutes

makes
4 servings

1 tablespoon extra virgin olive oil

½ cup chopped shallots

8 ounces sliced mixed wild mushrooms (shiitake, oyster, cremini)

2 cloves garlic, minced

2 tablespoons chopped fresh tarragon

¾ cup quick-cooking barley

1 can (14.5 ounces) reduced-sodium chicken broth

¼ cup grated Parmesan cheese

1 Heat the oil in a large saucepan over medium-high heat. Add the shallots and cook, stirring occasionally, for 2 to 3 minutes, or until starting to soften. Stir in the mushrooms and cook for 5 to 6 minutes, or until softened. Add the garlic and tarragon and cook for 1 minute.

2 Stir in the barley and cook, stirring, for 30 seconds. Pour in the broth and bring to a boil. Reduce the heat to medium-low, cover, and simmer for 10 to 12 minutes, or until the liquid is almost evaporated. Uncover and cook for 1 minute longer. Remove from the heat and stir in the cheese.

per serving 192 calories, 9 g protein, 29 g carbohydrates, 4 g fiber, 5.5 g fat (1.4 g saturated fat), 327 mg sodium

Sour Cream–Smashed Red Potatoes

RS: 6 g

prep time
5 minutes

total time
25 minutes

makes
4 servings

1¼ pounds red bliss potatoes, halved

¼ cup fat-free milk

1 tablespoon unsalted butter, melted

½ teaspoon salt

⅛ teaspoon freshly ground black pepper

⅓ cup light sour cream

Combine the potatoes in a medium saucepan with enough cold water to cover by 3". Bring to a boil over medium-high heat and cook for 17 to 18 minutes, or until tender. Drain. Return to the saucepan and add the milk, butter, salt, and pepper. Coarsely mash with a wooden spoon or fork. Gently stir in the sour cream.

per serving 157 calories, 5 g protein, 25 g carbohydrates, 2 g fiber, 4.8 g fat (2.9 g saturated fat), 319 mg sodium

Whole Grain
Blueberry Buttermilk
Pancakes *p. 56*

Grilled Vegetable and
Hummus Pitas *p. 93*

Potato, Red Pepper,
and Parmesan
Frittata *p. 51*

Egg and Bacon
Breakfast Sandwich *p. 53*

Israeli Couscous,
Chickpea, and Zucchini
Salad with Lemon-Agave
Dressing *p. 104*

Strawberry-Banana
Malted Milk *p. 190*

Dried Fruit and Oat Bran
Pretzel Trail Mix *p. 188*

Root Vegetable, Beef, and Barley Stew *p. 133*

Chicken and Potato
Panini with Basil-Lemon
Mayonnaise *p. 86*

Banana-Pecan
Oat Muffins *p. 62*

Spiced Corn Tortilla Crisps
with Pinto Bean Salsa *p. 184*

Chicken and
Whole Grain
Noodle Soup *p. 71*

Yam-Topped Turkey
and White Bean
Shepherd's Pie *p. 141*

Pizza
Margherita
p. 160

Glazed Mixed
Berry–Lemon
Bundt Cake *p. 198*

Sautéed Fruit Sundaes
with Sweet Tortilla
Crisps *p. 211*

Mixed Seafood
Risotto *p. 142*

Gingersnap-Crusted
Sweet Potato Pie
p. 199

Cranberry–Chocolate Chip Blondies *p. 197*
Chocolate Chip–Oatmeal Cookies *p. 195*

Colcannon

RS: 6 g

prep time
15 minutes

total time
30 minutes

makes
4 servings

1¼ **pounds baking potatoes, peeled and cut into 1" chunks**

7 **teaspoons unsalted butter**

½ **cup fat-free milk**

½ **teaspoon salt**

⅛ **teaspoon freshly ground black pepper**

3 **cups shredded cabbage (about ½ small head)**

1 Combine the potatoes in a medium saucepan with enough cold water to cover by 3". Bring to a boil over medium-high heat and cook for 11 to 12 minutes, or until tender. Drain and mash with a potato masher or put through a ricer. Return the potatoes to the saucepan and stir in 5 teaspoons of the butter, the milk, salt, and pepper until combined.

2 Meanwhile, melt the remaining 2 teaspoons butter in a medium nonstick skillet over medium-high heat. Add the cabbage and cook, stirring often, for 5 to 6 minutes, or until tender and starting to brown.

3 Stir the cabbage into the potato mixture until well combined.

per serving 157 calories, 4 g protein, 19 g carbohydrates, 3 g fiber, 6.9 g fat (4.3 g saturated fat), 321 mg sodium

Mashed Potatoes with Parmesan Aioli

RS: 6 g

prep time
10 minutes

total time
20 minutes

makes
4 servings

1¼ pounds baking potatoes, peeled and cut into 1" chunks

¼ cup fat-free milk

¼ cup grated Parmesan cheese

3 tablespoons light mayonnaise

1 tablespoon fresh lemon juice

1 clove garlic, minced

¼ teaspoon salt

⅛ teaspoon freshly ground black pepper

1 Combine the potatoes in a medium saucepan with enough cold water to cover by 3". Bring to a boil over medium-high heat and cook for 11 to 12 minutes, or until tender. Drain and mash with a potato masher or put through a ricer. Return the potatoes to the saucepan and stir in the milk until smooth.

2 Combine the cheese, mayonnaise, lemon juice, garlic, salt, and pepper in a bowl. Pour over the potato mixture and stir until well combined.

per serving 179 calories, 6 g protein, 28 g carbohydrates, 2 g fiber, 5.2 g fat (1.5 g saturated fat), 327 mg sodium

Bacon, Cheddar, and Chive Stuffed Potatoes

RS: 6 g

prep time
10 minutes

total time
25 minutes +
5 minutes
to stand

makes
4 servings

4 baking potatoes (5 to 6 ounces each), scrubbed

4 slices low-fat bacon (such as Oscar Mayer Center Cut Bacon, 30% Less Fat)

4 ounces low-fat sharp Cheddar cheese (such as Cabot 50% Less Fat Cheddar Cheese), shredded

2 tablespoons chopped fresh chives

¼ teaspoon salt

¼ teaspoon freshly ground black pepper

¼ cup fat-free sour cream

1 Prick the potatoes in several places with a fork. Set on a microwave-safe plate and microwave on high for 8 to 12 minutes, or until tender. Remove from the microwave and let stand for 5 minutes.

2 Meanwhile, cook the bacon in a medium non-stick skillet over medium-high heat, turning occasionally, for 5 to 6 minutes, or until crisp. Drain on a paper towel-lined plate. Crumble and reserve.

3 Halve each potato lengthwise. Using a spoon, scoop out the potato flesh, leaving a ¼"-thick shell. Coarsely mash the potato flesh in a medium bowl with a fork. Stir in the bacon, cheese, chives, salt, and pepper.

4 Divide the potato mixture among the 8 potato shells. Set on a microwave-safe plate and microwave on high for 1 to 2 minutes, or until hot. Top each potato half with sour cream and serve.

per serving 223 calories, 14 g protein, 28 g carbohydrates, 2 g fiber, 6.9 g fat (4.2 g saturated fat), 471 mg sodium

Note: If you have time, boil the potato in Step 1 instead of microwaving it. This will preserve even more RS.

Tex-Mex Potato Salad

RS: 8 g

prep time
20 minutes

total time
35 minutes +
time to cool

makes
4 servings

1 pound red potatoes
1 teaspoon corn oil
1 cup fresh or thawed frozen corn kernels
2 cloves garlic, minced
1 medium green bell pepper, chopped
½ cup chopped celery
⅓ cup chopped sweet onion
¼ cup light mayonnaise
1 tablespoon cider vinegar
¼ teaspoon ground chipotle pepper
¼ teaspoon salt

1 Combine the potatoes in a large saucepan with enough cold water to cover by 2". Bring to a boil over medium-high heat, reduce the heat to medium-low, and simmer for 10 to 12 minutes, or until tender. Drain and let cool for 15 minutes. Cut into ½" cubes and transfer to a large bowl.

2 Meanwhile, heat the oil in a medium nonstick skillet over medium-high heat. Add the corn and garlic and cook, stirring often, for 3 to 4 minutes, or until lightly browned.

3 Transfer the corn mixture to the bowl with the potatoes. Stir in the bell pepper, celery, onion, mayonnaise, vinegar, chipotle pepper, and salt.

per serving 191 calories, 4 g protein, 31 g carbohydrates, 4 g fiber, 6.6 g fat (1 g saturated fat), 293 mg sodium

Potato and Edamame with Sesame and Scallions

RS: 4 g

prep time
15 minutes

total time
30 minutes

makes
4 servings

12 ounces red bliss potatoes, cut into ½" cubes

1 cup frozen shelled edamame

1 tablespoon sesame oil

1 small onion, chopped

2 teaspoons grated fresh ginger

3 scallions, chopped

¼ teaspoon salt

1 Combine the potatoes in a medium saucepan with enough cold water to cover by 3". Bring to a boil over medium-high heat and cook for 8 minutes. Stir in the edamame, return to a boil, and cook for 2 to 3 minutes longer, or until the potatoes are tender. Drain.

2 Heat the oil in a large nonstick skillet over medium-high heat. Add the onion and ginger and cook, stirring occasionally, for 1 to 2 minutes, or until starting to soften. Stir in the potato mixture and cook, stirring, for 1 minute. Remove from the heat and stir in the scallions and salt.

per serving 151 calories, 6 g protein, 21 g carbohydrates, 4 g fiber, 5 g fat (0.5 g saturated fat), 168 mg sodium

Maple Whipped Sweet Potatoes

RS: 5 g

prep time
10 minutes

total time
20 minutes

makes
4 servings

1¼ pounds sweet potatoes, peeled and cut into 1" chunks

2 tablespoons unsalted butter

2 tablespoons maple syrup

½ teaspoon salt

⅛ teaspoon freshly ground black pepper

1 teaspoon grated fresh orange zest

Combine the potatoes in a medium saucepan with enough cold water to cover by 3". Bring to a boil over medium-high heat and cook for 10 to 12 minutes, or until tender. Drain. Transfer to the bowl of a food processor and add the butter, syrup, salt, and pepper. Process until smooth. Stir in the orange zest.

per serving 184 calories, 2 g protein, 32 g carbohydrates, 3.8 g fiber, 5.9 g fat (3.6 g saturated fat), 360 mg sodium

Curried Rice

RS: 5 g

prep time
15 minutes

total time
40 minutes +
5 minutes
to stand

makes
4 servings

2 teaspoons walnut oil
1 medium onion, chopped
1 tablespoon grated fresh ginger
1 teaspoon curry powder
1 cup long-grain white rice
2 cups water
¼ cup golden raisins
½ teaspoon salt
2 tablespoons chopped fresh basil
1 tablespoon chopped fresh mint

1 Heat the oil in a medium saucepan over medium-high heat. Add the onion and ginger and cook, stirring occasionally, for 1 to 2 minutes, or until starting to soften. Stir in the curry powder and cook for 30 seconds, or until fragrant. Add the rice and cook, stirring, for 1 minute.

2 Stir in the water, raisins, and salt. Bring to a boil, cover, and reduce the heat to medium-low. Simmer for 20 minutes, or until the water is absorbed. Remove from the heat and let stand for 5 minutes. Stir in the basil and mint.

per serving 236 calories, 4 g protein, 48 g carbohydrates, 2 g fiber, 2.8 g fat (0.4 g saturated fat), 297 mg sodium

Caramelized Onion and Pea Rice Pilaf

RS: 6 g

prep time
15 minutes

total time
35 minutes

makes
4 servings

¾ cup long-grain white rice

½ teaspoon salt

1 tablespoon walnut oil

2 cups chopped onions

1 teaspoon dried tarragon

2 cloves garlic, minced

¾ cup frozen peas

⅛ teaspoon freshly ground black pepper

1 Cook the rice per the package directions with ¼ teaspoon of the salt.

2 Meanwhile, heat the oil in a medium nonstick skillet over medium-high heat. Add the onions and tarragon and cook, stirring often, for 7 to 8 minutes, or until lightly browned. Stir in the garlic and cook for 2 minutes, or until softened and starting to brown. Add the peas, pepper, and the remaining ¼ teaspoon salt and cook for 2 minutes, or until heated through.

3 Stir the onion mixture into the rice and serve.

per serving 201 calories, 5 g protein, 38 g carbohydrates, 3 g fiber, 4 g fat (0.5 g saturated fat), 325 mg sodium

Brown Rice with Spinach, Peas, Lemon, and Parsley

RS: 8 g

prep time
15 minutes

total time
25 minutes

makes
4 servings

1 cup quick-cooking brown rice

4 teaspoons extra virgin olive oil

4 cloves garlic, sliced

1 large shallot, finely chopped

1 bag (6 ounces) baby spinach

1 cup frozen peas

⅓ cup chopped fresh parsley

1 tablespoon grated fresh lemon zest

½ teaspoon salt

¼ teaspoon freshly ground black pepper

1 Cook the rice per the package directions.

2 Meanwhile, heat the oil in a large nonstick skillet over medium-high heat. Add the garlic and shallot and cook, stirring occasionally, for 1 to 2 minutes, or until the garlic begins to brown. Add the spinach and cook, turning with kitchen tongs, for 1 to 2 minutes, or until wilted. Stir in the peas and cook for 2 minutes longer, or until heated through. Remove from the heat and stir in the rice, parsley, lemon zest, salt, and pepper. Serve hot.

per serving 171 calories, 5 g protein, 28 g carbohydrates, 5 g fiber, 5.3 g fat (0.7 g saturated fat), 405 mg sodium

Maduros
(Sautéed Sweet Plantains)

RS: 3 g

prep time
5 minutes

total time
10 minutes

makes
4 servings

1 tablespoon walnut oil

2 very ripe plantains (see note), peeled and cut diagonally into ½"-thick slices

2 tablespoons agave nectar

⅛ teaspoon salt

Heat the oil in a large nonstick skillet over medium-high heat. Add the plantains and cook, turning occasionally, for 5 to 6 minutes, or until well browned and tender. Remove from the heat and stir in the agave nectar and salt. Serve immediately.

per serving 169 calories, 1 g protein, 27 g carbohydrates, 2 g fiber, 3.7 g fat (0.4 g saturated fat), 76 mg sodium

NOTE: Very ripe plantains should have turned almost, if not completely, black.

Chilled Haricot Verts with Herbs, Lemon, and Olive Oil

RS: 10 g

prep time
15 minutes

total time
20 minutes +
1 hour to chill

makes
4 servings

1 pound haricot verts, trimmed

2 tablespoons chopped fresh parsley

2 tablespoons chopped fresh basil

1 tablespoon chopped fresh chives

1 tablespoon fresh lemon juice

1 tablespoon extra virgin olive oil

¼ teaspoon salt

⅛ teaspoon freshly ground black pepper

Bring a large pot of lightly salted water to a boil. Add the haricot verts, return to a boil, and cook for 2 minutes. Drain and rinse under cold water, then drain again. Transfer to a large bowl and add the parsley, basil, chives, lemon juice, oil, salt, and pepper and toss well. Refrigerate for at least 1 hour before serving.

per serving 81 calories, 1 g protein, 7 g carbohydrates, 2.8 g fiber, 3.5 g fat (0.5 g saturated fat), 147 mg sodium

Chapter

{9}

Meat, Poultry, and Seafood Entrées

Beef and Chipotle Two-Potato Skillet

RS: 6 g

prep time
20 minutes

total time
35 minutes

makes
4 servings

8 ounces baking potato, peeled and cut into ½" cubes

8 ounces sweet potato, peeled and cut into ½" cubes

12 ounces 93% lean ground beef

1 medium onion, chopped

1 small red bell pepper, chopped

2 cloves garlic, minced

1 teaspoon dried oregano

1 teaspoon chili powder

⅛–¼ teaspoon ground chipotle pepper

½ cup reduced-sodium beef broth

½ teaspoon salt

1 Combine the baking potato and sweet potato in a medium skillet with enough water to cover by 2". Bring to a boil and cook for 7 minutes. Drain.

2 Meanwhile, heat a large nonstick skillet over medium-high heat. Add the beef and cook, breaking it into smaller pieces with a wooden spoon, for 4 to 5 minutes, or until no longer pink. Stir in the onion, bell pepper, garlic, and oregano and cook, stirring occasionally, for 5 to 6 minutes, or until starting to brown.

3 Add the potatoes to the beef mixture, along with the chili powder and chipotle pepper. Cook for 3 to 4 minutes, or until the potatoes are starting to brown. Add the broth and salt and cook, tossing often, for about 1 minute, or until the liquid is mostly absorbed.

per serving 237 calories, 20 g protein, 25 g carbohydrates, 3 g fiber, 6.3 g fat (2.3 g saturated fat), 379 mg sodium

Spaghetti Pie Bolognese

RS: 6 g

prep time
15 minutes

total time
55 minutes

makes
4 servings

6 ounces spaghetti

1 large egg, lightly beaten

½ cup grated Parmesan cheese

1½ teaspoons dried basil

8 ounces 93% lean ground beef

1 cup chopped onion

2 cloves garlic, minced

1 can (14.5 ounces) no-salt-added diced tomatoes

1 tablespoon tomato paste

¼ teaspoon ground red pepper

1 cup frozen peas

¼ teaspoon salt

⅛ teaspoon freshly ground black pepper

1 Preheat the oven to 350°F. Coat a 9" deep-dish pie plate with cooking spray.

2 Bring a pot of lightly salted water to a boil. Add the spaghetti and cook per the package directions. Drain, rinse under cold water, and drain again.

3 Toss the spaghetti in a bowl with the egg, 6 tablespoons of the cheese, and 1 teaspoon of the basil. Press the spaghetti mixture onto the bottom and up the side of the prepared pie plate.

4 Heat a large nonstick skillet over medium-high heat. Add the beef and cook, stirring and breaking it into smaller pieces with a wooden spoon, for 3 to 4 minutes, or until no longer red. Stir in the onion, garlic, and the remaining ½ teaspoon basil and cook for 2 to 3 minutes, or until starting to soften. Add the tomatoes, tomato paste, and red pepper and cook for 3 to 4 minutes, or until starting to thicken. Add the peas, salt, and black pepper and cook for 1 minute.

5 Spoon the mixture over the spaghetti in the pie plate. Sprinkle with the remaining 2 tablespoons cheese. Cover with aluminum foil. Bake for 15 minutes. Remove the foil and bake for 5 minutes longer, or until the cheese melts. Cut into 4 wedges to serve.

per serving 376 calories, 26 g protein, 46 g carbohydrates, 5 g fiber, 9 g fat (3.8 g saturated fat), 436 mg sodium

Root Vegetable, Beef, and Barley Stew

RS: 5 g

prep time
20 minutes

total time
1 hour
35 minutes +
5 minutes
to stand

makes
6 servings

2 teaspoons olive oil

1 pound lean top round beef, trimmed and cut into ¾" chunks

12 ounces white turnips, peeled and cut into 24 pieces total

1 medium onion, chopped

3 medium carrots, cut into 1" chunks

2 ribs celery, cut into 1" pieces

8 cloves garlic, minced

½ teaspoon dried thyme

4 cups reduced-sodium beef broth

1 cup quick-cooking barley

½ teaspoon salt

¼ teaspoon freshly ground black pepper

1 Heat the oil in a large pot over medium-high heat. Add the beef and cook, turning occasionally, for about 4 minutes, or until browned. Stir in the turnips, onion, carrots, celery, garlic, and thyme and cook, stirring occasionally, for 4 minutes. Pour in the broth and bring to a boil. Reduce the heat to medium-low, cover, and simmer for 30 minutes.

2 Stir in the barley, cover, and return to a simmer. Cook for about 30 minutes, or until the barley is cooked through and the beef is tender. Remove from the heat, stir in the salt and pepper, and let stand for 5 minutes.

per serving 253 calories, 24 g protein, 29 g carbohydrates, 4.8 g fiber, 5 g fat (1.3 g saturated fat), 424 mg sodium

Tamale Pie with Red Beans and Corn

RS: 5 g

prep time
15 minutes

total time
40 minutes +
5 minutes
to cool

makes
4 servings

4 ounces 93% lean
ground beef

1 medium onion,
chopped

2 cloves garlic,
minced

1 cup frozen corn
kernels

1½ teaspoons chili
powder

¾ teaspoon ground
cumin

1 can (15 ounces)
no-salt-added
red kidney beans,
drained

1 can (14.5 ounces)
no-salt-added,
fire-roasted diced
tomatoes

¼ teaspoon salt

¾ ounce semisweet
chocolate

2½ ounces baked
tortilla chips, lightly
crushed (1 cup)

2 ounces shredded
low-fat sharp
Cheddar cheese
(such as Cabot
50% Less Fat
Cheddar Cheese)

1 Preheat the oven to 375°F. Coat an 8" × 8" baking dish with cooking spray.

2 Coat a nonstick skillet with cooking spray and heat over medium-high heat. Add the beef and cook, breaking it into smaller pieces with a wooden spoon, for 3 to 5 minutes, or until no longer pink. Stir in the onion, garlic, and corn and cook, stirring occasionally, for 3 to 4 minutes, or until starting to soften. Add the chili powder and cumin and cook for about 15 seconds, or until fragrant. Stir in the beans, tomatoes, and salt and cook for 2 minutes, or until heated through. Remove from the heat and stir in the chocolate until melted and combined.

3 Transfer the mixture to the prepared baking dish. Top with the tortilla chips and cheese. Bake for about 15 minutes, or until bubbly and the cheese has melted. Let cool for 5 minutes before serving.

per serving 315 calories, 19 g protein, 43 g carbohydrates, 10 g fiber, 8.6 g fat (3.7 g saturated fat), 649 mg sodium*

*Limit sodium intake to 2,300 mg per day.

Pork Tenderloin, Haricot Verts, and Pea Stir-Fry over Scallion Noodles

RS: 12 g

prep time
15 minutes

total time
40 minutes

makes
4 servings

4 ounces spaghetti

3 tablespoons reduced-sodium soy sauce

2 scallions, chopped

1 pound pork tenderloin, trimmed and cut into ¾" chunks

3 teaspoons toasted sesame oil

1 medium onion, chopped

8 ounces haricot verts, trimmed

¼ cup water

1 tablespoon grated fresh ginger

1 cup frozen peas

1 tablespoon honey

1 teaspoon garlic black bean sauce

1 Bring a large pot of lightly salted water to a boil over medium-high heat. Add the spaghetti and cook per the package directions. Drain, transfer to a bowl, and toss with 1 tablespoon of the soy sauce and the scallions. Keep warm.

2 Meanwhile, combine the pork and 1 tablespoon of the soy sauce in a bowl. Heat 1 teaspoon of the oil in a large nonstick skillet over medium-high heat. Add the pork and cook, stirring occasionally, for about 4 minutes, or until no longer pink. Transfer the pork to a bowl and reserve.

3 Return the skillet to the heat and add the remaining 2 teaspoons of oil. Add the onion and cook, stirring often, for about 1 minute, or until starting to soften slightly. Add the haricot verts and water and cook for 1 to 1½ minutes, or until the water evaporates. Stir in the ginger and cook for 30 seconds. Add the peas and cook for 1 minute, or until bright green. Stir in the pork, the remaining 1 tablespoon soy sauce, honey, and black bean sauce. Cook, stirring, for 1 to 2 minutes, or until hot. Serve over the spaghetti mixture.

per serving 349 calories, 31 g protein, 38 g carbohydrates, 4 g fiber, 6.5 g fat (1.4 g saturated fat), 568 mg sodium

Jerk Chicken with Mashed Sweet Plantains

RS: 4 g

prep time
10 minutes

total time
25 minutes

makes
4 servings

3 very ripe medium plantains (see note), cut into 1" chunks

¼ cup fat-free milk

1 teaspoon walnut oil

⅛ teaspoon salt

4 boneless, skinless chicken breast halves (6 ounces each)

1½ teaspoons jerk seasoning

1 Combine the plantains in a medium saucepan with enough cold water to cover by 2". Bring to a boil over medium-high heat and cook for 10 to 15 minutes, or until tender. Drain, return to the saucepan, and add the milk, oil, and salt. Mash until fairly smooth. Keep warm.

2 Meanwhile, coat a nonstick grill pan with cooking spray and heat on medium-high. Rub the chicken with the jerk seasoning and add to the pan. Cook for 5 to 6 minutes per side, or until the chicken is well marked and a thermometer inserted in the thickest portion registers 165°F. Serve with the plantains.

per serving 366 calories, 42 g protein, 44 g carbohydrates, 3 g fiber, 3.8 g fat (0.9 g saturated fat), 300 mg sodium

Note: Very ripe plantains should have turned almost, if not completely, black.

Sweet Potato and Black Bean Cakes with Chicken and Cumin-Cilantro Cream

RS: 6 g

prep time
15 minutes

total time
45 minutes

makes
4 servings
(2 cakes
each)

8 ounces sweet potato, peeled and cut into ¼" cubes

¾ cup all-purpose flour

1 teaspoon baking powder

1 teaspoon dried oregano

½ teaspoon salt

¾ teaspoon ground cumin

½ cup fat-free milk

1 large egg

1 can (15 ounces) no-salt-added black beans, rinsed and drained

4 teaspoons olive oil

½ cup fat-free sour cream

1 tablespoon chopped fresh cilantro

8 ounces cooked chicken breast, shredded

1 Combine the sweet potato in a small saucepan with enough water to cover by 2". Bring to a boil and cook for about 5 minutes, or until the potato is tender but still holds its shape. Drain, rinse under cold water, and drain again.

2 Combine the flour, baking powder, oregano, salt, and ½ teaspoon of the cumin in a bowl. Whisk together the milk and egg in a separate bowl. Add to the flour mixture, stirring until just moistened. Gently fold in the sweet potato and the beans.

3 Heat 2 teaspoons of the oil in a large nonstick skillet over medium heat. Add 4 scant ½ cups of the sweet potato batter. Cook for about 5 minutes, or until the tops are covered with bubbles. Turn and cook for 5 minutes longer. Remove from the skillet and keep warm. Repeat with the remaining oil and batter.

4 Meanwhile, combine the sour cream, cilantro, and remaining ¼ teaspoon of cumin in a bowl.

5 Place 2 cakes onto each of 4 plates. Top each serving with one-fourth of the chicken and 2 tablespoons of the cumin-cilantro cream and serve.

per serving 386 calories, 30 g protein, 44 g carbohydrates, 5.6 g fiber, 9 g fat (2.1 g saturated fat), 527 mg sodium

Arroz con Pollo

RS: 5 g

prep time
20 minutes

total time
1 hour
5 minutes +
5 minutes
to stand

makes
6 servings

2 teaspoons olive oil

1 pound boneless, skinless chicken thighs, trimmed and cut into ¾" chunks

½ teaspoon salt

¼ teaspoon freshly ground black pepper

1 medium onion, chopped

1 medium green bell pepper, chopped

4 cloves garlic, minced

1 teaspoon dried oregano

1 cup long-grain white rice

½ teaspoon ground turmeric

16 stuffed Manzanilla olives

2¼ cups reduced-sodium chicken broth

1 cup frozen peas

1 Heat 1 teaspoon of the oil in a Dutch oven over medium-high heat. Sprinkle the chicken with ¼ teaspoon of the salt and ⅛ teaspoon of the pepper. Add the chicken to the Dutch oven and cook, turning occasionally, for 5 to 6 minutes, or until the chicken is browned. Transfer to a plate.

2 Return the Dutch oven to the heat and add the remaining 1 teaspoon oil. Stir in the onion and bell pepper and cook, stirring occasionally, for 5 to 6 minutes, or until starting to brown. Add the garlic and oregano and cook for 1 minute. Stir in the rice and turmeric and cook for 1 minute longer. Add the olives, broth, and the reserved chicken. Bring to a boil and reduce the heat to medium-low. Cover and simmer for 30 minutes, or until the rice is tender.

3 Stir in the peas and the remaining ¼ teaspoon salt and ⅛ teaspoon pepper. Cook for 1 minute, or until the peas are heated through. Let stand for 5 minutes before serving.

per serving 287 calories, 21 g protein, 33 g carbohydrates, 2 g fiber, 7.2 g fat (1.3 g saturated fat), 529 mg sodium

Orecchiette with Garlic, Sausage, and Broccoli Rabe

RS: 5 g

prep time
15 minutes

total time
35 minutes

makes
4 servings

1 pound broccoli rabe, woody stems trimmed

8 ounces orecchiette

1 tablespoon extra virgin olive oil

8 ounces sweet Italian turkey sausage, removed from casings

1 medium onion, chopped

4 cloves garlic, minced

⅛ teaspoon crushed red-pepper flakes

½ teaspoon salt

1 Bring a large pot of lightly salted water to a boil. Add the broccoli rabe and cook for 3 minutes. Remove with kitchen tongs and drain well. Transfer to a cutting board and coarsely chop. Reserve.

2 Return the water to a boil, add the pasta, and cook per the package directions. Drain.

3 Heat the oil in a large nonstick skillet over medium-high heat. Add the sausage and cook, breaking it into smaller pieces with a wooden spoon, for 3 to 4 minutes, or until browned. Stir in the onion, garlic, and red-pepper flakes and cook, stirring occasionally, for 3 to 4 minutes, or until the onion begins to brown. Add the broccoli rabe and cook for 1 to 2 minutes, or until hot. Stir in the orecchiette and salt and cook for 1 minute.

per serving 385 calories, 21 g protein, 52 g carbohydrates, 10.5 g fiber, 10.5 g fat (0.7 g saturated fat), 694 mg sodium*

*Limit sodium intake to 2,300 mg per day.

Baked Penne with Ground Turkey, Ricotta, and Mozzarella

RS: 6 g

prep time
10 minutes

total time
50 minutes +
5 minutes
to stand

makes
6 servings

8 ounces penne

8 ounces ground turkey

2 cloves garlic, minced

1½ cups prepared tomato-basil pasta sauce

1 cup fat-free ricotta cheese

1 cup shredded reduced-fat mozzarella cheese

¼ cup grated Romano cheese

1 Preheat the oven to 350°F. Coat a 6-cup baking dish with cooking spray.

2 Bring a large pot of lightly salted water to a boil over medium-high heat. Add the penne and cook per the package directions. Drain.

3 Meanwhile, heat a large nonstick skillet over medium-high heat. Add the turkey and cook, breaking it into smaller pieces with a wooden spoon, for 3 to 4 minutes, or until no longer pink. Stir in the garlic and cook for 1 minute. Add the sauce, bring to a simmer, and cook for 2 minutes. Remove from the heat.

4 Combine the ricotta, ¾ cup of the mozzarella, and the Romano cheese in a bowl. Arrange half of the penne in the bottom of the prepared baking dish. Top with half of the turkey mixture, then spread with the cheese mixture. Top with the remaining penne and turkey mixture. Sprinkle with the remaining ¼ cup mozzarella.

5 Cover with foil that has been coated with cooking spray. Bake for 28 to 30 minutes, or until hot. Let stand for 5 minutes before serving.

per serving 298 calories, 27 g protein, 37 g carbohydrates, 1 g fiber, 5.4 g fat (3 g saturated fat), 471 mg sodium

Yam-Topped Turkey and White Bean Shepherd's Pie

RS: 11 g

prep time
15 minutes

total time
52 minutes +
10 minutes
to cool

makes
4 servings

1 pound yams, peeled and cut into chunks

1 cup 1% milk

½ teaspoon salt

¼ teaspoon freshly ground black pepper

1 pound lean ground turkey breast

1 medium onion, chopped

3 cloves garlic, minced

¼ teaspoon dried thyme

1½ cups frozen peas and carrots

1 cup rinsed and drained no-salt-added navy beans

2 tablespoons Hi-maize resistant starch

1 tablespoon cornstarch

2 teaspoons Dijon mustard

1 teaspoon Worcestershire sauce

1 Preheat the oven to 350°F. Coat a 6-cup baking dish with cooking spray.

2 Combine the yams in a medium saucepan with enough cold water to cover by 2". Bring to a boil over medium-high heat and cook for 10 minutes, or until tender. Drain and return the potatoes to the pan. Add ¼ cup of the milk, ¼ teaspoon of the salt, and ⅛ teaspoon of the pepper and mash. Reserve.

3 Meanwhile, coat a large nonstick skillet with cooking spray and heat over medium-high heat. Add the turkey and cook, breaking it into smaller pieces with a wooden spoon, for 4 to 5 minutes, or until no longer pink. Mix in the onion, garlic, and thyme and cook, stirring occasionally, for 4 to 5 minutes, or until the turkey starts to brown and the onion begins to soften. Add the peas and carrots and beans and cook for 1 minute. Remove from the heat and stir in the remaining ¾ cup milk, the resistant starch, cornstarch, mustard, Worcestershire sauce, and the remaining ¼ teaspoon salt and ⅛ teaspoon pepper.

4 Pour the mixture into the prepared baking dish. Spread the top with the mashed yams to cover. Bake for 20 to 25 minutes, or until the filling is bubbly and the top is very slightly browned. Cool for 10 minutes before serving.

per serving 347 calories, 37 g protein, 49 g carbohydrates, 11 g fiber, 2.7 g fat (0.5 g saturated fat), 563 mg sodium

Mixed Seafood Risotto

RS: 6 g

prep time
15 minutes

total time
57 minutes

makes
4 servings

5 cups reduced-sodium chicken broth

1 tablespoon extra virgin olive oil

½ cup finely chopped shallots

3 cloves garlic, minced

¾ cup Arborio rice

¼ teaspoon saffron threads, lightly crushed

⅓ cup dry vermouth

1 cup frozen peas

½ pound bay scallops

½ pound peeled, deveined medium shrimp

¼ teaspoon salt

¼ teaspoon freshly ground black pepper

1 Bring the broth to a simmer in a medium saucepan over medium-low heat.

2 Heat the oil in a 3-quart saucepan over medium heat. Add the shallots and garlic and cook, stirring with a wooden spoon, for about 2 minutes, or until softened. Add the rice and saffron and cook, stirring, for 1 minute. Pour in the vermouth and cook, stirring, for 1 to 1½ minutes, or until almost completely absorbed. Add ½ cup of the hot broth and cook, stirring constantly, until the broth is almost completely absorbed. Continue cooking and adding broth, about ½ cup at a time, for 27 to 32 minutes, or until the rice is creamy but still slightly toothsome.

3 Add the peas and cook for 1 minute. Stir in the scallops and shrimp and cook, stirring occasionally, for 3 to 4 minutes, or until the seafood is cooked through. Season with the salt and pepper. Serve immediately.

per serving 377 calories, 29 g protein, 41 g carbohydrates, 3.2 g fiber, 5.4 g fat (0.8 g saturated fat), 451 mg sodium

Creamy Smoked Salmon and Dill Fettuccine

RS: 4 g

prep time
10 minutes

total time
30 minutes

makes
4 servings

6 ounces fettuccine

1½ cups 1% milk

7 teaspoons all-purpose flour

¼ teaspoon salt

⅛ teaspoon freshly ground black pepper

3 ounces Neufchâtel cheese, softened

4 ounces smoked salmon, chopped

1 tablespoon chopped fresh dill

2 teaspoons grated fresh lemon zest

1 Bring a large pot of lightly salted water to a boil. Add the fettuccine and cook per the package directions. Drain, leaving slightly wet, and return to the pot.

2 Meanwhile, combine the milk, flour, salt, and pepper in a medium saucepan over medium heat. Cook, stirring constantly, for about 5 minutes, or until the mixture thickens and begins to boil. Stir in the cheese and cook for about 1 minute, or until melted. Stir in the salmon, dill, and lemon zest and cook for 30 seconds.

3 Pour the sauce over the fettuccine and toss well. Serve immediately.

per serving 322 calories, 22 g protein, 41 g carbohydrates, 2 g fiber, 8 g fat (4.2 g saturated fat), 449 mg sodium

Seared Salmon over Curried Lentils

RS: 5 g

prep time
15 minutes

total time
55 minutes

makes
4 servings

2½ cups water
½ cup brown lentils, picked over and rinsed
4 cloves garlic, peeled
1 bay leaf
½ teaspoon salt
1 teaspoon olive oil
1 cup chopped onion
½ cup chopped carrot
2 cloves garlic, minced
¾ teaspoon curry powder
1 tablespoon chopped fresh mint
4 salmon fillets (4 ounces each)
¼ teaspoon freshly ground black pepper
Lemon wedges (optional)

1 Combine the water, lentils, whole garlic cloves, bay leaf, and ¼ teaspoon of the salt in a medium saucepan over medium-high heat. Bring to a boil and reduce the heat to medium-low. Cover and simmer for 20 to 22 minutes, or until tender. Remove from the heat and discard the bay leaf and garlic cloves.

2 Heat the oil in a 10" nonstick skillet over medium-high heat. Add the onion and carrot and cook, stirring occasionally, for 2 to 3 minutes, or until starting to soften. Add the minced garlic and curry powder and cook, stirring, for 1 minute. Add the lentils and cook for 1 minute. Remove from heat and stir in the mint. Divide among 4 plates.

3 Using a paper towel, wipe the skillet clean. Coat with cooking spray and heat over medium-high heat. Sprinkle the salmon with the pepper and the remaining ¼ teaspoon salt. Add to the skillet, skin side up, and cook for 4 minutes per side, or until the fish is opaque. Serve the salmon over the lentils with the lemon wedges if desired.

per serving 304 calories, 28 g protein, 17 g carbohydrates, 6 g fiber, 13.6 g fat (2.7 g saturated fat), 374 mg sodium

Cornmeal-Crusted Potato Cod Cakes with Tartar Sauce

RS: 4 g

prep time
20 minutes

total time
55 minutes

makes
4 servings

¼ cup light mayonnaise

2 tablespoons sweet pickle relish, drained

12 ounces baking potato

1 pound skinless cod fillets

4 teaspoons olive oil

1 large shallot, finely chopped

2 cloves garlic, minced

¼ teaspoon dried thyme

1 large egg, lightly beaten

½ teaspoon salt

¼ teaspoon freshly ground black pepper

3 tablespoons cornmeal

1 To make the tartar sauce, combine the mayonnaise and relish in a bowl and reserve.

2 Prick the potato with a fork in several places. Microwave for 8 to 9 minutes, or until tender. Let cool for 5 minutes. Peel and mash in a bowl.

3 Meanwhile, fill a large skillet two-thirds full of water and bring to a boil over medium-high heat. Add the cod and reduce the heat to medium. Cook, turning once, for 8 to 10 minutes, or until the fish is cooked through. Remove with a slotted spoon or spatula and drain well. Add the cod to the bowl with the potatoes, breaking it into smaller pieces.

4 Meanwhile, heat 1 teaspoon of the oil in a large nonstick skillet over medium-high heat. Add the shallot, garlic, and thyme and cook, stirring often, for 2 minutes.

5 Stir the shallot mixture into the potato mixture. Add the egg, salt, and pepper and mix well. Divide the mixture into 4 portions, about ½ cup each, and form each into a patty that is 3½" in diameter and ¾" thick. Spread the cornmeal on a plate and dredge each patty in it to coat.

6 Place the nonstick skillet over medium heat and add the remaining 3 teaspoons oil. Add the patties and cook for 6 minutes per side, or until browned and cooked through. Serve with the tartar sauce.

per serving 310 calories, 24 g protein, 26 g carbohydrates, 2 g fiber, 12 g fat (1.9 g saturated fat), 556 mg sodium

Note: If you have time, boil the potato in Step 2 instead of microwaving it. This will preserve even more RS.

Shrimp and Clam Paella

RS: 3 g

prep time
15 minutes

total time
45 minutes

makes
4 servings

1 tablespoon extra virgin olive oil

1 medium onion, chopped

1 medium red bell pepper, chopped

2 cloves garlic, minced

¼ teaspoon saffron threads, lightly crushed

½ cup long-grain white rice

1 cup reduced-sodium chicken broth

⅔ cup frozen peas

12 stuffed Manzanilla green olives, halved crosswise

12 littleneck clams, scrubbed

1 pound peeled, deveined large shrimp

1 Heat the oil in a large nonstick skillet over medium-high heat. Add the onion, bell pepper, garlic, and saffron and cook, stirring occasionally, for about 2 minutes, or until the vegetables begin to soften. Stir in the rice and cook for 1 minute. Add the broth, bring to a boil, and reduce the heat to medium-low. Cover and simmer for 5 minutes.

2 Add the peas and olives and cook for 15 minutes. Stir in the clams and shrimp and cook for 5 to 7 minutes, or until the clams have opened and the shrimp are pink and cooked through. Serve immediately.

per serving 323 calories, 30 g protein, 29 g carbohydrates, 2 g fiber, 8 g fat (1 g saturated fat), 566 mg sodium

Shrimp and Haricot Vert Fajitas

RS: 5 g

prep time
15 minutes

total time
30 minutes

makes
4 servings

4 ounces haricot verts, trimmed

1 pound peeled, deveined large shrimp

1 teaspoon chili powder

3 teaspoons olive oil

1 medium onion, thinly sliced

1 jalapeño chile pepper, seeded and thinly sliced

2 plum tomatoes, cut into 4 wedges each

1 teaspoon Worcestershire sauce

¼ teaspoon salt

4 whole wheat flour tortillas (9"–10" each)

¼ cup fat-free corn and black bean salsa (such as Newman's Own)

1 Bring a large saucepan of lightly salted water to a boil. Add the haricot verts and cook for 2 minutes. Drain and reserve.

2 Toss the shrimp in a bowl with the chili powder. Heat 2 teaspoons of the oil in a large nonstick skillet over medium-high heat. Add the shrimp and cook for about 2 minutes per side, or until opaque and cooked through. Transfer to a plate and reserve.

3 Return the skillet to the stove and heat the remaining 1 teaspoon oil. Add the onion and chile pepper and cook, stirring occasionally, for 3 to 4 minutes, or until starting to brown. Add the haricot verts and tomatoes and cook, stirring occasionally, for 2 to 3 minutes, or until the tomatoes have wilted. Stir in the shrimp, Worcestershire sauce, and salt and cook for 1 minute, or until hot. Remove from the heat.

4 Heat the tortillas per the package directions. Top each with one-fourth of the shrimp mixture, then with 1 tablespoon salsa. Serve immediately.

per serving 317 calories, 28 g protein, 30 g carbohydrates, 5 g fiber, 8.1 g fat (0.9 g saturated fat), 706 mg sodium*

*Limit sodium intake to 2,300 mg per day.

Grilled Shrimp with Mango-Banana Salsa

RS: 3 g

prep time
20 minutes

total time
26 minutes

makes
4 servings

2 slightly green bananas, chopped

1 cup chopped mango

3 tablespoons finely chopped red onion

2 tablespoons chopped fresh cilantro

1 jalapeño chile pepper, finely chopped

1 tablespoon lime juice

½ teaspoon salt

1 pound peeled, deveined large shrimp

1 tablespoon walnut oil

1 Combine the bananas, mango, onion, cilantro, chile pepper, lime juice, and ¼ teaspoon of the salt in a bowl.

2 Coat a nonstick grill pan with cooking spray and heat on medium-high. Toss the shrimp with the oil and the remaining ¼ teaspoon salt. Add the shrimp to the grill and cook for 3 minutes per side, or until opaque.

3 Divide the shrimp among 4 plates and top each serving with ½ cup salsa.

per serving 212 calories, 21 g protein, 21 g carbohydrates, 2 g fiber, 5.4 g fat (0.7 g saturated fat), 440 mg sodium

Shrimp and Mixed Vegetable Fried Rice

RS: 4 g

prep time
20 minutes

total time
35 minutes

makes
4 servings

3 teaspoons walnut oil

¾ pound peeled, deveined medium shrimp

2 eggs, lightly beaten

1 cup chopped onion

2 teaspoons grated fresh ginger

2 cloves garlic, minced

1 cup frozen peas and carrots

2 cups cold, preferably day-old, white rice

4 medium scallions, chopped

2 tablespoons reduced-sodium soy sauce

1 Heat 1 teaspoon of the oil in a large nonstick skillet over medium-high heat. Add the shrimp and cook for 2 to 3 minutes per side, or until opaque. Transfer to a plate.

2 Return the skillet to the heat and add 1 teaspoon of the oil and the eggs. Cook, stirring occasionally, for 1 to 2 minutes, or until the eggs are cooked. Transfer to the plate with the shrimp.

3 Heat the remaining 1 teaspoon of oil in the skillet and add the onion, ginger, and garlic. Cook, stirring, for 1 minute. Add the peas and carrots and cook for 2 minutes. Add the reserved shrimp and eggs and cook for 1 minute. Stir in the rice and cook, stirring, for 2 to 3 minutes, or until heated through. Add the scallions and soy sauce and cook for 30 seconds longer, or until well combined.

per serving 306 calories, 25 g protein, 33 g carbohydrates, 3 g fiber, 7.8 g fat (1.5 g saturated fat), 496 mg sodium

Chapter

{10}

Vegetarian Entrées

Home-Style Macaroni and Cheese

RS: 4 g

prep time
10 minutes

total time
40 minutes +
5 minutes
to stand

makes
4 servings

6 ounces elbow macaroni

1 cup fat-free milk

2 tablespoons all-purpose flour

¼ teaspoon dry mustard

¼ teaspoon salt

⅛ teaspoon freshly ground black pepper

4 ounces shredded low-fat sharp Cheddar cheese (such as Cabot 50% Less Fat Cheddar Cheese)

¼ cup grated Romano cheese

2 slices multigrain bread

2 teaspoons unsalted butter, melted

1 Preheat the oven to 350°F. Coat a 6-cup baking dish with cooking spray.

2 Bring a large pot of lightly salted water to a boil. Add the macaroni and cook per the package directions. Drain and transfer to a bowl.

3 Combine the milk, flour, mustard, salt, and pepper in a medium saucepan over medium heat and cook, stirring, for 4 to 6 minutes, or until slightly thickened. Stir in the Cheddar and Romano cheeses and cook for about 30 seconds, or until melted. Pour over the macaroni and toss well to coat. Pour into the prepared baking dish.

4 Place the bread in the bowl of a food processor and process to crumbs. Transfer to a small bowl and stir in the butter. Sprinkle over the macaroni mixture.

5 Bake in the center of the oven for about 20 minutes, or until the topping is browned and the pasta is hot. Let stand for 5 minutes before serving.

per serving 398 calories, 20 g protein, 49 g carbohydrates, 2.6 g fiber, 13.9 g fat (8.2 g saturated fat), 542 mg sodium

Penne Pomodoro

RS: 5 g

prep time
10 minutes

total time
15 minutes

makes
4 servings

8 ounces penne

5 teaspoons extra virgin olive oil

3 cloves garlic, minced

1¼ pounds plum tomatoes, seeded and chopped

¼ teaspoon salt

¼ teaspoon freshly ground black pepper

⅓ cup grated Romano cheese

¼ cup chopped fresh basil

1 Bring a large pot of lightly salted water to a boil. Add the penne and cook per the package directions. Drain.

2 Meanwhile, heat the oil in a large nonstick skillet over medium-high heat. Add the garlic and cook for 45 seconds, or until starting to brown. Mix in the tomatoes, salt, and pepper and cook, stirring occasionally, for 2 to 3 minutes, or until starting to soften.

3 Stir the penne and cheese into the sauce and cook for 1 minute. Remove from the heat and stir in the basil.

per serving 324 calories, 12 g protein, 49 g carbohydrates, 4 g fiber, 9.8 g fat (2.8 g saturated fat), 307 mg sodium

Ratatouille Lasagna

RS: 5 g

prep time
30 minutes

total time
2 hours +
15 minutes
to cool

makes
8 servings

2 tablespoons extra virgin olive oil

1 pound eggplant, trimmed and cut into ½" cubes

2 medium onions, chopped

1½ teaspoons dried basil

1 large red bell pepper, chopped

1 large (12-ounce) zucchini, trimmed and cut into ½" cubes

2 cans (14.5 ounces each) no-salt-added diced tomatoes

½ teaspoon salt

1 container (15 ounces) fat-free ricotta cheese

1½ cups shredded part-skim mozzarella cheese (6 ounces)

½ cup grated Romano cheese

1 large egg white

12 no-boil lasagna noodles (about 8 ounces)

1 To make the ratatouille: Heat 1 tablespoon of the oil in a large nonstick skillet over medium-high heat. Add the eggplant and cook, stirring occasionally, for 9 to 10 minutes, or until softened. Transfer to a bowl. Return the skillet to the heat and add the remaining 1 tablespoon oil, the onions, and basil. Cook, stirring occasionally, for 2 to 3 minutes, or until starting to soften. Add the bell pepper and zucchini and cook for 5 to 6 minutes, or until tender. Stir in the diced eggplant, tomatoes, and ¼ teaspoon of the salt. Cook, stirring occasionally, for 6 to 7 minutes, or until slightly thickened.

2 Meanwhile, combine the ricotta cheese, 1 cup of the mozzarella cheese, the Romano cheese, egg white, and the remaining ¼ teaspoon salt in a bowl.

3 Preheat the oven to 375°F. Coat a 13" × 9" pan with cooking spray.

4 Arrange 4 lasagna noodles in the bottom of the prepared pan. Spread with half of the ricotta mixture, then top with 2 cups of the ratatouille. Repeat the layering with 4 lasagna noodles, the remaining ricotta mixture, and 2 cups ratatouille. Top with the remaining 4 lasagna noodles. Spread the top layer of noodles with the remaining ratatouille then sprinkle with the remaining ½ cup mozzarella.

5 Cover with foil that has been coated with cooking spray. Bake for 45 minutes. Uncover and continue baking for 15 minutes, or until bubbly and the mozzarella on top is melted. Let cool for 15 minutes before cutting.

per serving 312 calories, 20 g protein, 33 g carbohydrates, 5 g fiber, 9.3 g fat (3.0 g saturated fat), 467 mg sodium

Lentil and Tomato Pasta Toss

RS: 6 g

prep time
15 minutes

total time
45 minutes

makes
4 servings

½ cup French lentils, picked over and rinsed

6 ounces penne

4 teaspoons extra virgin olive oil

1 medium onion, chopped

3 ribs celery, chopped

5 cloves garlic, thinly sliced

12 ounces plum tomatoes, chopped

½ teaspoon salt

¼ teaspoon freshly ground black pepper

¼ cup grated Parmesan cheese

1 Combine the lentils in a large saucepan with enough water to cover by 3". Bring to a boil and reduce the heat to medium-low. Cover and simmer for 20 to 22 minutes, or until the lentils are tender but hold their shape. Drain.

2 Meanwhile, bring a large pot of lightly salted water to a boil. Add the penne and cook per the package directions. Drain.

3 Heat the oil in a large nonstick skillet over medium-high heat. Add the onion, celery, and garlic and cook, stirring occasionally, for 4 to 5 minutes, or until the vegetables are crisp-tender and the garlic has started to brown. Add the lentils and tomatoes and cook for 2 to 3 minutes, or until the tomatoes soften.

4 Stir the penne, salt, and pepper into the sauce and cook, tossing, for 1 minute. Divide among 4 bowls and top each with 1 tablespoon of the cheese. Serve immediately.

per serving 330 calories, 15 g protein, 54 g carbohydrates, 7 g fiber, 6.9 g fat (1.7 g saturated fat), 407 mg sodium

Fettuccine Alfredo

RS: 8 g

prep time
5 minutes

total time
13-17 minutes

makes
4 servings

6 ounces fettuccine

1¼ cups fat-free milk

3 tablespoons Hi-maize resistant starch

2 tablespoons all-purpose flour

1 tablespoon unsalted butter

⅛ teaspoon ground nutmeg

¼ teaspoon salt

⅛ teaspoon freshly ground black pepper

½ cup grated Parmesan cheese

1 Bring a pot of lightly salted water to a boil. Add the fettuccine and cook per the package directions. Drain and transfer to a large bowl.

2 Meanwhile, combine the milk, resistant starch, flour, butter, nutmeg, salt, and pepper in a saucepan over medium-low heat. Cook, stirring constantly, for 1 to 2 minutes, or until the mixture thickens and begins to boil. Remove from the heat and stir in the cheese until smooth.

3 Pour the sauce over the fettuccine and toss.

per serving 270 calories, 13 g protein, 43 g carbohydrates, 5 g fiber, 6.4 g fat (3.8 g saturated fat), 333 mg sodium

Fusilli Salsa Cruda

RS: 5 g

prep time
10 minutes

total time
20-25
minutes

makes
4 servings

8 ounces fusilli

1 pound plum
tomatoes, chopped

12 pitted kalamata
olives, sliced

⅓ cup thinly sliced
fresh basil

2 tablespoons fresh
lemon juice

2 tablespoons extra
virgin olive oil

1 tablespoon capers,
drained and
chopped

½ teaspoon salt

¼ teaspoon freshly
ground black
pepper

1 Bring a large pot of lightly salted water to a boil. Add the fusilli and cook per the package directions. Drain and transfer to a bowl.

2 Meanwhile, combine the tomatoes, olives, basil, lemon juice, oil, capers, salt, and pepper in a bowl.

3 Pour the tomato mixture over the hot fusilli and toss well to combine. Serve hot or at room temperature.

per serving 321 calories, 8 g protein, 48 g carbohydrates, 4 g fiber, 11.2 g fat (1.4 g saturated fat), 544 mg sodium

Linguine with Parsley-Basil Pesto

RS: 6 g

prep time
10 minutes

total time
23 minutes

makes
4 servings

8 ounces linguine

1 cup fresh basil leaves

½ cup fresh parsley

3 tablespoons walnuts, toasted

3 tablespoons grated Romano cheese

2 tablespoons water

1 tablespoon fresh lemon juice

1 clove garlic

¼ teaspoon salt

4 teaspoons extra virgin olive oil

1 Bring a large pot of lightly salted water to a boil. Add the linguine and cook per the package directions. Drain and return to the pot.

2 Meanwhile, combine the basil, parsley, walnuts, cheese, water, lemon juice, garlic, and salt in a blender and puree. Add the oil and process until blended.

3 Toss the pesto with the linguine to coat and serve immediately.

per serving 311 calories, 10 g protein, 44 g carbohydrates, 3 g fiber, 10.5 g fat (2.2 g saturated fat), 238 mg sodium

Pizza Margherita

RS: 5 g

prep time
20 minutes +
1 hour for
dough to rise

total time
1 hour
45 minutes

makes
6 servings

1 package (0.75 ounce) active dry yeast

1 teaspoon sugar

1 cup warm water (105°–110°F)

4 teaspoons extra virgin olive oil

1½ cups all-purpose flour

½ cup Hi-maize resistant starch

2 tablespoons vital wheat gluten

1 teaspoon salt

2 large tomatoes, thinly sliced

1 cup shredded part-skim mozzarella cheese

⅓ cup grated Parmesan cheese

14 fresh basil leaves

1 Combine the yeast and sugar in a bowl with the warm water. Stir well and let stand in a warm place for 10 minutes, or until frothy. Stir in 3 teaspoons of the oil.

2 Combine the flour, resistant starch, vital wheat gluten, and salt in a large bowl. Add the yeast mixture and stir with a wooden spoon until a rough dough forms. Knead the dough in the bowl for about 5 minutes, or until fairly smooth. Coat a separate bowl with cooking spray and add the dough. Also coat the dough with cooking spray, cover with plastic wrap, and let stand in a warm place (85°F) free from drafts for about 1 hour, or until doubled in bulk.

3 Preheat the oven to 425°F. Coat a 16" pizza pan with cooking spray.

4 Gently press on the dough to deflate. Turn out onto a lightly floured surface and stretch or roll, then fit into the prepared pan. Spread the dough with the remaining 1 teaspoon oil. Starting at the outer edge, make concentric circles with the tomato slices working in toward the center. Sprinkle with the mozzarella and Parmesan cheeses.

5 Bake the pizza for 22 to 24 minutes, or until the crust is golden and the cheese is melted and lightly browned. Top with the basil leaves, cut into 6 slices, and serve.

per serving 250 calories, 13 g protein, 37 g carbohydrates, 7.1 g fiber, 7.5 g fat (3.0 g saturated fat), 595 mg sodium

Rosemary and Potato Pizza

RS: 9 g

prep time
30 minutes +
1 hour for
dough to rise

total time
2 hours
5 minutes

makes
6 servings

1 package (0.75 ounce) active dry yeast

1 teaspoon sugar

1 cup warm water (100°–110°F)

4 teaspoons extra virgin olive oil

1½ cups all-purpose flour

½ cup Hi-maize resistant starch

2 tablespoons vital wheat gluten

1 teaspoon salt

8 ounces baking potato, peeled and cut into thin slices

8 slices reduced-fat provolone cheese

1 jar (7.5 ounces) roasted red peppers, rinsed, drained, patted dry, and cut into strips

6 cloves garlic, thinly sliced

5 teaspoons fresh rosemary leaves

1 Combine the yeast and sugar in a bowl with the warm water. Stir well and let stand in a warm place for 10 minutes, or until frothy. Stir in 1 teaspoon of the oil.

2 Combine the flour, resistant starch, vital wheat gluten, and salt in a large bowl. Add the yeast mixture and stir with a wooden spoon until a rough dough forms. Knead the dough in the bowl for about 5 minutes, or until fairly smooth. Coat a separate bowl with cooking spray and add the dough. Also coat the dough with cooking spray, cover with plastic wrap, and let stand in a warm place (85°F) free from drafts for about 1 hour, or until doubled in bulk.

3 Meanwhile, combine the potato in a small saucepan with enough water to cover by 2". Bring to a boil and cook for 4 minutes, or until tender but firm. Drain and let cool.

4 Preheat the oven to 425°F. Coat a 16" pizza pan with cooking spray.

5 Gently press on the dough to deflate. Turn out onto a lightly floured surface and stretch or roll, then fit into the prepared pan. Spread the dough with 2 teaspoons of the oil. Top with the cheese. Starting at the outer edge, make concentric circles with the potato slices, working in toward the center.

6 Toss the pepper strips and garlic with the remaining 1 teaspoon oil in a small bowl. Top the pizza with the pepper strips, garlic, and rosemary.

7 Bake the pizza for 24 to 25 minutes, or until the crust is golden and the garlic is lightly browned. Cut into 6 slices and serve.

per serving 280 calories, 13 g protein, 44 g carbohydrates, 8 g fiber, 8.2 g fat (3.1 g saturated fat), 595 mg sodium

Hoisin Tofu and Snap Pea Stir-Fry over Brown Rice

RS: 5 g

prep time
15 minutes

total time
40 minutes

makes
4 servings

⅔ cup quick-cooking brown rice

3 tablespoons hoisin sauce

2 tablespoons oyster-flavored sauce

3 teaspoons sesame oil

1 package (14 ounces) light firm tofu (such as Nasoya), drained and cut into ½" cubes

4 ounces sliced shiitake mushrooms

1 tablespoon grated fresh ginger

8 ounces sugar snap peas

2 medium carrots, sliced

1 cup frozen peas

3 scallions, chopped

1 Cook the rice per the package directions, omitting any salt or fat.

2 Meanwhile, combine the hoisin and oyster sauces in a small bowl.

3 Heat 2 teaspoons of the sesame oil in a large nonstick skillet over medium-high heat. Add the tofu and cook, stirring occasionally, for 4 to 5 minutes, or until just beginning to brown. Transfer to a bowl.

4 Heat the remaining 1 teaspoon oil in the skillet and add the mushrooms and ginger. Cook, stirring occasionally, for 3 to 5 minutes, or until softened. Stir in the snap peas, carrots, and peas and cook for 3 minutes, or until crisp-tender. Add the reserved tofu and hoisin mixture and cook, stirring, for 2 to 3 minutes, or until heated through. Remove from the heat and stir in the scallions. Serve over the rice.

per serving 252 calories, 14 g protein, 36 g carbohydrates, 6.2 g fiber, 6.2 g fat (0.8 g saturated fat), 546 mg sodium

North African Spiced Chickpeas and Rice

RS: 10 g

prep time
15 minutes

total time
35 minutes

makes
4 servings

½ cup long-grain white rice

1½ tablespoons olive oil

1 large onion, thinly sliced

4 cloves garlic, sliced

1 teaspoon ground cumin

½ teaspoon ground turmeric

¼ teaspoon ground ginger

3 plum tomatoes, coarsely chopped

2 cans (15 ounces each) no-salt-added chickpeas, rinsed and drained

½ teaspoon salt

¼ teaspoon freshly ground black pepper

2 tablespoons chopped fresh basil

1 Cook the rice per the package directions, omitting any salt or fat.

2 Meanwhile, heat the oil in a large nonstick skillet over medium-high heat. Add the onion and cook, stirring occasionally, for 6 to 7 minutes, or until starting to brown. Stir in the garlic and cook for 1 to 2 minutes, or until starting to brown. Add the cumin, turmeric, and ginger and cook for 15 seconds, or until fragrant. Add the tomatoes and cook for 2 to 3 minutes, or until starting to soften. Add the chickpeas, salt, and pepper and cook, stirring occasionally, for 2 to 3 minutes, or until hot. Remove from the heat and stir in the basil.

3 Serve the chickpeas over the rice.

per serving 310 calories, 11 g protein, 52 g carbohydrates, 8 g fiber, 6.7 g fat (0.8 g saturated fat), 332 mg sodium

Cuban Black Beans and Rice

RS: 11 g

prep time
20 minutes

total time
42 minutes

makes
4 servings

¾ cup long-grain white rice

1 tablespoon olive oil

1 cup chopped white onion

1 cup chopped red bell pepper

1 cup chopped green bell pepper

4 cloves garlic, minced

1 teaspoon dried oregano

1 teaspoon ground cumin

1 tablespoon red-wine vinegar

2 cans (15 ounces each) no-salt-added black beans, drained (not rinsed)

½ cup water

½ teaspoon salt

1 Cook the rice per the package directions, omitting any salt or fat.

2 Meanwhile, heat the oil in a large saucepan over medium-high heat. Add the onion, red and green bell peppers, garlic, oregano, and cumin and cook, stirring occasionally, for 5 to 6 minutes, or until starting to soften. Stir in the vinegar and cook for 1 minute. Add the beans and water and bring to a boil. Reduce the heat to medium-low and simmer, covered, for 15 minutes. Remove from the heat and stir in the salt. Serve over the rice.

per serving 343 calories, 14 g protein, 63 g carbohydrates, 11 g fiber, 4 g fat (0.6 g saturated fat), 319 mg sodium

Potato and Pea Samosas

RS: 10 g

prep time
20 minutes +
1 hour
30 minutes
for dough
to rise

total time
2 hours
40 minutes +
20 minutes
to cool

makes
4 servings

1 package (0.75 ounce) active dry yeast

1 cup warm water (100°–110°F)

3 teaspoons olive oil

1 cup all-purpose flour

¼ cup Hi-maize resistant starch

1 tablespoon vital wheat gluten

1 teaspoon salt

1 medium onion, chopped

2 teaspoons curry powder

1 cup frozen peas

1 large (12 ounces) potato, cooked, peeled, and mashed

2 tablespoons chopped fresh cilantro

⅛ teaspoon freshly ground black pepper

1 Combine the yeast with the warm water in a bowl. Stir well and let stand in a warm place for 10 minutes, or until frothy. Stir in 1 teaspoon of the oil.

2 Combine the flour, resistant starch, vital wheat gluten, and ½ teaspoon of the salt in a large bowl. Add the yeast mixture and stir with a wooden spoon until a rough dough forms. Knead for about 5 minutes, or until fairly smooth. Coat a separate bowl with cooking spray and add the dough. Also coat the dough with cooking spray, cover with plastic wrap, and let stand in a warm place (85°F) free from drafts for about 1 hour, or until doubled in bulk. Gently deflate the dough. Cover and let rise again for 30 minutes.

3 Heat the remaining 2 teaspoons oil in a small nonstick skillet over medium-high heat. Add the onion and stir occasionally, for about 5 minutes. Stir in the curry powder and cook for 15 seconds. Add the peas and cook for 1 minute. Add the potato and let cool for 10 minutes. Stir in the cilantro, pepper, and the remaining ½ teaspoon salt.

4 Turn out the dough onto a lightly floured surface and divide into 4 pieces. Roll 1 piece out to a 6½" circle. Top half with one-fourth of the potato mixture (about ½ cup) and fold the other half over. Crimp the edges to seal. Transfer to a baking sheet coated with cooking spray. Repeat with the remaining dough and potato mixture. Let stand in a warm place for 20 minutes.

5 Preheat the oven to 425°F. Bake the samosas for 18 to 20 minutes, or until golden. Cool for 10 minutes.

per serving 278 calories, 9 g protein, 55 g carbohydrates, 9 g fiber, 4.2 g fat (0.6 g saturated fat), 629 mg sodium

Bean and Corn Burgers with Chipotle Mayonnaise

RS: 5 g

prep time
15 minutes

total time
23 minutes

makes
4 servings

¼ cup reduced-fat mayonnaise

1 tablespoon ketchup

¼ teaspoon ground chipotle pepper

1 can (15 ounces) no-salt-added black beans, rinsed and drained

1 large egg

½ cup fresh or thawed frozen corn kernels

¼ cup finely chopped red onion

3 tablespoons plain dry bread crumbs

1 teaspoon chili powder

¼–½ teaspoon salt

1 tablespoon olive oil

4 whole wheat hamburger rolls

Sliced tomatoes (optional)

Lettuce leaves (optional)

1 Combine the mayonnaise, ketchup, and chipotle pepper in a small bowl, mix well, and reserve.

2 Partially mash the black beans with a fork in a medium bowl. Stir in the egg, corn, onion, bread crumbs, chili powder, and salt. Form the mixture into four ½"-thick patties (about ½ cup each).

3 Heat the oil in a large nonstick skillet over medium-high heat. Add the patties and cook for about 4 minutes per side, or until crisp and heated through. Serve on the rolls with the chipotle mayonnaise, adding the sliced tomato and lettuce leaves, if desired.

per serving 321 calories, 11 g protein, 44 g carbohydrates, 8 g fiber, 12.1 g fat (2 g saturated fat), 587 mg sodium

Marinated Grilled Portobello Burgers on Whole Grain Rolls

RS: 1 g

prep time
15 minutes

total time
27 minutes

makes
4 servings

2 tablespoons balsamic vinegar

1 tablespoon extra virgin olive oil

2 teaspoons honey

3 teaspoons Dijon mustard

¼ teaspoon salt

¼ teaspoon freshly ground black pepper

4 portobello mushroom caps (3½–4 ounces each)

2 ounces goat cheese, softened

2 teaspoons water

4 whole grain hamburger rolls

4 Boston lettuce leaves

4 tomato slices

4 thin red onion slices

1 Combine the vinegar, oil, honey, 1 teaspoon of the mustard, salt, and pepper in a bowl. Brush both sides of the mushroom caps with the mixture. Let stand for 5 minutes.

2 Coat a nonstick grill pan with cooking spray and heat on medium-high. Add the mushroom caps and grill for 5 to 6 minutes per side, or until well marked and tender.

3 Mash the cheese in a small bowl with the water. Spread the cut side of the top of each roll with the cheese mixture. Brush the cut side of the bottoms with the remaining mustard then top each with 1 lettuce leaf, 1 tomato slice, 1 onion slice, 1 mushroom cap, and the top half of the bun. Serve hot, warm, or at room temperature.

per serving 265 calories, 12 g protein, 30 g carbohydrates, 4 g fiber, 9.9 g fat (3.9 g saturated fat), 509 mg sodium

Soft Corn Tacos with Refried Beans, Salsa, and Cheese

RS: 5 g

prep time
10 minutes

total time
13 minutes

makes
4 servings
(2 tacos
each)

1 small white onion, thinly sliced

2 tablespoons chopped fresh cilantro

1 tablespoon fresh lime juice

1 teaspoon olive oil

1 can (16 ounces) fat-free refried beans

½ teaspoon chili powder

8 corn tortillas (6" each)

½ cup shredded low-fat sharp Cheddar cheese (such as Cabot 50% Less Fat Cheddar Cheese)

⅓ cup prepared fat-free black bean and corn salsa (such as Newman's Own)

1 Combine the onion, cilantro, and lime juice in a bowl.

2 Heat the oil in a medium nonstick skillet over medium-high heat. Add the beans and chili powder and cook, stirring, for 2 to 3 minutes, or until hot.

3 Warm the tortillas per the package directions. Top each tortilla with 3 tablespoons of the refried beans, 1 tablespoon of the onion mixture, 2 table-spoons of the cheese, and 2 teaspoons of the salsa. Serve immediately.

per serving 395 calories, 16 g protein, 65 g carbohydrates, 12 g fiber, 7.4 g fat (1.7 g saturated fat), 837 mg sodium*

*Limit sodium intake to 2,300 mg per day.

Curried Cauliflower, Chickpeas, and Peas

RS: 5 g

prep time
20 minutes

total time
45 minutes

makes
4 servings

2 tablespoons olive oil

2 tablespoons grated fresh ginger

2 medium onions, chopped

2 teaspoons sugar

1 teaspoon ground cumin

1 teaspoon curry powder

⅛ teaspoon ground red pepper

6 cups cauliflower florets

1 can (15 ounces) no-salt-added chickpeas, rinsed and drained

¾ cup reduced-sodium chicken broth

1 cup frozen peas

¼ teaspoon salt

¾ cup couscous

1 Heat the oil in a Dutch oven over medium-high heat. Add the ginger and cook for 30 seconds, or until fragrant. Stir in the onions and sugar and cook for 8 to 9 minutes, or until starting to brown. Add the cumin, curry powder, and red pepper and cook for 15 seconds, or until fragrant. Stir in the cauliflower and chickpeas and cook for 2 minutes. Pour in the broth and bring to a boil. Reduce the heat to medium-low and simmer for 8 to 10 minutes, or until the cauliflower is tender. Stir in the peas and salt, cover, and cook for 2 minutes, or until hot.

2 Meanwhile, cook the couscous per the package directions.

3 Divide the couscous among 4 bowls and top each with 2 cups of the cauliflower mixture.

per serving 353 calories, 14 g protein, 58 g carbohydrates, 11 g fiber, 8 g fat (1 g saturated fat), 333 mg sodium

Two-Bean Chili

RS: 9 g

prep time
15 minutes

total time
50 minutes

makes
4 servings

2 teaspoons olive oil

1 cup chopped onion

1 cup chopped red
bell pepper

3 cloves garlic,
minced

1 teaspoon dried
oregano

1 can (15 ounces)
no-salt-added
black beans,
drained (not
rinsed)

1 can (15 ounces)
no-salt-added
red kidney
beans, drained
(not rinsed)

1 can (14.5 ounces)
no-salt-added,
fire-roasted diced
tomatoes

1 cup reduced-
sodium vegetable
broth

1 tablespoon chili
powder

½ ounce semisweet
chocolate

½ teaspoon salt

3 ounces elbow
macaroni

Optional Garnishes

½ cup low-fat
shredded Cheddar
cheese (such as
Cabot 50% Less
Fat Cheddar
Cheese)

¼ cup fat-free sour
cream

1 Heat the oil in a Dutch oven over medium-high heat. Add the onion, bell pepper, garlic, and oregano and cook, stirring occasionally, for 4 to 5 minutes, or until slightly softened. Stir in the black beans, kidney beans, tomatoes, broth, and chili powder. Bring to a boil and reduce the heat to medium-low. Cover and simmer for 28 to 30 minutes, or until slightly thickened. Remove from the heat and stir in the chocolate and salt.

2 Meanwhile, bring a large saucepan of lightly salted water to a boil. Add the macaroni and cook per the package directions. Drain.

3 Serve the chili over the macaroni. Garnish with cheese and sour cream, if desired.

per serving 277 calories, 13 g protein, 48 g carbohydrates, 12 g fiber, 4 g fat (1 g saturated fat), 349 mg sodium

African Yam and Vegetable Stew

RS: 9 g

prep time
20 minutes

total time
1 hour
5 minutes

makes
4 servings

2 teaspoons olive oil

1 medium onion, chopped

1 jalapeño chile pepper, seeded and finely chopped

1 tablespoon grated fresh ginger

1 teaspoon ground cumin

1 pound yams, peeled and cut into ½" cubes

1 can (15 ounces) no-salt-added chickpeas, rinsed and drained

3 cups reduced-sodium vegetable broth

⅓ cup raisins

1 bag (6 ounces) prewashed spinach

3 tablespoons creamy natural peanut butter

1 Heat the oil in a Dutch oven over medium-high heat. Add the onion and chile pepper and cook, stirring occasionally, for 2 to 3 minutes, or until starting to soften. Stir in the ginger and cumin and cook for 1 minute. Add the yams, chickpeas, and broth and bring to a boil. Reduce the heat to medium-low, cover, and simmer for 30 minutes, or until the yams are tender.

2 Stir in the raisins and cook for 5 minutes. Stir in the spinach and cook for 2 minutes longer. Remove from the heat and stir in the peanut butter until dissolved.

per serving 337 calories, 10 g protein, 55 g carbohydrates, 11 g fiber, 9 g fat (1 g saturated fat), 299 mg sodium

Chapter

Snacks

Tomatoes and White Beans on Multigrain Crostini

RS: 4 g

prep time
15 minutes

total time
15 minutes +
5 minutes
to cool

makes
4 servings

1 multigrain baguette (6 ounces), cut into 12 slices

1 clove garlic, halved

1 can (15 ounces) no-salt-added cannellini beans, rinsed and drained

3 medium plum tomatoes, seeded and chopped

3 tablespoons chopped fresh basil

1½ tablespoons balsamic vinegar

1 tablespoon extra virgin olive oil

¼ teaspoon salt

⅛ teaspoon freshly ground black pepper

1 Preheat the oven to 425°F. Coat a baking sheet with cooking spray.

2 Arrange the bread slices in a single layer on the prepared baking sheet. Bake in the center of the oven for 6 to 7 minutes, or until lightly browned and crisp. Let cool for 5 minutes, then rub 1 side of each slice with the garlic halves.

3 Meanwhile, combine the beans, tomatoes, basil, vinegar, oil, salt, and pepper in a bowl.

4 To serve, spoon the bean mixture onto the garlic-rubbed side of the bread slices.

per serving 285 calories, 8 g protein, 45 g carbohydrates, 6 g fiber, 8.6 g fat (1.3 g saturated fat), 426 mg sodium

Edamame, Tomato, and Cheese on Multigrain Pita

RS: 1 g

prep time
5 minutes

total time
17 minutes +
5 minutes
to cool

makes
4 servings

3 multigrain or whole wheat pitas (9"–10" each), split in half horizontally

¼ teaspoon garlic powder

1 cup shelled frozen edamame

½ cup frozen corn kernels

2 plum tomatoes, seeded and chopped

3 tablespoons grated Pecorino Romano cheese

1 tablespoon extra virgin olive oil

1 Preheat the oven to 425°F.

2 Arrange the pita halves on a work surface and coat lightly with cooking spray. Sprinkle with the garlic powder. Cut each pita half into 2 half-moons and set on a baking sheet. Bake for 6 to 7 minutes, or until lightly browned and crisp. Cool for 5 minutes on the baking sheet.

3 Meanwhile, bring 1 cup of lightly salted water to a boil in a small saucepan over medium-high heat. Add the edamame and cook for 4 minutes. Stir in the corn, return to a boil, and cook for 1 minute longer. Drain, transfer to a bowl, and cool for 5 minutes. Stir in the tomatoes, cheese, and oil.

4 Serve the edamame mixture with the toasted pita crisps.

per serving 254 calories, 11 g protein, 37 g carbohydrates, 7 g fiber, 7.9 g fat (1.6 g saturated fat), 366 mg sodium

Potato Focaccia Squares with Tomato and Parmesan

RS: 7 g

prep time
30 minutes +
1 hour
45 minutes
for standing
and rising

total time
3 hours
10 minutes +
20 minutes
to cool

makes
8 servings

8 ounces baking potato
1 package (0.75 ounce) active dry yeast
1 cup warm water (100°–110°F),
2 tablespoons extra virgin olive oil
1½ cups all-purpose flour
½ cup Hi-maize resistant starch
2 tablespoons vital wheat gluten
1½ teaspoons salt
1 large tomato, cut into 9 slices
¼ cup grated Parmesan cheese

1 Prick the potato with a fork in several places. Microwave for 8 to 9 minutes, or until tender. Let cool for 5 minutes. Peel and mash in a bowl.

2 Combine the yeast in a bowl with the warm water. Stir well and let stand in a warm place for 10 minutes, or until frothy. Stir in 1 tablespoon of the oil.

3 Combine the flour, resistant starch, vital wheat gluten, and 1 teaspoon of the salt in a large bowl. Add the potato and yeast mixture and stir with a wooden spoon until a rough dough forms. Knead the dough in the bowl for about 5 minutes, or until fairly smooth. Coat a separate bowl with cooking spray and add the dough. Also coat the dough with cooking spray, cover with plastic wrap, and let stand in a warm place (85°F) free from drafts for about 1 hour, or until doubled in bulk.

4 Spread 2 teaspoons of the oil in a 9" × 9" baking pan. Press the dough into the pan to fit. Cover and let stand in a warm place until risen, 30 minutes.

5 Preheat the oven to 350°F.

6 Brush the top of the dough with the remaining 1 teaspoon oil. Top with the tomato slices, cheese, and the remaining ½ teaspoon salt. Bake for 50 to 55 minutes, or until golden. Cool in the pan for 10 minutes. Transfer to a rack and cool for 10 minutes longer before cutting into 8 squares. Serve warm or at room temperature.

per serving 175 calories, 6 g protein, 31 g carbohydrates, 6 g fiber, 4.6 g fat (0.98 g saturated fat), 478 mg sodium

Note: If you have time, boil the potato in Step 1 instead of microwaving it. This will preserve even more RS.

Black Pepper Biscuits with Chive Cream Cheese

RS: 3 g

prep time
20 minutes

total time
32-34
minutes +
2 minutes
to cool

makes
6 servings

¼ cup fat-free cream cheese, softened

2 tablespoons chopped fresh chives

1 cup all-purpose flour

¼ cup Hi-maize resistant starch

1 teaspoon sugar

1 teaspoon baking powder

½ teaspoon coarsely ground black pepper

¼ teaspoon salt

3 tablespoons cold unsalted butter, cut into small pieces

6 tablespoons fat-free milk

1 Preheat the oven to 400°F. Coat a large baking sheet with cooking spray.

2 Combine the cream cheese and chives. Mix well and reserve.

3 Combine the flour, resistant starch, sugar, baking powder, pepper, and salt in a medium bowl. Cut in the butter with a pastry blender or 2 knives until the mixture resembles coarse meal. Stir in the milk until just moist.

4 Turn out the dough onto a lightly floured surface and knead gently 4 or 5 times. Roll the dough into a ½"-thick, 6" × 4" rectangle. Dust the top lightly with flour. Fold the dough crosswise into thirds (like folding a sheet of paper). Roll or pat to a ¾" thickness. Cut the dough with a 2¼" biscuit cutter to make 6 dough rounds, rerolling scraps if necessary.

5 Set the rounds on the prepared baking sheet. Bake for 12 to 14 minutes, or until lightly golden. Transfer to a rack and cool for 2 minutes. Halve and spread each with the cream cheese mixture.

per serving 152 calories, 4 g protein, 22 g carbohydrates, 3 g fiber, 6.1 g fat (3.8 g saturated fat), 226 mg sodium

English Muffin Grilled Cheese

RS: 1 g

prep time
5 minutes

total time
6 minutes

makes
1 serving

1 multigrain 100-calorie English muffin, split

1 teaspoon Dijon mustard

1 tomato slice

⅕ Hass avocado, peeled, pitted, and mashed

⅛ teaspoon salt

1 ounce shredded low-fat Cheddar cheese (such as Cabot 50% Less Fat Cheddar Cheese)

1 Preheat the broiler.

2 Toast the English muffin. Spread the cut side of half with the mustard. Top with the tomato slice. Spread the avocado over the cut side of the remaining muffin half. Sprinkle the tomato and avocado with the salt. Top both halves with the cheese.

3 Set on a baking sheet and broil for 45 seconds to 1 minute, or until the cheese melts. Fold the two halves together to form a sandwich.

per serving 224 calories, 15 g protein, 29 g carbohydrates, 10 g fiber, 10.2 g fat (3.6 g saturated fat), 463 mg sodium

The King's Mini Peanut Butter and Banana Sandwiches

RS: 3 g

prep time
10 minutes

total time
15 minutes

makes
4 servings
(3 triangles
each)

6 slices whole grain
bread

3 tablespoons
natural peanut
butter

2 small bananas,
sliced

1 Spread 1 side of each slice of bread with peanut butter. Top 3 of the slices with the banana, then top with the remaining 3 slices.

2 Heat a large nonstick skillet over medium heat until hot. Lightly coat the sandwiches with cooking spray. Add to the skillet and cook for 2 to 3 minutes per side, or until the outside of the sandwiches are toasted and the middles are warm. Transfer to a cutting board and cut each into 4 triangles. Serve warm.

per serving 210 calories, 6 g protein, 35 g carbohydrates, 9.6 g fiber, 6.9 g fat (0.8 g saturated fat), 166 mg sodium

Note: This was one of Elvis Presley's favorite foods, which his mother made for him when he was a boy (although his were cooked in tons of butter). Later in life he would enjoy these sandwiches along with mini hamburgers and other goodies from his childhood.

Fresh Corn, Pepper, and Avocado Salad

RS: 3 g

prep time
10 minutes

total time
13 minutes +
5 minutes
to cool

makes
4 servings

5 **large corn on the cob, shucked**

1 **medium red bell pepper, chopped**

¾ **Hass avocado, peeled, pitted, and chopped**

½ **cup finely chopped red onion**

2 **tablespoons chopped fresh cilantro**

2 **tablespoons fresh lime juice**

2 **teaspoons olive oil**

½ **teaspoon salt**

1 Bring a large pot of lightly salted water to a boil. Add the corn and cook for 3 minutes (the water doesn't need to return to a boil). Drain the corn and cool for 5 minutes.

2 With a sharp knife, cut the corn kernels from the cobs and transfer to a bowl. Stir in the bell pepper, avocado, onion, cilantro, lime juice, oil, and salt and toss well. Serve warm or at room temperature.

per serving 214 calories, 6 g protein, 36 g carbohydrates, 8.8 g fiber, 8.1 g fat (1.1 g saturated fat), 318 mg sodium

Marinated Roasted Pepper and Red Potato Salad

RS: 11 g

prep time
15 minutes

total time
30 minutes +
5 minutes
to cool

makes
4 servings

1 pound tiny red potatoes, halved

1 jar (7 ounces) roasted red peppers, rinsed, drained, patted dry, and cut into strips

3 scallions, chopped

3 tablespoons chopped fresh basil

1 tablespoon balsamic vinegar

1 tablespoon extra virgin olive oil

2 teaspoons drained nonpareil capers

¼ teaspoon salt

⅛ teaspoon freshly ground black pepper

1 Combine the potatoes in a small saucepan with enough water to cover by 2". Bring to a boil and cook for 12 to 14 minutes, or until tender. Drain and let cool for 5 minutes.

2 Transfer the potatoes to a bowl. Add the peppers, scallions, basil, vinegar, oil, capers, salt, and pepper and toss well. Serve warm or at room temperature.

per serving 129 calories, 2 g protein, 23 g carbohydrates, 3.3 g fiber, 3.7 g fat (0.5 g saturated fat), 227 mg sodium

Toasted Orzo with Feta

RS: 6 g

prep time
10 minutes

total time
25 minutes +
15 minutes
to stand

makes
4 servings

6 ounces orzo

¾ cup crumbled
reduced-fat feta
cheese

2 navel oranges, cut
into segments

⅓ cup finely chopped
red onion

1 tablespoon extra
virgin olive oil

2 teaspoons chopped
fresh oregano

1 teaspoon grated
fresh orange zest

½ teaspoon salt

¼ teaspoon freshly
ground black
pepper

1 Bring a pot of lightly salted water to a boil.

2 Heat a large nonstick skillet over medium-high heat. Add the orzo and cook, shaking the skillet often, for 3 to 4 minutes, or until the orzo is lightly browned. Add the orzo to the boiling water and cook per the package directions. Drain and transfer to a bowl.

3 Add the cheese, oranges, onion, oil, oregano, orange zest, salt, and pepper to the orzo and mix well. Let stand for 15 minutes to allow the flavors to blend.

per serving 278 calories, 12 g protein, 43 g carbohydrates, 4 g fiber, 7.5 g fat (2.9 g saturated fat), 647 mg sodium

Spiced Corn Tortilla Crisps with Pinto Bean Salsa

RS: 5 g

prep time
20 minutes

total time
20 minutes +
time to cool

makes
4 servings

8 corn tortillas (6" each)

1½ teaspoons walnut oil

1 teaspoon ground cumin

½ teaspoon ground coriander

½ teaspoon salt

⅛ teaspoon ground red pepper

1 can (15 ounces) no-salt-added pinto beans, rinsed and drained

1 large tomato, chopped

¼ cup finely chopped red bell pepper

¼ cup finely chopped white onion

2 tablespoons chopped fresh cilantro

2 tablespoons fresh lime juice

1 Preheat the oven to 400°F. Coat a baking sheet with cooking spray.

2 Brush 1 side of each tortilla with oil. Sprinkle with the cumin, coriander, ¼ teaspoon of the salt, and the red pepper. Cut each into 8 wedges and arrange on the prepared baking sheet in a single layer. Bake, in 2 batches if necessary, for 8 to 9 minutes, or until crisp. Let cool.

3 Meanwhile, combine the beans, tomato, bell pepper, onion, cilantro, lime juice, and the remaining ¼ teaspoon salt in a bowl.

4 Serve the salsa with the tortilla crisps.

per serving 202 calories, 7 g protein, 37 g carbohydrates, 7.9 g fiber, 3.3 g fat (0.4 g saturated fat), 326 mg sodium

Hot Artichoke-Bean Dip with Multigrain Crisps

RS: 2 g

prep time
15 minutes

total time
50 minutes

makes
6 servings

1 multigrain baguette (6 ounces), cut into 12 slices

2 teaspoons olive oil

¼ cup chopped onion

1 clove garlic, minced

1 package (9 ounces) frozen artichoke hearts, thawed

¾ cup no-salt-added cannellini beans, rinsed and drained

1 cup fat-free ricotta cheese

¼ cup fat-free cream cheese

⅓ cup grated Parmesan cheese

3 tablespoons reduced-fat mayonnaise

1 tablespoon fresh lemon juice

¼ teaspoon salt

⅛ teaspoon freshly ground black pepper

1 Preheat the oven to 425°F. Coat an 8" × 8" baking dish with cooking spray.

2 Arrange the bread slices on a large baking sheet coated with cooking spray. Bake for 6 to 7 minutes, or until lightly browned and crisp. Let cool.

3 Meanwhile, heat the oil in a medium nonstick skillet over medium-high heat. Add the onion and garlic and cook for 1 to 2 minutes, or until starting to soften. Stir in the artichoke hearts and cook, stirring occasionally, for 5 to 6 minutes, or until starting to brown. Transfer to the bowl of a food processor and add the beans, ricotta, cream cheese, Parmesan, mayonnaise, lemon juice, salt, and pepper. Pulse until well blended but still chunky.

4 Transfer the mixture to the prepared baking dish. Bake for 28 to 30 minutes, or until hot and the top is browned. Serve warm with the crisps.

per serving 235 calories, 8 g protein, 32 g carbohydrates, 6 g fiber, 8.9 g fat (1.9 g saturated fat), 463 mg sodium

Chipotle–Red Bean Dip with Pita Wedges

RS: 5 g

prep time
5 minutes

makes
4 servings

1 can (15 ounces) no-salt-added red kidney beans, rinsed and drained

2 tablespoons fresh lemon juice

2 tablespoons water

4 teaspoons canola oil

½ teaspoon ground coriander

½ teaspoon salt

⅛ teaspoon ground chipotle pepper

2 tablespoons chopped fresh cilantro

3 small (4") whole wheat pitas, cut into 8 wedges each

Combine the beans, lemon juice, water, oil, coriander, salt, and chipotle pepper in a food processor and puree. Transfer to a bowl and stir in the cilantro. Serve with the pita wedges.

per serving 157 calories, 7 g protein, 23 g carbohydrates, 7 g fiber, 5.2 g fat (0.5 g saturated fat), 411 mg sodium

Corn Flake and Puffed Rice Marshmallow Treats

RS: 1 g

prep time
10 minutes

total time
16 minutes +
1 hour to cool

makes
12 servings

2 tablespoons
unsalted butter

1 bag (10 ounces)
marshmallows

½ teaspoon vanilla
extract

6 cups corn flakes

2 cups puffed rice

½ cup sweetened
coconut flakes,
toasted

1 Coat an 8" × 8" baking dish with cooking spray.

2 Melt the butter in a large saucepan over medium heat. Add the marshmallows and vanilla extract and cook, stirring, for 6 to 7 minutes, or until melted. Remove from the heat and stir in the corn flakes, puffed rice, and coconut flakes, stirring until well coated.

3 Pour the marshmallow mixture into the prepared pan, using a rubber spatula if needed. Place a piece of wax paper over the mixture and press down firmly with the palms of your hands to flatten. Let cool in the pan for 30 minutes. Remove from the pan and transfer to a cutting board and cool completely, about 30 minutes. Cut into 12 pieces.

per serving 167 calories, 2 g protein, 35 g carbohydrates, 1 g fiber, 2.8 g fat (2 g saturated fat), 167 mg sodium

Dried Fruit and Oat Bran Pretzel Trail Mix

RS: <1 g

prep time
5 minutes

makes
6 servings

2 cups corn flakes

4 ounces oat bran pretzels (about 2 cups)

¼ cup golden raisins

¼ cup dried pineapple, cut into ½" dice

¼ cup dried cranberries

¼ cup sliced almonds, toasted

¼ cup semisweet chocolate chips

Combine the corn flakes, pretzels, raisins, pineapple, cranberries, almonds, and chocolate chips in a bowl. Store in an airtight plastic container.

per serving 218 calories, 4 g protein, 43 g carbohydrates, 3 g fiber, 4 g fat (1.4 g saturated fat), 94 mg sodium

Spicy Snack Mix

RS: <1 g

prep time
10 minutes

total time
50 minutes +
time to cool

makes
10 servings

4 multigrain pitas (6" each), each cut into 32 pieces

3 cups corn Chex cereal

1 cup wheat Chex cereal

2 cups unsalted mini pretzel twists

¼ cup canola oil

2 tablespoons honey

2 teaspoons Worcestershire sauce

1 tablespoon ground cumin

1 teaspoon garlic powder

½ teaspoon salt

¼ teaspoon ground red pepper

½ cup dried cranberries

1 Preheat the oven to 400°F. Coat a baking sheet with cooking spray.

2 Combine the pitas, corn cereal, wheat cereal, and pretzels in a large bowl.

3 Heat the oil in a small skillet over low heat until warm. Add the honey, Worcestershire sauce, cumin, garlic powder, salt, and red pepper. Cook, stirring, for 15 seconds or until well combined. Stir into the cereal mixture in several additions to better distribute the seasonings.

4 Pour the cereal mixture onto the prepared baking sheet. Place in the oven and reduce the heat to 200°F. Bake for 40 minutes, or until just golden. Transfer to a large bowl, stir in the cranberries, and let cool completely.

per serving 237 calories, 5 g protein, 42 g carbohydrates, 4 g fiber, 6.9 g fat (0.6 g saturated fat), 432 mg sodium

Strawberry-Banana Malted Milk

RS: 3 g

prep time
5 minutes

makes
1 serving

½ banana

½ cup frozen strawberries

½ cup fat-free milk

1 tablespoon natural flavor malt powder

2 teaspoons honey

3 ice cubes

Combine the banana, strawberries, milk, malt powder, honey, and ice cubes in a blender. Process for 1 to 2 minutes, or until smooth. Serve immediately in a tall glass.

per serving 218 calories, 7 g protein, 50 g carbohydrates, 0.5 g fiber, 0.5 g fat (0.2 g saturated fat), 104 mg sodium

Peanut Butter–Banana Smoothie

RS: 5 g

prep time
5 minutes

makes
1 serving

1 small banana
¼ cup fat-free milk
1 tablespoon natural
peanut butter
1 tablespoon honey
3 ice cubes

Combine the banana, milk, peanut butter, honey, and ice cubes in a blender. Process until smooth.

per serving 260 calories, 7 g protein, 43 g carbohydrates, 3 g fiber, 8.3 g fat (1.1 g saturated fat), 29 mg sodium

Chapter

{12}

Desserts

Chocolate Chip–Oatmeal Cookies

RS: 3 g

prep time
15 minutes

total time
25 minutes +
time to cool

makes
14 servings
(3 cookies
each)

1¼ cups all-purpose flour

½ cup old-fashioned rolled oats

½ cup Hi-maize resistant starch

¾ teaspoon baking soda

¼ teaspoon salt

6 tablespoons unsalted butter, softened

½ cup packed dark brown sugar

¼ cup granulated sugar

2 large egg whites

1½ teaspoons vanilla extract

½ cup mini semisweet chocolate chips

1 Preheat the oven to 350°F. Coat 2 large baking sheets with cooking spray.

2 Combine the flour, oats, resistant starch, baking soda, and salt in a bowl. Combine the butter and brown and granulated sugars in the bowl of an electric mixer and beat at medium speed until well blended, stopping occasionally to scrape down the side of the bowl. With the mixer running, add the egg whites and vanilla extract and beat for 2 minutes. Reduce the speed to low and beat in the flour mixture until blended. Add the chocolate chips and beat for 30 seconds.

3 Drop the dough by level tablespoons 2" apart onto the prepared baking sheets. Lightly press down on the top of each mound of dough to flatten very slightly. Bake for 10 to 12 minutes, or until lightly browned. Cool on the baking sheets for 2 minutes. Transfer to racks and cool completely.

per serving 178 calories, 2 g protein, 29 g carbohydrates, 3 g fiber, 7 g fat (4.2 g saturated fat), 34 mg sodium

Cranberry Oatmeal Cookies

RS: 3 g

prep time
20 minutes

total time
35 minutes +
time to cool

makes
12 servings
(3 cookies
each)

1 cup old-fashioned rolled oats

1 cup all-purpose flour

½ cup Hi-maize resistant starch

1½ teaspoons baking powder

¼ teaspoon baking soda

½ teaspoon ground cinnamon

¼ teaspoon salt

½ cup packed dark brown sugar

6 tablespoons unsalted butter, softened

1 large egg

2 teaspoons vanilla extract

½ cup dried cranberries

1 Preheat the oven to 350°F. Coat 2 baking sheets with cooking spray.

2 Combine the oats, flour, resistant starch, baking powder, baking soda, cinnamon, and salt in a bowl. Combine the sugar and butter in the bowl of an electric mixer and beat at medium speed until well blended, stopping occasionally to scrape down the side of bowl. With the mixer running, add the egg and vanilla extract and beat for 2 minutes. Reduce the speed to low and beat in the oat mixture until blended. Add the cranberries and beat for 30 seconds, or until well combined.

3 Drop the batter in 36 level tablespoons 2" apart onto the prepared baking sheets. Lightly press down on each cookie to form a disc about 2" in diameter. Bake for 12 to 14 minutes, or until lightly browned. Cool on the baking sheets for 2 minutes. Transfer to racks and cool completely.

per serving 181 calories, 3 g protein, 30 g carbohydrates, 4 g fiber, 6.7 g fat (3.8 g saturated fat), 134 mg sodium

Cranberry–Chocolate Chip Blondies

RS: 3 g

prep time
15 minutes

total time
40 minutes +
30 minutes
to cool

makes
12 servings

1½ cups all-purpose flour

½ cup Hi-maize resistant starch

2 teaspoons baking powder

¼ teaspoon salt

1½ cups packed light brown sugar

6 tablespoons unsalted butter, melted

2 large eggs, lightly beaten

2 teaspoons vanilla extract

⅓ cup dried cranberries

⅓ cup semisweet mini chocolate chips

2 tablespoons confectioners' sugar (optional)

1 Preheat the oven to 350°F. Coat a 9" × 9" baking pan with cooking spray, then lightly dust with flour.

2 Combine the flour, resistant starch, baking powder, and salt in a bowl. Combine the sugar, butter, eggs, and vanilla extract in a large bowl. Add to the flour mixture and stir until just combined. Fold in the cranberries and chocolate chips.

3 Spread or press the batter into the prepared pan. Bake for 25 to 26 minutes, or until a wooden pick inserted into the center comes out with moist crumbs attached. Cool in the pan on a rack for 30 minutes. Cut into 12 bars and sprinkle with confectioners' sugar, if desired.

per serving 249 calories, 3 g protein, 44 g carbohydrates, 3.5 g fiber, 8 g fat (4.8 g saturated fat), 135 mg sodium

Glazed Mixed Berry–Lemon Bundt Cake

RS: 4 g

prep time
15 minutes

total time
1 hour
10 minutes +
1 hour
15 minutes
to cool
and stand

makes
16 servings

3 cups all-purpose flour

1 cup Hi-maize resistant starch

1 cup sugar

1½ teaspoons baking powder

½ teaspoon baking soda

¼ teaspoon salt

1 cup low-fat buttermilk

3 large eggs

½ cup walnut oil

⅓ cup + 2½ tablespoons fresh lemon juice

2 cups fresh or thawed frozen mixed berries (raspberries, blueberries, blackberries)

1 cup confectioners' sugar

1 Preheat the oven to 350°F. Coat a 10" tube pan with cooking spray, then dust with flour.

2 Combine the flour, resistant starch, sugar, baking powder, baking soda, and salt in the bowl of an electric mixer. Mix on low to combine. Add the buttermilk, eggs, oil, and ⅓ cup of the lemon juice. Mix on low speed for 3 minutes, or until well combined. Stir in the berries.

3 Pour the batter into the prepared pan. Bake in the center of the oven for 50 to 55 minutes, or until a wooden pick inserted into the center of the cake comes out clean. Cool in the pan on a rack for 15 minutes. Remove the cake from the pan and cool on a rack for 45 minutes.

4 Combine the confectioners' sugar with the remaining 2½ tablespoons lemon juice and stir until a thick glaze forms. Using a spoon, drizzle the glaze over the cake. Let stand for 15 minutes to set before serving.

per serving 264 calories, 4 g protein, 47 g carbohydrates, 5.7 g fiber, 8.2 g fat (1 g saturated fat), 144 mg sodium

Gingersnap-Crusted Sweet Potato Pie

RS: 6 g

prep time
12 minutes

total time
1 hour
20 minutes +
time to cool

makes
8 servings

2 pounds sweet potatoes

4 tablespoons unsalted butter, melted

15 gingersnap cookies (¾ cup fine crumbs)

2 tablespoons sugar

2 large eggs

½ cup 1% milk

½ cup agave nectar

1 teaspoon ground cinnamon

1 teaspoon vanilla extract

¼ teaspoon ground allspice

¼ teaspoon ground nutmeg

¼ teaspoon salt

1 Preheat the oven to 350°F.

2 Prick the sweet potatoes with a fork in several places. Microwave for 8 to 10 minutes on high, or until tender. Let cool for 5 minutes. Peel the potatoes and transfer to a bowl. Add 2 tablespoons of the melted butter and mash.

3 Meanwhile, place the cookies in the bowl of a food processor and process to fine crumbs. Transfer to a bowl, stir in the sugar, and mix well. Add the remaining 2 tablespoons melted butter and stir until well blended. Press the mixture into the bottom and up the side of a 9" glass pie plate. Bake for 5 minutes. Remove from the oven and let cool.

4 Beat the eggs, milk, agave nectar, cinnamon, vanilla extract, allspice, nutmeg, and salt into the sweet potatoes with an electric mixer on medium speed until well blended.

5 Pour the filling into the pie plate. Bake for 45 to 50 minutes, or until a knife inserted into the center comes out clean. Cool the pie completely on a rack before cutting.

per serving 281 calories, 4 g protein, 48 g carbohydrates, 3.1 g fiber, 8.5 g fat (4.5 g saturated fat), 232 mg sodium

Note: If you have time, boil the potato in Step 2 instead of microwaving it. This will preserve even more RS.

Coconut-Macadamia Banana Bread

RS: 3 g

prep time
10 minutes

total time
55 minutes +
50 minutes
to cool

makes
12 servings

1 large egg

½ cup sugar

2 tablespoons walnut oil

3 very ripe large bananas, mashed

½ cup fat-free milk

1 teaspoon vanilla extract

¼ teaspoon coconut extract

1½ cups all-purpose flour

⅓ cup Hi-maize resistant starch

2 teaspoons baking powder

½ teaspoon salt

⅓ cup sweetened coconut flakes

⅓ cup macadamia nuts, chopped

1 Preheat the oven to 350°F. Coat a 9" × 5" baking pan with cooking spray.

2 Combine the egg, sugar, and oil in a large bowl and mix well. Add the bananas, milk, and vanilla and coconut extracts and mix until smooth. Combine the flour, resistant starch, baking powder, and salt in a bowl. Stir into the banana mixture until just moistened. Fold in the coconut flakes and nuts.

3 Pour the batter into the prepared baking pan. Bake for 40 to 45 minutes, or until a wooden pick inserted into the center comes out clean. Cool in the pan for 5 minutes. Remove from the pan and cool on a rack for 45 minutes before slicing.

per serving 191 calories, 3 g protein, 33 g carbohydrates, 4 g fiber, 6.4 g fat (1.5 g saturated fat), 182 mg sodium

Banana-Chocolate Turnovers

RS: 4 g

prep time
10 minutes

total time
30 minutes +
time to cool

makes
4 servings

3 medium bananas, sliced

¼ cup mini semisweet chocolate chips

1 tablespoon granulated sugar

8 sheets phyllo dough

⅓ cup confectioners' sugar

1¼ teaspoons water

1 Preheat the oven to 350°F. Coat a baking sheet with cooking spray.

2 Combine the bananas, chocolate chips, and granulated sugar in a bowl and mix well.

3 Place 1 sheet of phyllo on a work surface with a short side nearest you. Coat lightly with cooking spray and top with a second sheet. Repeat with 2 more sheets. Cut the phyllo vertically into 2 equal strips.

4 Center one-fourth of the banana mixture at the bottom of a strip. Fold from the bottom right corner over the filling to the left side to form a right triangle. Continue folding from corner to side all the way up to the top of the strip. Place the triangle seam side down on the prepared baking sheet. Repeat with the other strip and place on the baking sheet. Repeat the process with the remaining 4 phyllo sheets and filling.

5 Lightly coat the turnovers with cooking spray. Bake for 18 to 20 minutes, or until lightly golden. Let cool for 10 minutes.

6 Combine the confectioners' sugar with the water to form a glaze. Drizzle in a back-and-forth motion over the turnovers. Let cool completely before serving.

per serving 295 calories, 4 g protein, 60 g carbohydrates, 3.7 g fiber, 5.8 g fat (2.6 g saturated fat), 0 mg sodium

Whole Cornbread Pudding

RS: 3 g

prep time
15 minutes

total time
1 hour
35 minutes +
45 minutes
to cool

makes
6 servings

½ cup enriched yellow cornmeal

½ cup all-purpose flour

¼ cup Hi-maize resistant starch

1 teaspoon baking powder

¼ teaspoon salt

3 cups low-fat buttermilk

2 tablespoons unsalted butter, melted

1 cup fresh or thawed frozen corn kernels

3 large eggs, lightly beaten

½ cup sugar

1 tablespoon vanilla extract

1 Preheat the oven to 400°F. Coat an 8" × 8" baking dish with cooking spray.

2 Combine the cornmeal, flour, resistant starch, baking powder, and salt in a bowl. Stir in ¾ cup of the buttermilk and the butter until just combined. Fold in the corn. Pour the batter into the prepared baking dish. Bake for 18 to 20 minutes, or until the cornbread has pulled away from the sides of the pan. Turn onto a rack and cool for 15 minutes.

3 Combine the remaining 2¼ cups buttermilk, the eggs, sugar, and vanilla extract in a bowl. Coat an 8" × 8" baking dish with cooking spray then crumble the cornbread into it. Pour the buttermilk mixture over the cornbread and place the baking dish in a large roasting pan. Pour enough hot water to come halfway up the sides of the baking dish. Reduce the oven temperature to 350°F and bake for 55 to 60 minutes, or until the pudding is set but still very moist. Let cool for 30 minutes before cutting.

per serving 311 calories, 10 g protein, 51 g carbohydrates, 4 g fiber, 8 g fat (4 g saturated fat), 338 mg sodium

Coconut Rice Pudding

RS: 5 g

prep time
5 minutes

total time
53 minutes +
40 minutes
to stand

makes
5 servings

2 cups water

1 cup light
   unsweetened
   coconut milk

½ cup long-grain
   white rice

⅓ cup sugar

2 tablespoons honey

½ teaspoon coconut
   extract

¼ teaspoon salt

Combine the water, coconut milk, rice, sugar, honey, coconut extract, and salt in a medium saucepan over medium-high heat. Bring to a boil, stirring occasionally, to help dissolve the sugar. Reduce the heat to medium-low, cover, and simmer for 45 minutes, or until the rice is tender and creamy. Remove from the heat and let stand for 40 minutes. Serve warm or cold.

per serving 236 calories, 3 g protein, 47 g carbohydrates, 0.5 g fiber, 4 g fat (3 g saturated fat), 166 mg sodium

Creamy Peach-Cranberry Rice Pudding

RS: 3 g

prep time
10 minutes

total time
1 hour
10 minutes +
time to cool

makes
4 servings

2 cups water

1 can (12 ounces) evaporated skim milk

6 tablespoons sugar

1 teaspoon vanilla extract

¾ cup quick-cooking brown rice

⅛ teaspoon salt

1 cup frozen sliced peaches, thawed and chopped

¼ cup dried cranberries

1 Combine the water, milk, sugar, and vanilla extract in a medium saucepan over medium-high heat. Bring to a boil and add the rice and salt. Cover, reduce the heat to medium-low, and simmer for 20 minutes. Uncover, increase the heat to medium, and simmer for about 20 minutes, or until the rice is almost tender.

2 Stir in the peaches and cranberries, cover, and reduce the heat to medium-low. Return to a simmer and cook, stirring occasionally, for 5 to 6 minutes, or until the rice is creamy and tender. Remove from the heat and let stand for 10 minutes before serving, or cool completely and chill until ready to serve.

per serving 265 calories, 7 g protein, 58 g carbohydrates, 1 g fiber, 0.2 g fat (0 g saturated fat), 181 mg sodium

Pear-Cranberry Barley Pudding

RS: 5 g

prep time
10 minutes

total time
1 hour +
time to cool

makes
4 servings

1⅓ cups water

¾ cup quick-cooking barley

⅓ cup dried cranberries

2 large eggs

1 cup 1% milk

½ cup sugar

1 teaspoon vanilla extract

¼ teaspoon salt

1 medium (8-ounce) pear, peeled, cored, and cut into ½" cubes

1 Preheat the oven to 350°F. Coat a 6-cup baking dish with cooking spray.

2 Bring the water to a boil in a small saucepan over medium-high heat. Add the barley and cranberries and cook per the barley package directions. Let cool for 10 minutes.

3 Whisk together the eggs, milk, sugar, vanilla extract, and salt. Stir in the barley mixture and the pear. Pour into the prepared baking dish. Bake in the center of the oven for 43 to 45 minutes, or until set. Cool for 10 minutes before serving. Serve warm, at room temperature, or chilled.

per serving 309 calories, 8 g protein, 65 g carbohydrates, 5 g fiber, 3.4 g fat (1.1 g saturated fat), 208 mg sodium

Southern Baked Sweet Potato Pudding

RS: 6 g

prep time
15 minutes

total time
50 minutes +
30 minutes
to cool

makes
6 servings

1½ pounds sweet
potatoes

2 tablespoons
unsalted butter,
softened

2 large eggs

1 can (12 ounces)
evaporated skim
milk

½ cup sugar

2 teaspoons grated
fresh orange zest

¾ teaspoon ground
cinnamon

¼ teaspoon ground
allspice

¼ teaspoon ground
nutmeg

1 Preheat the oven to 375°F. Coat a 6-cup baking dish with cooking spray.

2 Prick the sweet potatoes with a fork in several places. Microwave for 8 to 9 minutes, or until tender. Let cool for 5 minutes. Peel the potatoes, transfer to a bowl, and mash with the butter. Beat in the eggs with an electric mixer on medium. Add the milk, sugar, orange zest, cinnamon, allspice, and nutmeg and beat until combined.

3 Pour into the prepared baking dish. Bake for 33 to 35 minutes, or until the pudding is just set and the tip of a knife inserted into the center comes out clean. Cool for 30 minutes before serving.

per serving 239 calories, 8 g protein, 40 g carbohydrates, 3 g fiber, 5.7 g fat (3 g saturated fat), 138 mg sodium

Note: If you have time, boil the potato in Step 2 instead of microwaving it. This will preserve even more RS.

Apple–Raisin Bread Pudding with Bourbon Sauce

RS: 3 g

prep time
25 minutes +
1 hour
to stand

total time:
1 hour
40 minutes +
time to stand
and cool

makes
8 servings

12 slices cinnamon raisin swirl bread (such as from Pepperidge Farm), cut into ½" cubes

2 large Golden Delicious apples, peeled, cored, and cut into ½" cubes

3 cups fat-free milk

¼ cup Hi-maize resistant starch

4 large eggs, lightly beaten

¾ cup sugar

3 teaspoons vanilla extract

½ teaspoon ground cinnamon

2 tablespoons water

2 tablespoons bourbon

2 tablespoons unsalted butter

1 Set the bread cubes on a large baking sheet and let stand for 1 hour or more.

2 Preheat the oven to 350°F. Coat a 2-quart (8-cup) baking dish with cooking spray. Place the bread cubes in the dish.

3 Combine the apples, milk, resistant starch, eggs, ½ cup of the sugar, 2 teaspoons of the vanilla extract, and the cinnamon in a bowl. Pour over the bread and let stand, occasionally pressing down on the bread to help saturate, for 10 to 15 minutes.

4 Place the baking dish in a large roasting pan and add enough hot water to come halfway up the sides of the baking dish. Bake for 55 to 60 minutes, or until a knife inserted into the center comes out clean. Let cool for 10 minutes.

5 Combine the remaining ¼ cup sugar and the water in a small skillet over medium-high heat and bring to a boil, stirring. Carefully add the bourbon and the remaining 1 teaspoon vanilla extract and cook for 1 minute. Remove from the heat and whisk in the butter until melted.

6 When ready to serve, spoon the sauce over the bread pudding and cut into 8 portions.

per serving 328 calories, 11 g protein, 55 g carbohydrates, 5 g fiber, 7.7 g fat (2.7 g saturated fat), 233 mg sodium

Grilled Pineapple Salsa on Cinnamon Tostadas

RS: 3 g

prep time
10 minutes

total time
25 minutes +
time to cool

makes
4 servings

4 corn tortillas
(6" each)

1½ teaspoons walnut
oil

4 teaspoons sugar

¼ teaspoon ground
cinnamon

3 (¾"-thick)
pineapple slices
(about ¼ medium
pineapple)

2 bananas, cut into
½" cubes

1 medium mango,
cut into ½" cubes

2 tablespoons
chopped fresh mint

1 tablespoon agave
nectar

2 teaspoons fresh
lime juice

1 Preheat the oven to 400°F.

2 Brush the tortillas with the oil and arrange in a single layer on a large baking sheet. Combine the sugar and cinnamon in a bowl and sprinkle over the tortillas. Bake the tortillas for 10 to 12 minutes, or until crisp. Let cool completely, 10 minutes.

3 Meanwhile, coat a grill pan with cooking spray and heat on medium-high. Add the pineapple slices and cook for 3 to 4 minutes per side, or until well marked and crisp-tender. Transfer to a cutting board and cool for 5 minutes. Cut into ½" cubes. Transfer to a bowl and add the bananas, mango, mint, agave nectar, and lime juice.

4 Place 1 tortilla on each of 4 serving plates. Top each with ¾ cup of the pineapple mixture.

per serving 236 calories, 2 g protein, 53 g carbohydrates, 5 g fiber, 3 g fat (0.3 g saturated fat), 38 mg sodium

Mango-Berry Crisp

RS: 3 g

prep time
20 minutes

total time
50 minutes +
time to cool

makes
6 servings

4 cups fresh or
thawed frozen
mango chunks

2 cups fresh or
thawed frozen
raspberries

¼ cup agave nectar

4 tablespoons
Hi-maize resistant
starch

¼ teaspoon ground
ginger

¾ cup old-fashioned
rolled oats

¼ cup all-purpose
flour

¼ cup packed light
brown sugar

¼ teaspoon ground
cinnamon

3 tablespoons
unsalted butter

1 Preheat the oven to 400°F. Coat an 11" × 7" baking dish with cooking spray.

2 Combine the mango, raspberries, agave nectar, 2 tablespoons of the resistant starch, and the ground ginger in a bowl. Pour into the prepared baking dish.

3 Combine the remaining 2 tablespoons resistant starch, the oats, flour, sugar, and cinnamon in a separate bowl. Add the butter and rub in with your fingertips until the mixture resembles coarse crumbs and clumps together when pressed.

4 Sprinkle the oat mixture evenly over the fruit to cover. Bake for 28 to 30 minutes, or until the filling is bubbly and the topping is lightly browned. Serve warm or at room temperature.

per serving 291 calories, 4 g protein, 60 g carbohydrates, 9 g fiber, 6.7 g fat (3.7 g saturated fat), 4 mg sodium

Pineapple Bananas Foster

RS: 3 g

prep time
5 minutes

total time
10-12
minutes

makes
4 servings

4 teaspoons unsalted butter

½ cup packed light brown sugar

1 tablespoon fresh lemon juice

⅛ teaspoon ground cinnamon

2 bananas, cut into ¼"-thick slices

1 cup fresh pineapple chunks

2 cups fat-free vanilla ice cream

1 Melt the butter in a medium nonstick skillet over medium heat. Add the sugar, lemon juice, and cinnamon and cook, stirring, for about 1 minute, or until the sugar dissolves. Stir in the bananas and pineapple and cook, stirring occasionally, for 4 to 5 minutes, or until starting to soften. Remove from the heat.

2 Place ½ cup of the ice cream into each of 4 wine glasses. Top each with ½ cup of the banana mixture. Serve immediately.

per serving 306 calories, 3 g protein, 67 g carbohydrates, 6 g fiber, 5.6 g fat (3.5 g saturated fat), 59 mg sodium

Sautéed Fruit Sundaes with Sweet Tortilla Crisps

RS: 2 g

prep time
15 minutes

total time
25 minutes

makes
4 servings

3 corn tortillas (6" each)

2 tablespoons sugar

1 tablespoon unsalted butter

1 large mango, peeled, pitted, and cut into ½" cubes

1 cup sliced fresh strawberries

2 medium bananas, cut into ½"-thick slices

1 tablespoon fresh lime juice

1 tablespoon chopped fresh cilantro

2 cups fat-free vanilla ice cream

½ cup fat-free nondairy whipped topping

1 Preheat the oven to 425°F. Coat a large baking sheet with cooking spray.

2 Coat the tortillas with cooking spray. Cut each into 4 wedges and place in a single layer on the prepared baking sheet. Sprinkle each wedge with ½ teaspoon sugar. Bake for 8 to 9 minutes, or until crisp. Cool on the sheet.

3 Meanwhile, melt the butter in a medium nonstick skillet over medium-high heat. Add the mango, strawberries, and banana and cook, stirring occasionally, for 3 minutes, or until the fruit is softened but still holds its shape. Add the lime juice and cook for 30 seconds. Remove from the heat and stir in the cilantro. Cool for 3 minutes.

4 Scoop ½ cup of the ice cream into each of 4 sundae glasses. Top each with ½ cup of the fruit mixture. Dollop 2 tablespoons of the whipped topping on top of each sundae. Insert 3 tortilla crisps into the top of each so that they are standing up. Serve immediately.

per serving 308 calories, 5 g protein, 63 g carbohydrates, 8 g fiber, 7 g fat (4.4 g saturated fat), 60 mg sodium

Granola-Topped Strawberry Banana Split

RS: 3 g

total time
12 minutes +
5 minutes
to cool

makes
4 servings

2 cups strawberries, sliced

2 tablespoons orange juice

2 teaspoons agave nectar

2 cups fat-free vanilla ice cream

2 bananas, halved lengthwise and again crosswise, making 8 pieces

½ cup Maple, Oat, Raisin, and Walnut Granola (page 64)

4 maraschino cherries, rinsed

1 Combine the strawberries, orange juice, and agave nectar in a small saucepan over medium-high heat. Cook, stirring occasionally, for 2 to 2½ minutes, or until softened. Let cool for 5 minutes.

2 To assemble, scoop ½ cup of the ice cream into each of 4 bowls. Add 2 banana pieces, ¼ cup of the strawberry mixture, and 2 tablespoons of the granola, and top with a cherry. Serve immediately.

per serving 239 calories, 5 g protein, 53 g carbohydrates, 8 g fiber, 3 g fat (1 g saturated fat), 62 mg sodium

Ice Cream Bombes with Chocolate Drizzle

RS: 2 g

prep time
10 minutes +
30 minutes
to freeze

makes
4 servings

4 slices whole wheat cinnamon raisin swirl bread (such as from Pepperidge Farm)

2 cups fat-free vanilla, chocolate, or strawberry ice cream, slightly softened

1 medium banana, sliced

½ cup nondairy whipped topping

¼ cup chocolate syrup

4 strawberries, sliced

1 Working 1 slice at a time, roll the bread slices with a rolling pin to flatten and slightly enlarge. With a long side of the bread closest to you, spread ½ cup of the ice cream across the center. Top with one-fourth of the banana slices. Place a large piece of plastic wrap under the bread slice, then roll up the bread to form a cylinder. Wrap the plastic around the cylinder and twist the ends tightly to help keep the cylinder shape. Place in the freezer. Repeat with remaining ingredients.

2 To serve, remove the bombes from the freezer and unwrap. Cut each on an angle into 5 slices and arrange on small plates. Dollop with the whipped topping, then drizzle with the chocolate syrup. Garnish with the strawberry slices.

per serving 280 calories, 6 g protein, 57 g carbohydrates, 6 g fiber, 4.7 g fat (2.5 g saturated fat), 168 mg sodium

6-Week
Skinny Carbs
Diet Menus

So just what will you eat on a day on the Skinny Carbs Diet? You grab a Banana-Pecan Oat Muffin (page 62) for a quick breakfast on the way out the door, tote your Chicken Tortilla Soup with Avocado (page 72) and a Warm Succotash Salad with Bacon (page 97) to the office for a filling lunch, nosh on Chipotle–Red Bean Dip with Pita Wedges (page 186) for a simple midday snack, head home for some comforting Home-Style Macaroni and Cheese (page 153)—and end your day with some Chocolate Chip–Oatmeal Cookies (page 195). That's right, this is no ordinary diet!

As described in Chapter 3, the diet guidelines are simple and focus on helping you gradually increase the amount of RS and fiber you eat. To summarize:

Phase 1 Daily Goals: approximately 1,400 calories (for women) or 1,800 calories (for men), at least 20 grams of fiber, and 5 grams of RS

Phase 2 Daily Goals: approximately 1,600 calories (for women) or 2,000 (for men), at least 25 grams of fiber, and 10 grams of RS

Phase 3 Daily Goals: approximately 1,600 calories (for women) or 2,000 (for men), at least 30 grams of fiber, and 20 grams of RS

For those of you who like flexibility, you simply may add the RS-rich foods listed in Chapter 3 to what you're already eating. Our 150 recipes will give you a lot of delicious ways to do this, but feel free to experiment! Just track what you're eating to make sure that you're reaching the optimum levels of RS and fiber. A food diary or online health tracker, such as the one found at www.prevention.com/healthtracker, can help. Once you compare what you're eating with the list of RS-rich foods, you might even find you already are meeting some of these daily goals.

For those of you who don't want to spend a lot of time planning or calculating grams of RS or fiber, here are 6 weeks of Skinny Carbs Diet menus for you. You'll see that we've supplemented the RS-rich recipes in this book with others that might have less RS but plenty of deliciousness, just to add some variety to your diet. These bonus recipes appear immediately after the weekly meal plans; you can find other good recipe ideas at www.prevention.com/recipefinder.

But remember that these menus are just suggestions. If you want to swap meals within any given phase of the diet, please do. You also can tweak these meals to your tastes—for example, feel free to substitute Salmon with Ginger-Soy Butter for tuna with teriyaki sauce. If you feel there's too much cooking involved on any given day, by all means, pour yourself a bowl of store-bought granola rather than making your own. Just pay attention to the calorie, fiber, and RS counts. And don't forget to count calories from beverages and other drinks; for meals that don't include beverages, try water or tea or coffee.

Phase 1: Week 1

Daily Goal: approximately 1,400 calories, at least 20 g fiber, and 5g RS

Monday TOTAL 1,377 calories, 19 g fiber, 5 g RS

Breakfast	Lunch	Dinner	Dessert
▪ Peanut Butter Breakfast Shake (page 250)	▪ Spinach and Goat Cheese Salad ▪ Grilled Eggplant (page 245)	▪ Steak and 'Shrooms ▪ Zucchini and Carrots with Walnuts (page 262)	▪ Coconut Rice Pudding (page 203)
391 calories, 5 g fiber	*272 calories, 6 g fiber*	*478 calories, 7 g fiber*	*236 calories, 1 g fiber, 5 g RS*

Tuesday TOTAL 1,399 calories, 22 g fiber, 5 g RS

Breakfast	Lunch	Dinner	Dessert
▪ Yogurt, Granola, and Banana-Strawberry Parfait (page 65) ▪ Chai tea with 3 Tbsp vanilla soy milk	▪ Turkey- Avocado Cobb Salad (page 261) ▪ Pumpkin-Ginger Soup (page 252)	▪ Grilled Shrimp with Mango-Banana Salsa (page 148) ▪ Stir-Fry of Asparagus and Bell Pepper with Ginger and Sesame (page 258)	▪ Banana Ice Cream
405 calories, 5 g fiber, 5 g RS	*390 calories, 9 g fiber*	*484 calories, 6 g fiber*	*119 calories, 2 g fiber*

Wednesday TOTAL 1,382 calories, 21 g fiber, 5 g RS

Breakfast	Lunch	Dinner	Dessert
▪ Organic Green Omelet (page 248)	▪ Roasted Garlic Soup with Pork and Broccoli (page 253) ▪ Avocado, Grapefruit, and Papaya Salad (page 231)	▪ Hoisin Tofu and Snap Pea Stir-Fry over Brown Rice (page 162)	▪ Chocolate Mousse (page 239)
448 calories, 3 g fiber	*412 calories, 9 g fiber*	*252 calories, 6 g fiber, 5 g RS*	*270 calories, 3 g fiber*

Thursday TOTAL 1,406 calories, 20 g fiber, 5 g RS

Breakfast	Lunch	Dinner	Dessert
■ Breakfast Smoothie with Flax (page 233)	■ Seared Scallops with Pumpkin Soup (page 255)	■ Arroz con Pollo (page 138) ■ Broccoli Spears with Goat Cheese (page 235)	■ Apple Strudel (page 228)
382 calories, 7 g fiber	*426 calories, 7 g fiber*	*445 calories, 5 g fiber, 5 g RS*	*153 calories, 1 g fiber*

Friday TOTAL 1,406 calories, 22 g fiber, 5 g RS

Breakfast	Lunch	Dinner	Dessert
■ Frittata ■ Coffee with 2 tsp sugar and 4 Tbsp soy milk	■ California Wrap (page 91) ■ Citrusy Red-Pepper Soup (page 240)	■ Creamy Smoked Salmon and Dill Fettuccine (page 143) ■ Creamy Garlic Spinach (page 241)	■ Caramel Flan with Fresh Fruit (page 236)
298 calories, 1 g fiber	*387 calories, 10 g fiber, 1 g RS*	*485 calories, 9 g fiber, 4 g RS*	*252 calories, 2 g fiber*

Saturday TOTAL 1,400 calories, 20 g fiber, 5 g RS

Breakfast	Lunch	Dinner	Dessert
■ Whole Grain Blueberry Buttermilk Pancakes (page 56) ■ 8 oz cranberry juice cocktail	■ Spiced Butternut Soup with Crab (page 257) ■ Watercress and Radicchio Salad with Honey-Mustard Vinaigrette (page 261)	■ Pan-Fried Chicken with Tarragon (page 249) ■ Asparagus with Pine Nuts (page 230)	■ Choco Espresso Soufflés (page 238)
446 calories, 6 g fiber, 5 g RS	*391 calories, 6 g fiber*	*367 calories, 7 g fiber*	*196 calories, 1 g fiber*

Sunday TOTAL 1,403 calories, 20 g fiber, 5 g RS

Breakfast	Lunch	Dinner	Dessert
■ Asparagus and Goat Cheese Omelets (page 229) ■ 8 oz orange juice	■ Seared Salmon over Curried Lentils (page 144)	■ Peaches and Pork Chops (page 249) ■ Roasted Brussels Sprouts and Onions with Thyme (page 252)	■ Mocha Tofu Pudding (page 247)
405 calories, 2 g fiber	*304 calories, 6 g fiber, 5 g RS*	*544 calories, 10 g fiber*	*160 calories, 2 g fiber*

Phase 2: Week 2

Daily Goal: approximately 1,600 calories, at least 25 g fiber, and 10 g RS

Monday   TOTAL 1,606 calories, 26 g fiber, 16 g RS

Breakfast	Lunch	Snack	Dinner	Dessert
■ Asparagus and Goat Cheese Omelets (page 229) ■ 6 oz orange juice	■ Chicken and Potato Panini with Basil-Lemon Mayonnaise (page 86) ■ Big Broiled Balsamic Mushrooms (page 233)	■ Fresh Corn, Pepper, and Avocado Salad (page 181)	■ Home-Style Macaroni and Cheese (page 153)	■ Southern Baked Sweet Potato Pudding (page 206)
377 calories, 2 g fiber	*378 calories, 9 g fiber, 3 g RS*	*214 calories, 9 g fiber, 3 g RS*	*398 calories, 3 g fiber, 4 g RS*	*239 calories, 3 g fiber, 6 g RS*

Tuesday   TOTAL 1, 589 calories, 25 g fiber, 19 g RS

Breakfast	Lunch	Snack	Dinner	Dessert
■ Hot Barley with Apples, Raisins, Milk, and Honey (page 49) ■ 8 oz cranberry juice	■ Baked Halibut with Onions and Peppers (page 231)	■ Strawberry-Banana Malted Milk (page 190)	■ Jerk Chicken with Mashed Sweet Plantains (page 136) ■ Stir-Fried Kale with Almonds (page 258)	■ Glazed Mixed Berry–Lemon Bundt Cake (page 198)
405 calories, 6 g fiber, 8 g RS	*235 calories, 1 g fiber,*	*193 calories, 6 g fiber, 3 g RS*	*492 calories, 6 g fiber, 4 g RS*	*264 calories, 6 g fiber, 4 g RS*

Wednesday   TOTAL 1,600 calories, 28 g fiber, 15 g RS

Breakfast	Lunch	Snack	Dinner	Dessert
■ Potato Pancakes with Eggs (page 55) ■ Soy Milk Berry Smoothie (page 256)	■ Grilled Vegetable and Hummus Pitas (page 93)	■ Berries in a Cloud (page 232)	■ Lentil and Tomato Pasta Toss (page 156) ■ Okra with Tomatoes, Ginger, and Basil (page 248)	■ Caramel Flan with Fresh Fruit (page 236)
409 calories, 6 g fiber, 5 g RS	*314 calories, 9 g fiber, 4 g RS*	*221 calories, 1 g fiber,*	*404 calories, 20 g fiber, 6 g RS*	*252 calories, 2 g fiber*

Thursday TOTAL 1,590 calories, 29 g fiber, 16 g RS

Breakfast	Lunch	Snack	Dinner	Dessert
■ Creamy Cheddar and Corn-Studded Grits (page 48) ■ 4 oz cranberry juice	■ California Wrap (page 91) ■ Spicy Snack Mix (page 189)	■ Caramelized Onion and Pea Rice Pilaf (page 124)	■ Root Vegetable, Beef, and Barley Stew (page 133)	■ Apple–Raisin Bread Pudding with Bourbon Sauce (page 207)
281 calories, 4 g fiber, 1 g RS	*527 calories, 12 g fiber, 2 g RS*	*201 calories, 3 g fiber, 6 g RS*	*253 calories, 5 g fiber, 4 g RS*	*328 calories, 5 g fiber, 3 g RS*

Friday TOTAL 1,601 calories, 30 g fiber, 19 g RS

Breakfast	Lunch	Snack	Dinner	Dessert
■ Sweet Breakfast Porridge (page 45) ■ Coffee with 1 tsp sugar and 4 Tbsp soy milk	■ Curried Apple and Pear Soup (page 241)	■ Potato Focaccia Squares with Tomato and Parmesan (page 177)	■ Sweet Potato and Black Bean Cakes with Chicken and Cumin-Cilantro Cream (page 137) ■ Zucchini and Carrots with Walnuts (page 262)	■ Pineapple Bananas Foster (page 210)
317 calories, 1 g fiber, 4 g RS	*272 calories, 8 g fiber*	*175 calories, 6 g fiber, 7 g RS*	*542 calories, 9 g fiber, 6 g RS*	*306 calories, 6 g fiber, 3 g RS*

Saturday TOTAL 1,627 calories, 26 g fiber, 15 g RS

Breakfast	Lunch	Snack	Dinner	Dessert
■ Banana-Pecan Oat Muffins (page 62)	■ Chicken Tortilla Soup with Avocado (page 72) ■ Warm Succotash Salad with Bacon (page 97)	■ Chipotle–Red Bean Dip with Pita Wedges (page 186)	■ Salmon with Ginger-Soy Butter (page 254) ■ Asian Sesame Coleslaw (page 229)	■ Creamy Peach-Cranberry Rice Pudding (page 204)
194 calories, 4 g fiber, 4 g RS	*535 calories, 11 g fiber, 7 g RS*	*157 calories, 7 g fiber, 1 g RS*	*456 calories, 3 g fiber*	*265 calories, 1 g fiber, 3 g RS*

Sunday TOTAL 1,605 calories, 27 g fiber, 19 g RS

Breakfast	Lunch	Snack	Dinner	Dessert
■ Spiced Yam Waffles with Maple Syrup (page 59) ■ Coffee with 1 tsp sugar and 4 Tbsp soy milk	■ Chicken and Potato Panini with Basil-Lemon Mayonnaise (page 86)	■ Watermelon Salad (page 262) ■ Chilled Mango-Lime Soup (page 237)	■ Linguine with Parsley-Basil Pesto (page 159)	■ Sautéed Fruit Sundaes with Sweet Tortilla Crisps (page 211)
386 calories, 8 g fiber, 8 g RS	*325 calories, 5 g fiber, 3 g RS*	*275 calories, 3 g fiber*	*311 calories, 3 g fiber, 6 g RS*	*308 calories, 8 g fiber, 2 g RS*

Phase 2: Week 3

Daily Goal: approximately 1,600 calories, at least 25g fiber, and 10 g RS

Monday TOTAL 1,602 calories, 29 g fiber, 12 g RS

Breakfast	Lunch	Snack	Dinner	Dessert
■ Get Up and Go Veggie Omelet (page 244) ■ 4 oz cranberry juice	■ Teriyaki Tofu Wraps with Brown Rice (page 90) ■ Citrusy Red-Pepper Soup (page 240)	■ English Muffin Grilled Cheese (page 179)	■ Ratatouille Lasagna (page 155) ■ Sautéed Yellow Squash, Zucchini, and Onions (page 254)	■ Coconut-Macadamia Banana Bread (page 200)
312 calories, 1 g fiber	*410 calories, 6 g fiber, 3 g RS*	*224 calories, 10 g fiber, 1 g RS*	*465 calories, 8 g fiber, 5 g RS*	*191 calories, 4 g fiber, 3 g RS*

Tuesday TOTAL 1,601 calories, 26 g fiber, 18 g RS

Breakfast	Lunch	Snack	Dinner	Dessert
■ Savory Breakfast Porridge (page 46) ■ Soy Hot Chocolate (page 256)	■ Black Bean and Cheddar Burritos (page 92)	■ Chicken and Whole Grain Noodle Soup (page 71)	■ Seasoned Pepper Turkey with Portuguese Tomatoes (page 255) ■ Balsamic Bell Peppers with Pine Nuts (page 232)	■ Granola-Topped Strawberry Banana Split (page 212)
391 calories, 2 g fiber, 4 g RS	*329 calories, 9 g fiber, 6 g RS*	*278 calories, 4 g fiber, 3 g RS*	*364 calories, 3 g fiber*	*239 calories, 8 g fiber, 5 g RS*

Wednesday TOTAL 1,614 calories, 25 g fiber, 18 g RS

Breakfast	Lunch	Snack	Dinner	Dessert
■ Sautéed Banana-Filled Crepes (page 60) ■ 8 oz cranberry juice	■ Warm Succotash Salad with Bacon (page 97)	■ Soy Milk Berry Smoothie (page 256)	■ Home-Style Macaroni and Cheese (page 153) ■ Zucchini and Red Pepper in Lemon-Herb Butter (page 263)	■ Whole Cornbread Pudding (page 202)
386 calories, 6 g fiber, 5 g RS	*241 calories, 6 g fiber, 6 g RS*	*169 calories, 4 g fiber*	*507 calories, 5 g fiber, 4 g RS*	*311 calories, 4 g fiber, 3 g RS*

Thursday TOTAL 1,575 calories, 25 g fiber, 13 g RS

▪Maple, Oat, Raisin, and Walnut Granola (page 64) ▪8 oz grapefruit juice	▪Turkey-Avocado Cobb Salad (page 261)	▪Potato, Corn, and Clam Chowder (page 73)	▪Creamy Smoked Salmon and Dill Fettuccine (page 143) ▪Creamy Garlic Spinach (page 241)	▪Banana-Chocolate Turnovers (page 201)
345 calories, 4 g fiber, 1 g RS	*288 calories, 5 g fiber*	*162 calories, 3 g fiber, 4 g RS*	*485 calories, 9 g fiber, 4 g RS*	*295 calories, 4 g fiber, 4 g RS*

Friday TOTAL 1,604 calories, 26 g fiber, 19 g RS

Breakfast	Lunch	Snack	Dinner	Dessert
▪Corn Tortilla Huevos Rancheros (page 54)	▪Salade Niçoise (page 100) ▪Cream of Roasted Red Pepper and Tomato Soup (page 241)	▪Hot Artichoke-Bean Dip with Multigrain Crisps (page 185)	▪Spaghetti Pie Bolognese (page 132)	▪A Trip to the Peach (page 231)
256 calories, 5 g fiber, 3 g RS	*452 calories, 9 g fiber, 8 g RS*	*235 calories, 6 g fiber, 2 g RS*	*376 calories, 5 g fiber, 6 g RS*	*285 calories, 1 g fiber*

Saturday TOTAL 1,599 calories, 25 g fiber, 15 g RS

Breakfast	Lunch	Snack	Dinner	Dessert
▪Creamy Cheddar and Corn-Studded Grits (page 48) ▪8 oz orange juice	▪White Bean Panzanella (page 101)	▪Edamame, Tomato, and Cheese on Multigrain Pita (page 176)	▪Mixed Seafood Risotto (page 142) ▪Tossed Romaine and Radish Salad (page 260)	▪Chocolate Chip-Oatmeal Cookie (page 195)
326 calories, 4 g fiber, 1 g RS	*273 calories, 7 g fiber, 4 g RS*	*254 calories, 7 g fiber, 1 g RS*	*568 calories, 4 g fiber, 6 g RS*	*178 calories, 3 g fiber, 3 g RS*

Sunday TOTAL 1,598 calories, 25 g fiber, 15 g RS

Breakfast	Lunch	Snack	Dinner	Dessert
▪Deviled Egg and Spinach Casserole (page 242)	▪Chicken, Corn, and Black Bean Salad with Lime and Cilantro (page 99)	▪Peanut Butter-Banana Smoothie (page 191)	▪Seared Salmon over Curried Lentils (page 144) ▪Asparagus with Orange-Walnut Vinaigrette (page 230)	▪Apple-Ginger Fool (page 228)
405 calories, 4 g fiber	*311 calories, 8 g fiber, 5 g RS*	*260 calories, 3 g fiber, 5 g RS*	*418 calories, 9 g fiber, 5 g RS*	*206 calories, 1 g fiber*

Phase 2: Week 4

Daily Goal: approximately 1,600 calories, at least 25 g fiber, and 10 g RS

Monday TOTAL 1,597 calories, 25 g fiber, 15 g RS

Breakfast	Lunch	Snack	Dinner	Dessert
Bacon and Red Pepper Strata (page 52) 8 oz grapefruit juice	Ratatouille Lasagna (page 155)	Honey-Pecan Smoothie (page 246)	Cornmeal-Crusted Potato Cod Cakes with Tartar Sauce (page 145) Broccoli and Napa Cabbage Salad with Miso Dressing (page 234)	Pear-Cranberry Barley Pudding (page 205)
340 calories, 6 g fiber, 1 g RS	312 calories, 5 g fiber, 5 g RS	214 calories, 2 g fiber	422 calories, 7 g fiber, 4 g RS	309 calories, 5 g fiber, 5 g RS

Tuesday TOTAL 1,626 calories, 25 g fiber, 18 g RS

Breakfast	Lunch	Snack	Dinner	Dessert
Whole Grain Blueberry Buttermilk Pancakes (page 56)	Hawaiian Chicken Salad (page 246)	Peanut Butter–Banana Smoothie (page 191)	Seared Salmon over Curried Lentils (page 144) Zucchini with Garlic and Oregano (page 263)	Whole Cornbread Pudding (page 202)
309 calories, 6 g fiber, 5 g RS	386 calories, 3 g fiber	260 calories, 3 g fiber, 5 g RS	360 calories, 9 g fiber, 5 g RS	311 calories, 4 g fiber, 3 g RS

Wednesday TOTAL 1,617 calories, 26 g fiber, 20 g RS

Breakfast	Lunch	Snack	Dinner	Dessert
Yogurt, Granola, and Banana-Strawberry Parfait (page 65)	Fennel Salad with Olives, Eggs, and Tuna (page 243) Cream of Mushroom Soup (page 240)	Black Pepper Biscuits with Chive Cream Cheese (page 178)	Rosemary and Potato Pizza (page 161) Broccoli with Tahini Sauce (page 235)	Coconut-Macadamia Banana Bread (page 200) Peachy Frozen Yogurt (page 250)
385 calories, 5 g fiber, 5 g RS	412 calories, 3 g fiber	152 calories, 3 g fiber, 3 g RS	376 calories, 11 g fiber, 9 g RS	292 calories, 4 g fiber, 3 g RS

Thursday TOTAL 1,614 calories, 30 g fiber, 15 g RS

Breakfast	Lunch	Snack	Dinner	Dessert
■Apple Dutch-Baby Pancake (page 58) ■1 cup hot cocoa	■Grilled Jerk Chicken with Pineapple and Red Pepper (page 245)	■Caramelized Leek and Potato Soup (page 81)	■Orecchiette with Garlic, Sausage, and Broccoli Rabe (page 139)	■Pineapple Smoothie (page 250)
386 calories, 9 g fiber, 4 g RS	288 calories, 1 g fiber	272 calories, 4 g fiber, 6 g RS	385 calories, 11 g fiber, 5 g RS	283 calories, 2 g fiber

Friday TOTAL 1,605 calories, 25 g fiber, 18 g RS

Breakfast	Lunch	Snack	Dinner	Dessert
■Potato Pancakes with Eggs (page 55) ■8 oz cranberry juice cocktail	■Black Bean and Cheddar Burritos (page 92)	■Peanut Noodle Salad (page 107)	■Grilled Chicken Burgers with Vegetable Salsa (page 244)	■Mango-Berry Crisp (page 209)
377 calories, 2 g fiber, 5 g RS	329 calories, 9 g fiber, 6 g RS	329 calories, 4 g fiber, 4 g RS	279 calories, 1 g fiber	291 calories, 9 g fiber, 3 g RS

Saturday TOTAL 1,619 calories, 26 g fiber, 13 g RS

Breakfast	Lunch	Snack	Dinner	Dessert
■Lemon-Barley Silver Dollar Pancakes (page 57) ■8 oz orange juice	■California Wrap (page 91)	■Kiwifruit Shakes (page 247) ■4 oz cranberry juice	■Ratatouille Lasagna (page 155)	■Pineapple Bananas Foster (page 210)
430 calories, 6 g fiber, 7 g RS	290 calories, 8 g fiber, 1 g RS	281 calories, 1 g fiber	312 calories, 5 g fiber, 5 g RS	306 calories, 6 g fiber, 3 g RS

Sunday TOTAL 1,612 calories, 25 g fiber, 16 g RS

Breakfast	Lunch	Snack	Dinner	Dessert
■Scrambled Eggs with Two-Potato Hash (page 50)	■Shrimp Lettuce Wraps (page 256) ■Chilled Tomato and Dill Soup (page 237)	■Chicken Tortilla Soup with Avocado (page 72)	■Spaghetti Pie Bolognese (page 132) ■Broiled Asparagus (page 236)	■Apple–Raisin Bread Pudding with Bourbon Sauce (page 207)
213 calories, 3 g fiber, 6 g RS	340 calories, 6 g fiber	294 calories, 5 g fiber, 1 g RS	435 calories, 6 g fiber, 6 g RS	328 calories, 5 g fiber, 3 g RS

Phase 2: Week 5

Daily Goal: approximately 1,600 calories, at least 25 g fiber, and 10 g RS

Monday TOTAL 1,605 calories, 26 g fiber, 17 g RS

Breakfast	Lunch	Snack	Dinner	Dessert
■ Apple Dutch-Baby Pancake (page 58)	■ Chicken and Potato Panini with Basil-Lemon Mayonnaise (page 86)	■ Tomatoes and White Beans on Multigrain Crostini (page 175)	■ Pork Loin with Apple Cider Glaze (page 251)	■ Gingersnap-Crusted Sweet Potato Pie (page 199)
306 calories, 9 g fiber, 4 g RS	325 calories, 5 g fiber, 3 g RS	285 calories, 6 g fiber, 4 g RS	408 calories, 3 g fiber	281 calories, 3 g fiber, 6 g RS

Tuesday TOTAL 1,601 calories, 27 g fiber, 19 g RS

Breakfast	Lunch	Snack	Dinner	Dessert
■ Creamy Cheddar and Corn-Studded Grits (page 48)	■ Home-Style Macaroni and Cheese (page 153)	■ Pasta Fagioli (page 70) ■ Garlic-Soy Spinach (page 243)	■ Jerk Chicken with Mashed Sweet Plantains (page 136)	■ Glazed Mixed Berry–Lemon Bundt Cake (page 198)
214 calories, 4 g fiber, 1 g RS	398 calories, 3 g fiber, 4 g RS	359 calories, 11 g fiber, 6 g RS	366 calories, 3 g fiber, 4 g RS	264 calories, 6 g fiber, 4 g RS

Wednesday TOTAL 1,600 calories, 25 g fiber, 17 g RS

Breakfast	Lunch	Snack	Dinner	Dessert
■ Hot Barley with Apples, Raisins, Milk, and Honey (page 49) ■ 8 oz cranberry juice	■ Chicken and Potato Panini with Basil-Lemon Mayonnaise (page 86)	■ Broccoli Rabe and Roasted Red Pepper Wraps (page 234)	■ Smoked Salmon on Multigrain Bread with Lemon-Dill Cream Cheese (page 89)	■ Coconut Rice Pudding (page 203)
405 calories, 6 g fiber, 8 g RS	325 calories, 5 g fiber, 3 g RS	189 calories, 2 g fiber	445 calories, 11 g fiber, 1 g RS	236 calories, 1 g fiber, 5 g RS

Thursday TOTAL 1,593 calories, 25 g fiber, 16 g RS

Breakfast	Lunch	Snack	Dinner	Dessert
▪Bacon and Red Pepper Strata (page 52) ▪1 cup hot cocoa	▪Summer Tomato and Arugula Salad (page 259) ▪Tropical Smoothie (page 260)	▪Grilled Shrimp with Mango-Banana Salsa (page 148)	▪Linguine with Parsley-Basil Pesto (page 159) ▪Roasted Carrots and Parsnips (page 252)	▪Southern Baked Sweet Potato Pudding (page 206)
324 calories, 6 g fiber, 1 g RS	386 calories, 4 g fiber	212 calories, 2 g fiber, 3 g RS	432 calories, 10 g fiber, 6 g RS	239 calories, 3 g fiber, 6 g RS

Friday TOTAL 1,598 calories, 26 g fiber, 17 g RS

Breakfast	Lunch	Snack	Dinner	Dessert
▪Yogurt, Granola, and Banana-Strawberry Parfait (page 65)	▪Tuscan Bread and White Bean Soup (page 76)	▪Tuna Salad (page 260)	▪Seared Salmon over Curried Lentils (page 144)	▪Whole Cornbread Pudding (page 202)
385 calories, 5 g fiber, 5 g RS	292 calories, 8 g fiber, 4 g RS	306 calories, 3 g fiber	304 calories, 6 g fiber, 5 g RS	311 calories, 4 g fiber, 3 g RS

Saturday TOTAL 1,599 calories, 26 g fiber, 20 g RS

Breakfast	Lunch	Snack	Dinner	Dessert
▪Whole Grain Blueberry Buttermilk Pancakes (page 56) ▪8 oz cranberry juice cocktail	▪Chicken Tortilla Soup with Avocado (page 72)	▪Spicy Snack Mix (page 189)	▪Beef and Chipotle Two-Potato Skillet (page 131) ▪Mushrooms and Broccoli (page 247)	▪Pineapple Bananas Foster (page 210)
446 calories, 6 g fiber, 5 g RS	294 calories, 5 g fiber, 1 g RS	237 calories, 4 g fiber, 5 g RS	318 calories, 5 g fiber, 6 g RS	306 calories, 6 g fiber, 3 g RS

Sunday TOTAL 1,600 calories, 29 g fiber, 15 g RS

Breakfast	Lunch	Snack	Dinner	Dessert
▪Multigrain French Toast with Honeyed Strawberries and Bananas (page 63)	▪Beef and Mushroom-Barley Soup (page 69) ▪Watercress and Radicchio Salad with Honey-Mustard Vinaigrette (page 261)	▪Soy Milk Berry Smoothie (page 256)	▪Baked Penne with Ground Turkey, Ricotta, and Mozzarella (page 140) ▪Romaine and Watercress Salad with Anchovy Vinaigrette (page 253)	▪Ice Cream Bombes with Chocolate Drizzle (page 213)
285 calories, 9 g fiber, 4 g RS	431 calories, 6 g fiber, 4 g RS	169 calories, 4 g fiber	435 calories, 2 g fiber, 6 g RS	280 calories, 6 g fiber, 3 g RS

Phase 3: Week 6

Daily Goal: approximately 1,600 calories, at least 30 g fiber, and 20 g RS

Monday TOTAL 1,632 calories, 32 g fiber, 25 g RS

Breakfast	Lunch	Snack	Dinner	Dessert
■ Savory Breakfast Porridge (page 46) ■ 4 oz orange juice	■ Chicken Soft Tacos with Fast Bean Salsa (page 87)	■ French Lentil Salad (page 102) ■ ½ serving Corn Flake–Crusted Noodle Kugel (page 113)	■ Orecchiette with Garlic, Sausage, and Broccoli Rabe (page 139)	■ Gingersnap-Crusted Sweet Potato Pie (page 199)
323 calories, 1 g fiber, 4 g RS	257 calories, 7 g fiber, 4 g RS	386 calories, 10 g fiber, 6 g RS	385 calories, 11 g fiber, 5 g RS	281 calories, 3 g fiber, 6 g RS

Tuesday TOTAL 1,586 calories, 32 g fiber, 35 g RS

Breakfast	Lunch	Snack	Dinner	Dessert
■ Banana-Pecan Oat Muffins (page 62)	■ Potato, Corn, and Clam Chowder (page 73) ■ Orzo Salad with Grape Tomatoes, Mozzarella, and Basil (page 106)	■ Strawberry-Banana Malted Milk (page 190)	■ Navy Bean Gumbo over Rice (page 75) ■ Corn-Studded Jalapeño Corn Bread (page 111)	■ Coconut Rice Pudding (page 203)
194 calories, 4 g fiber, 4 g RS	455 calories, 6 g fiber, 10 g RS	194 calories, 6 g fiber, 3 g RS	507 calories, 15 g fiber, 13 g RS	236 calories, 1 g fiber, 5 g RS

Wednesday TOTAL 1,597 calories, 34 g fiber, 26 g RS

Breakfast	Lunch	Snack	Dinner	Dessert
■ Egg and Bacon Breakfast Sandwich (page 53) ■ English Breakfast tea with 3 Tbsp milk and 1 tsp sugar	■ Chicken and Whole Grain Noodle Soup (page 71) ■ Salade Niçoise (page 100)	■ Hot Artichoke-Bean Dip with Multigrain Crisps (page 185)	■ African Yam and Vegetable Stew (page 171)	■ Chocolate Chip–Oatmeal Cookies (page 195)
250 calories, 8 g fiber, 1 g RS	597 calories, 8 g fiber, 11 g RS	235 calories, 6 g fiber, 2 g RS	337 calories, 11 g fiber, 9 g RS	178 calories, 3 g fiber, 3 g RS

Thursday TOTAL 1,600 calories, 31 g fiber, 38 g RS

Breakfast	Lunch	Snack	Dinner	Dessert
■Hot Barley with Apples, Raisins, Milk, and Honey (page 49) ■Hot spiced chai	■Penne Pomodoro (page 154) ■Green Pea Soup with Whole Grain Croutons (page 79)	■Marinated Roasted Pepper and Red Potato Salad (page 182)	■Mixed Seafood Risotto (page 142)	■Coconut- Macadamia Banana Bread (page 200)
336 calories, 6 g fiber, 8 g RS	567 calories, 15 g fiber, 10 g RS	129 calories, 3 g fiber, 11 g RS	377 calories, 3 g fiber, 6 g RS	191 calories, 4 g fiber, 3 g RS

Friday TOTAL 1,605 calories, 37 g fiber, 21 g RS

Breakfast	Lunch	Snack	Dinner	Dessert
■Corn Tortilla Huevos Rancheros (page 54)	■Pizza Margherita (page 160) ■Summer Salad with Green Goddess Dressing (page 259)	■Shrimp Salad Rolls (page 88)	■Tamale Pie with Red Beans and Corn (page 134) ■Steamed Spinach (page 258)	■Creamy Peach- Cranberry Rice Pudding (page 204)
256 calories, 5 g fiber, 3 g RS	400 calories, 9 g fiber, 5 g RS	294 calories, 4 g fiber, 5 g RS	390 calories, 18 g fiber, 5 g RS	265 calories, 1 g fiber, 3 g RS

Saturday TOTAL 1,602 calories, 39 g fiber, 25 g RS

Breakfast	Lunch	Snack	Dinner	Dessert
■Multigrain French Toast with Honeyed Strawberries and Bananas (page 63)	■Beef and Mushroom-Barley Soup (page 69)	■Spiced Corn Tortilla Crisps with Pinto Bean Salsa (page 184)	■Shrimp and Haricot Vert Fajitas (page 147) ■Tuscan Bread and White Bean Soup (page 76)	■Cranberry- Chocolate Chip Blondies (page 197)
285 calories, 9 g fiber, 4 g RS	262 calories, 5 g fiber, 4 g RS	202 calories, 8 g fiber, 5 g RS	609 calories, 13 g fiber, 9 g RS	249 calories, 4 g fiber, 3 g RS

Sunday TOTAL 1,594 calories, 37 g fiber, 36 g RS

Breakfast	Lunch	Snack	Dinner	Dessert
■Sautéed Banana- Filled Crepes (page 60) ■4 oz orange juice	■Wheat Berry and Barley Salad with Dried Fruit and Goat Cheese (page 103) ■Smoky Lentil Soup (page 77)	■Farfalle Salad with Chicken, Almonds, and Grapes (page 98)	■Arroz con Pollo (page 138) ■Maduros (Sautéed Sweet Plantains) (page 126)	■Granola-Topped Strawberry Banana Split (page 212)
305 calories, 6 g fiber, 5 g RS	464 calories, 18 g fiber, 16 g RS	338 calories, 3 g fiber, 4 g RS	456 calories, 4 g fiber, 8 g RS	239 calories, 8 g fiber, 3 g RS

Bonus Recipes

(Listed in alphabetical order.)

Apple-Ginger Fool

prep time 6 minutes ■ **total time** 6 minutes ■ **makes** 6 servings

2 cups applesauce

¼ cup + 1 tablespoon confectioners' sugar

1 tablespoon applejack or brandy (optional)

½ tablespoon minced crystallized ginger

1 cup heavy cream

1 Combine the applesauce, ¼ cup of the sugar, the applejack or brandy (if using), and ginger.

2 Using an electric mixer on medium speed, beat the cream and the remaining 1 tablespoon sugar in a medium bowl until soft peaks form. Gently fold the applesauce mixture into the whipped cream just until blended. Serve immediately.

Apple Strudel

prep time 30 minutes ■ **total time** 45 minutes ■ **makes** 12 servings

2 Granny Smith or Golden Delicious apples, peeled, cored, and thinly sliced (about 3 cups)

2 tablespoons golden raisins

¼ cup packed brown sugar

½ teaspoon ground cinnamon

¼ teaspoon freshly ground nutmeg

⅓ cup dried bread crumbs

¼ cup granulated sugar

12 sheets (17" x 11") frozen phyllo dough, thawed

½ cup butter, melted

½ cup apricot all-fruit spread, warmed

1 tablespoon confectioners' sugar

1 Preheat the oven to 400°F. Line a baking sheet with parchment paper. Cover the phyllo with a damp towel.

2 Combine the apples, raisins, brown sugar, cinnamon, and nutmeg in a large bowl.

3 Combine the bread crumbs and granulated sugar in a small bowl.

4 Place 1 sheet of the phyllo dough on a work surface. Generously brush the phyllo with the melted butter. Sprinkle with 1 scant tablespoon of the crumb mixture. Repeat layering with 5 of the remaining phyllo sheets, topping the last sheet of phyllo with the butter only.

5 Spread the top sheet of phyllo with ¼ cup of the all-fruit spread to within 1" of the edges. Spoon half of the apple mixture over the fruit spread to within 1" of the edges. Fold 1" of each long edge of the phyllo over the apple mixture. Starting with the short edge, roll up as tightly as possible. Gently place the strudel seam side down on the prepared baking sheet.

6 Repeat to make a second strudel. Place on the baking sheet.

7 Brush both strudels with any remaining butter and sprinkle with any remaining crumbs. Using a sharp knife, make several slashes in the top of each.

8 Bake for 15 minutes, or until crisp and golden brown. Sprinkle with the confectioners' sugar. Serve warm.

Asian Sesame Coleslaw

prep time 5 minutes ■ total time 15 minutes ■ makes 4 servings

3 cups shredded carrot-and-cabbage coleslaw

1 can (11 ounces) mandarin oranges, drained

¼ cup rice vinegar

2 teaspoons reduced-sodium soy sauce

1 teaspoon dark sesame oil

2 tablespoons honey

Combine the coleslaw, oranges, vinegar, soy sauce, oil, and 1 tablespoon of the honey in a large bowl. Toss well. Let the salad marinate for 10 minutes at room temperature. Add up to 1 tablespoon more honey to taste, if desired.

Asparagus and Goat Cheese Omelets

prep time 5 minutes ■ total time 29 minutes ■ makes 4 servings

16 asparagus spears (10 ounces), trimmed and cut into ½" lengths

8 large eggs

¾ cup 1% milk

¼ cup chopped fresh basil

½ teaspoon salt

½ teaspoon freshly ground black pepper

4 teaspoons butter

1 garlic clove, minced

½ cup (3 ounces) crumbled goat cheese

1 Cook the asparagus in boiling water over high heat for 2 to 5 minutes, or until crisp-tender. Drain.

2 Break 2 eggs into a small bowl. Add 3 tablespoons of the milk and lightly beat with a fork. Stir in 1 tablespoon of the basil and ⅛ teaspoon each of the salt and pepper.

3 Melt 1 teaspoon of the butter in an 8" nonstick skillet over medium heat. Add one-fourth of the garlic and cook for 2 minutes, or until soft. Add one-fourth of the asparagus, then pour in the egg mixture. Cook for 4 minutes, or until the eggs are almost set, lifting the edge occasionally to let the raw eggs flow under. Spoon 2 tablespoons of the cheese along the center. Fold the omelet in half, and place in a warm oven on a baking sheet coated with cooking spray.

4 Prepare 3 more omelets.

Asparagus with Orange-Walnut Vinaigrette

prep time 11 minutes ▪ **total time** 18 minutes ▪ **makes** 4 servings

¼ teaspoon salt

1 bunch (16 ounces) asparagus, ends trimmed

5 teaspoons apple cider vinegar

2 tablespoons walnut or olive oil

2 teaspoons grated orange zest

⅛ teaspoon freshly ground black pepper

2 tablespoons walnuts, coarsely chopped

1 Pour water to ½" deep in a large skillet. Add ⅛ teaspoon of the salt and bring to a boil over high heat. Add the asparagus and cook for 4 to 7 minutes, or until tender-firm. Drain in a colander and cool under cold running water. Drain and lay on a paper towel-lined plate to dry.

2 Whisk the vinegar, oil, orange zest, pepper, and the remaining ⅛ teaspoon salt in a small bowl. Remove the asparagus to a platter, spoon the vinaigrette over the top, and sprinkle with the nuts. Serve at room temperature or chilled.

Asparagus with Pine Nuts

prep time 14 minutes ▪ **total time** 25 minutes ▪ make 4 servings

2 pounds asparagus, trimmed and cut into 2½" pieces

½ cup pine nuts

2 garlic cloves, minced

¼ cup freshly squeezed orange juice

¼ teaspoon salt

1 Bring 1" water to a boil in a large pot over high heat. Add the asparagus and cook for 2 minutes, or until bright green. Drain and pat dry.

2 Toast the nuts in a large nonstick skillet over medium heat, stirring often, for 3 to 4 minutes, or until lightly browned and fragrant. Tip onto a plate and set aside. Wipe out the skillet with a paper towel.

3 Coat the same skillet with olive oil cooking spray. Add the asparagus and garlic and cook over medium-high heat, stirring, for 2 minutes, or until the garlic is lightly browned.

4 Add the juice and salt and cook, stirring, for 3 minutes, or until thickened and the asparagus is tender.

5 Sprinkle with the reserved nuts before serving.

A Trip to the Peach

prep time 5 minutes ■ **total time** 5 minutes ■ **makes** 1 serving

1 cup vanilla yogurt

⅓ cup frozen or canned peaches (drain the syrup)

1 tablespoon sliced almonds

Just mix the ingredients and eat.

Avocado, Grapefruit, and Papaya Salad

prep time 5 minutes ■ **total time** 1 hour 5 minutes ■ **makes** 4 servings

1 tablespoon olive oil

2 teaspoons lemon or lime juice

1 avocado, peeled and sliced

2 pink grapefruit, peeled and sectioned

1 small ripe papaya, peeled and sliced

2 scallions, thinly sliced

4 cups mixed baby greens

1 tablespoon cilantro, finely chopped

1 Whisk together the oil and juice in a medium bowl. Add the avocado, grapefruit, papaya, and scallions. Toss gently to combine.

2 Cover and refrigerate for 1 hour. Serve over a bed of the greens, sprinkled with the cilantro.

Baked Halibut with Onions and Peppers

prep time 5 minutes ■ **total time** 1 hour 25 minutes ■ **makes** 6 servings

3 tablespoons lemon juice

1 teaspoon salt

½ teaspoon paprika

6 halibut steaks (5 to 6 ounces each)

2 tablespoons trans-free margarine

½ cup chopped onion

1 large bell pepper, cut into strips

1 Combine the lemon juice, salt, and paprika in a shallow bowl. Add the fish, cover, and refrigerate for 1 hour, turning once.

2 Preheat the oven to 450°F. Coat a 13" x 9" baking dish with cooking spray.

3 Melt the margarine in a medium skillet over medium-high heat and cook the onion for 5 to 10 minutes, or until brown. Place the fish in the prepared baking dish and top with the onion and pepper.

4 Bake for 10 minutes, or until the fish is just opaque.

Balsamic Bell Peppers with Pine Nuts

prep time 5 minutes ▪ **total time** 11 minutes ▪ **makes** 4 servings

2 teaspoons olive oil, preferably extra virgin

1 pound orange or yellow bell peppers, cut into strips

⅛ teaspoon salt

2 teaspoons minced fresh garlic

1 teaspoon balsamic vinegar

1 tablespoon pine nuts, toasted and chopped

Set a skillet over medium heat for 1 minute. Add the oil and heat for 30 seconds. Add the peppers and salt and toss to combine. Cover and cook, tossing occasionally, about 3 minutes, or until the peppers are starting to soften. Add the garlic and cook, tossing, about 1 minute, or until the garlic is fragrant. Drizzle with the vinegar to taste. Toss to heat through. Serve sprinkled with the nuts.

Banana Ice Cream

prep time 30 minutes ▪ **total time** 5 hours ▪ **makes** 4 servings

2 large frozen bananas, sliced

2 tablespoons sugar

1½ cups fat-free milk

½ teaspoon cinnamon

½ teaspoon vanilla extract

⅛ teaspoon ground nutmeg

1 Combine the bananas, sugar, and ½ cup of the milk in a food processor or blender. Puree until smooth. Add the cinnamon, vanilla extract, and remaining 1 cup milk. Puree until smooth.

2 Transfer the mixture to a metal or plastic container. Cover and freeze for 4 hours or overnight. Remove from the freezer and break up the mixture with a knife. Process briefly in a food processor or blender.

3 Return to the container, cover, and freeze for at least 30 minutes before serving. Sprinkle with the nutmeg and serve.

Berries in a Cloud

prep time 20 minutes ▪ **total time** 1 hour 15 minutes ▪ **makes** 8 servings

4 large egg whites, at room temperature

Pinch of salt

2 cups sugar

2 cups mixed seasonal berries

1 Preheat the oven to 200°F. Line 2 baking sheets with parchment paper.

2 Beat the egg whites and salt in a large bowl with an electric mixer at medium speed until frothy. With the mixer at high speed, beat in the sugar in a steady stream. Continue beating until the whites stand in stiff, glossy peaks when the beaters are lifted.

3 Spoon the meringue into a piping bag or large zip-top bag with a corner snipped off. Pipe 16 circles (4½" round) onto the parchment paper. Pipe 2 or 3 layers of meringue around each circle to make cups.

4 Bake the meringues about 55 minutes, or until dried out but not beginning to brown. Let cool for 2 to 3 minutes. Transfer to wire racks to cool completely. Spoon the berries into the cups just before serving.

Big Broiled Balsamic Mushrooms

prep time 5 minutes ■ **total time** 9 minutes ■ **makes** 4 servings

2 tablespoons balsamic vinegar

2 tablespoons water

2 teaspoons olive oil

½ teaspoon dried thyme

12 ounces portobello mushrooms, trimmed and thickly sliced

1 Preheat the broiler. Line a broiler-pan rack with foil.

2 Whisk the vinegar, water, oil, and thyme in a large bowl. Add the mushrooms and toss gently to coat. Arrange in a single layer on the rack and broil 3" from the heat for 2 minutes. Turn and broil for 2 minutes longer, or until golden.

Breakfast Smoothie with Flax

prep time 5 minutes ■ **total time** 5 minutes ■ **makes** 1 serving

1 cup fat-free milk or low-fat, calcium-enriched soy or rice beverage

¾ cup (6 ounces) fat-free plain yogurt

½ cup strawberries, banana, or other fresh fruit, sliced

2 tablespoons walnuts

2 tablespoons flaxseed meal

Ground cinnamon and/or sugar substitute to taste

Combine the milk or milk substitute, yogurt, fruit, walnuts, and flaxseed meal in a blender. Add the cinnamon and/or sugar substitute and blend for 15 seconds.

Broccoli and Napa Cabbage Salad with Miso Dressing

prep time 5 minutes ■ **total time** 25 minutes ■ **makes** 4 servings

1 tablespoon sesame seeds

2 cups small broccoli florets

1½ tablespoons mellow white miso

1½ tablespoons rice wine vinegar

1 tablespoon canola oil

2 teaspoons reduced-sodium soy sauce

1 teaspoon flax oil

¾ teaspoon finely grated fresh ginger

½ teaspoon brown sugar

4 cups sliced Napa cabbage or iceberg lettuce (1"-thick slices)

½ cup thinly sliced radishes

1 Kirby cucumber, thinly sliced

2 scallions, thinly sliced

1 large carrot, peeled

1 Cook the sesame seeds in a small skillet over medium heat, tossing, for 2 minutes, or until light golden. Tip out onto a plate and let cool.

2 Bring ½" water to a boil in a medium saucepan. Add the broccoli, cover, and cook, stirring several times, for 4 minutes, or until crisp-tender. Drain and cool briefly under cold running water.

3 Whisk the miso, vinegar, canola oil, soy sauce, flax oil, ginger, and sugar in a salad bowl until well blended.

4 Add the cabbage or lettuce, radishes, cucumber, scallions, and broccoli. With a vegetable peeler, peel long, curly strands from the carrot, letting them drop into the salad bowl. Toss the salad to mix, sprinkle with the toasted sesame seeds, and serve.

Broccoli Rabe and Roasted Red Pepper Wraps

prep time 10 minutes ■ **total time** 18 minutes ■ **makes** 4 servings

1 pound broccoli rabe, woody stems trimmed (trimmed weight about 8 ounces)

1 tablespoon extra virgin olive oil

3 garlic cloves, thinly sliced

⅛ teaspoon red-pepper flakes (optional)

¼ teaspoon salt

1 tablespoon balsamic vinegar

2 multigrain wraps (10" diameter), such as Mission brand

1 roasted red pepper (from a jar), drained, patted dry, and cut into strips

½ cup shredded reduced-fat mozzarella cheese

1 Bring a large pot of lightly salted water to a boil. Add the broccoli rabe, return to a boil, and cook for 3 minutes. Drain, rinse with cold water, and drain again.

2 Heat the oil in a large nonstick skillet over medium-high heat. Add the garlic and red-pepper flakes, if using, and cook about 1 minute, or until the garlic begins to brown slightly. Stir in the broccoli rabe and salt and cook for 1 to 2 minutes, or until hot. Add the vinegar and cook for 1 minute longer. Remove from the heat.

3 Place the wraps on a work surface and make a line across the center of each, leaving a 1½" border on each end, with the broccoli rabe, pepper strips, and cheese. Fold the right and left sides of the wrap so that they just cover the very edges of the filling, and then fold the bottom over and roll up jelly roll-style. Cut each in half on an angle.

Broccoli Spears with Goat Cheese

prep time 10 minutes ▪ **total time** 20 minutes ▪ **makes** 4 servings

1 pound broccoli, cut into long spears
¾ cup milk
2 teaspoons flour
½ garlic clove, crushed
1 tablespoon white wine
2 ounces goat cheese
½ cup (2 ounces) shredded low-fat sharp Cheddar cheese

1 Fill a large bowl with ice cubes and water to cover. Bring a large saucepan of salted water to a boil. Add the broccoli and cook about 4 minutes, or just until crisp-tender. Drain and immediately transfer the broccoli to the cold water to stop the cooking. When cool, drain well and blot dry.

2 Combine the milk, flour, and garlic in a small saucepan and whisk to blend. Heat over medium heat, stirring constantly, until boiling. Boil for 3 to 4 minutes, or until creamy and thickened. Add the wine and cook for 1 minute. Add the goat cheese and Cheddar and stir until melted.

3 Transfer to a small bowl or fondue pot over a low flame and serve immediately with the broccoli spears.

Broccoli with Tahini Sauce

prep time 3 minutes ▪ **total time** 10 minutes ▪ **makes** 2 servings

2 large stalks broccoli
1 tablespoon tahini
1 tablespoon balsamic vinegar
Pinch of salt

1 Remove the broccoli stem and cut or break the top into bite-size florets. Peel the stem with a sharp knife, then slice it into 2"-thick rounds. Transfer to a vegetable steamer. Steam over boiling water about 5 minutes, or until the broccoli is bright green and tender.

2 While the broccoli cooks, mix the tahini, vinegar, and salt in a small bowl. Add just enough water to make a thick sauce. When the broccoli is cooked, place it in a medium serving bowl and drizzle with the sauce.

Broiled Asparagus

prep time 3 minutes ■ **total time** 11 minutes ■ **makes** 8 servings

2 pounds asparagus, trimmed
3 tablespoons olive oil
Salt

1 Heat the broiler, putting the rack in the middle position.

2 Put the asparagus in a roasting pan and toss with the oil to coat. Arrange the asparagus evenly in a single layer. Sprinkle with salt to taste.

3 Broil the asparagus for 5 minutes, or until nearly done. Shake the pan to turn the spears and broil about 3 minutes longer.

Caramel Flan with Fresh Fruit

prep time 20 minutes ■ **total time** 40 minutes ■ **makes** 4 servings

1 tablespoon water
$\frac{2}{3}$ cup sugar
3 large eggs
$1\frac{1}{2}$ cups 1% milk
$1\frac{1}{2}$ teaspoons vanilla extract
2 cups mixed raspberries, blackberries, and sliced kiwifruit

1 Preheat the oven to 325°F.

2 Combine the water and $\frac{1}{3}$ cup of the sugar in a heavy medium skillet. Heat over medium-high heat until the sugar is melted and caramelized (golden in color), stirring often. Carefully pour the caramelized sugar (it will be very hot) evenly into four or six 4- to 6-ounce ramekins or custard cups. Tilt the ramekins to coat the bottoms. Let stand for 10 minutes.

3 Whisk the eggs and remaining $\frac{1}{3}$ cup sugar in a medium bowl until well blended. Whisk in the milk and vanilla extract. Transfer to a large glass measuring cup or pitcher for easier handling. Pour evenly into the ramekins. Place the ramekins in a baking pan just large enough to hold them without touching. Place the pan on the oven rack and pour hot water into the pan to a depth of $\frac{1}{2}$".

4 Bake the flans for 20 to 25 minutes, or until a knife inserted near the center comes out clean. Carefully lift the ramekins from the hot water onto a wire rack. Serve warm or cool completely, cover, and refrigerate for up to 24 hours. Garnish with the fresh fruit.

Chilled Mango-Lime Soup

prep time 10 minutes ■ **total time** 1 hour 10 minutes ■ **makes** 4 servings

2 ripe mangoes, cut into chunks
½ cup (4 ounces) low-fat plain yogurt
½ cup orange juice
½ cup ginger ale
¼ cup lime juice
1 tablespoon honey

Combine the mangoes, yogurt, orange juice, ginger ale, lime juice, and honey in a blender or food processor. Blend or process until pureed. Add some ice water if a thinner soup is desired. Cover and refrigerate for 1 hour.

Chilled Tomato and Dill Soup

prep time 12 minutes ■ **total time** 54 minutes ■ **makes** 4 servings

1 onion, finely chopped
1 tablespoon olive oil
1 tablespoon water
2 garlic cloves, minced
3 cups peeled and chopped tomatoes (about 1½ pounds)
4 tablespoons stemmed and chopped fresh dill
3 cups low-sodium chicken or vegetable broth
Salt and freshly ground black pepper
4 dill fronds, for garnish

1 Combine the onion, oil, and water in a medium saucepan over low heat. Cook, stirring occasionally, for 12 minutes, or until soft (do not let the onion burn). Add the garlic and cook for 5 minutes longer.

2 Increase the heat to medium. Add the tomatoes, dill, and broth. Simmer for 25 minutes. Season with salt and pepper to taste.

3 Chill in the refrigerator for 2 hours. Serve garnished with the dill fronds.

Choco Espresso Soufflés

prep time 17 minutes ■ **total time** 40 minutes ■ **makes** 6 servings

1 tablespoon unsalted butter, at room temperature

¼ cup + 1 tablespoon granulated sugar

¼ cup cornstarch

3 tablespoons brown sugar

3 tablespoons unsweetened cocoa powder

1½ teaspoons instant espresso powder

¼ teaspoon ground cinnamon

1¼ cups half-and-half

6 large egg whites

⅛ teaspoon salt

2 teaspoons vanilla extract

Espresso beans (optional)

1 Preheat the oven to 400°F. Coat six 7-ounce ovenproof coffee cups, soufflé dishes, or custard cups with the butter. Dust evenly with 2 tablespoons of the granulated sugar, turning the cups or dishes to coat the sides completely. Place the cups on a baking sheet.

2 Whisk the cornstarch, brown sugar, cocoa, espresso, cinnamon, and 2 tablespoons of the remaining granulated sugar in a heavy medium saucepan. Gradually whisk in the half-and-half until smooth.

3 Cook over medium heat, whisking frequently and then constantly as the mixture gets hotter, until it comes to a boil and thickens. Remove the pan from the heat. Place a sheet of plastic wrap directly on the surface of the mixture to prevent a skin from forming. Set aside.

4 Beat the egg whites and salt at high speed in the bowl of an electric mixer until foamy. Gradually beat in the remaining 1 tablespoon granulated sugar and continue beating until stiff peaks form.

5 Whisk the vanilla extract into the half-and-half mixture. Stir in a big spoonful of the beaten whites to lighten it, then pour the half-and-half mixture into the beaten whites. With a large rubber spatula, fold it into the whites until no white streaks remain. Divide the mixture evenly among the prepared cups or dishes.

6 Bake the soufflés for 13 to 15 minutes, or until puffed and firm to the touch. Remove from the oven and serve immediately, garnished with the espresso beans, if desired.

Chocolate Mousse

prep time 20 minutes ■ **total time** 2 hours 20 minutes ■ **makes** 8 servings

¾ cup 1% milk

1 tablespoon instant coffee powder

⅔ cup unsweetened cocoa powder

¼ cup packed brown sugar

1 egg, lightly beaten

2 tablespoons coffee liqueur or strong brewed coffee

1 teaspoon unflavored gelatin

2 ounces bittersweet chocolate, coarsely chopped

1 tablespoon vanilla extract

4 egg whites

½ cup sugar

½ teaspoon cream of tartar

1 cup fat-free nondairy whipped topping

1 Combine the milk and coffee powder in a medium saucepan. Cook over medium heat, stirring occasionally, for 2 to 3 minutes, or until steaming. Whisk in the cocoa and brown sugar until smooth. Remove from the heat and slowly whisk in the egg. Reduce the heat to low and whisk constantly for 5 minutes, or until thickened. Remove from the heat.

2 Place the coffee liqueur or brewed coffee in a cup. Sprinkle with the gelatin. Let stand for 1 minute to soften. Stir into the cocoa mixture until dissolved. Add the chocolate and vanilla extract. Stir until the chocolate is melted. Transfer to a large bowl and set aside for 30 minutes, or until cooled to room temperature.

3 Pour about 2" water into another medium saucepan and bring to a simmer.

4 In a large heatproof bowl that will fit over the saucepan, combine the egg whites, sugar, and cream of tartar. Whisk well to combine. Set the bowl over the simmering water and gently whisk for 2 minutes, or until an instant-read thermometer registers 140°F (the mixture will be too hot to touch). Remove from the heat. Using an electric mixer, beat on medium-high speed for 5 minutes, or until cool.

5 Fold the egg-white mixture into the chocolate mixture. Fold in the whipped topping. Divide among dessert glasses and refrigerate for at least 2 hours or up to 24 hours.

Citrusy Red-Pepper Soup

prep time 15 minutes ■ **total time** 1 hour 20 minutes ■ **makes** 6 servings

2 large red bell peppers, halved and seeded

2 small onions, minced

¼ cup diced carrots

2 tablespoons canned, diced mild green chili peppers

2 garlic cloves, minced

2 teaspoons olive oil

4 cups frozen fat-free chicken stock, thawed

1 large navel orange, peeled and chopped

2 tablespoons chopped fresh parsley or cilantro

½ teaspoon ground red pepper

½ teaspoon salt

¼ teaspoon freshly ground black pepper

½ cup reduced-fat sour cream

1 Preheat the broiler. Line a broiler pan with foil. Place the bell peppers cut side down on the pan and broil 4" from the heat for 15 minutes, or until blackened. Place the peppers in a brown paper bag and roll the top to seal. Let stand for 20 minutes. Remove the peppers from the bag. Peel off the blackened skin and discard. Set the peppers aside.

2 Combine the onions, carrots, chili peppers, garlic, and oil in a Dutch oven. Cook, stirring, over medium-high heat for 10 minutes, or until the onions are soft but not browned. Add the stock, orange, parsley or cilantro, ground red pepper, salt, and black pepper. Bring to a boil. Reduce the heat to medium, cover, and cook for 10 minutes, or until the carrots are very soft.

3 Let the soup cool slightly. Add the reserved red peppers and the sour cream. Place the soup in a blender or food processor and puree or process until smooth. Return to the pot and heat through.

Cream of Mushroom Soup

prep time 10 minutes ■ **total time** 25 minutes ■ **makes** 4 servings

1 tablespoon olive oil

1 tablespoon dry or nonalcoholic white wine

12 ounces mushrooms, sliced

¼ cup finely chopped onion

1 garlic clove, minced

1 tablespoon chopped fresh thyme

2 teaspoons chopped fresh parsley

2 cups fat-free chicken broth

1 cup fat-free evaporated milk

2 tablespoons cornstarch

¼ teaspoon freshly ground black pepper

⅛ teaspoon ground nutmeg

1 Warm the oil and wine in a medium saucepan over medium heat. Add the mushrooms, onion, garlic, thyme, and parsley. Cook, stirring frequently, for 5 minutes, or until the mushrooms release their liquid and the vegetables are soft.

2 Add the broth, cover, and simmer for 5 minutes over low heat. Place the mixture in a food processor or blender and puree. Return to the saucepan.

3 Meanwhile, whisk together ¼ cup of the milk and the cornstarch in a small bowl until smooth. Slowly add to the mushroom mixture, stirring constantly, over medium heat. Stir in the pepper, nutmeg, and the remaining ¾ cup milk. Cook and stir until thickened and bubbly. Cook and stir for 2 minutes more.

Cream of Roasted Red Pepper and Tomato Soup

prep time 5 minutes ▪ **total time** 10 minutes ▪ **makes** 4 servings

¾ cup roasted red peppers
1 container (32 ounces) ready-to-serve creamy tomato soup (not condensed)
½ cup chicken broth
⅛ teaspoon dried basil

Puree the peppers, soup, and broth in a food processor or blender. Pour into a saucepan and bring to a boil. Add the basil and reduce the heat to medium-low. Simmer for 5 minutes.

Creamy Garlic Spinach

prep time 6 minutes ▪ **total time** 6 minutes ▪ **makes** 6 servings

2 tablespoons butter
2 tablespoons chopped onion
½ teaspoon minced oil-packed garlic
2 bags (20 ounces total) baby spinach leaves
2 ounces herbed cream cheese

1 Melt the butter in a large skillet over medium heat. Add the onion and garlic and cook about 4 minutes, or until soft.

2 Add the spinach and cook about 2 minutes, or just until wilted. Stir in the cream cheese until melted.

Curried Apple and Pear Soup

prep time 15 minutes ▪ **total time** 45 minutes ▪ **makes** 4 servings

2 tablespoons olive oil
1 large onion, chopped
2 carrots, chopped
1 celery rib, chopped
2 teaspoons sugar
2 teaspoons mild or hot curry powder
½ teaspoon ground cumin
½ teaspoon salt
2 pears, peeled, cored, and coarsely chopped
2 Granny Smith apples, peeled, cored, and coarsely chopped
2 cups low-sodium vegetable broth
2 cups water
½ cup fat-free Greek-style yogurt
½ cup sliced almonds, toasted

1 Heat the oil in a large pot or Dutch oven over medium heat. Add the onion, carrots, and celery and sprinkle with the sugar. Cook, stirring often, for 8 to 10 minutes, or until tender and the onion is lightly golden and caramelized.

2 Add the curry powder, cumin, and salt. Cook and stir for 30 seconds, or until fragrant.

3 Add the pears and apples and stir to coat. Add the broth and water, cover, and bring to a boil. Reduce the heat to low and simmer for 15 minutes, or until the fruit is very tender.

4 Transfer the soup to a food processor fitted with a metal blade or a blender. Process until smooth. Return the soup to the pot and warm through.

5 Ladle into 4 bowls and top each with 2 tablespoons of the yogurt and 2 tablespoons of the almonds.

Deviled Egg and Spinach Casserole

prep time 15 minutes ▪ **total time** 55 minutes ▪ **makes** 10 servings

12 hard-boiled eggs

6 tablespoons mayonnaise

¼ teaspoon dry mustard

⅛ teaspoon freshly ground black pepper

4 packages (10 ounces each) frozen chopped spinach

½ cup butter

¼ cup flour

4 cups milk

2 cups grated sharp cheese

1 teaspoon Worcestershire sauce

1 teaspoon salt

¼ teaspoon hot-pepper sauce

1 Coat a 3-quart baking dish or casserole dish with cooking spray. Cut the eggs in half lengthwise and remove the yolks. Mash the yolks with the mayonnaise, mustard, and pepper. Blend until smooth and fill the egg whites with the mixture.

2 Cook the spinach, drain, and squeeze out all the moisture. Melt the butter in a saucepan and blend in the flour.

3 Add the milk gradually to the flour-and-butter paste, stirring constantly while cooking over medium heat until the sauce thickens. Measure ¼ cup of the cheese and set it aside, then stir the remaining cheese into the sauce until the cheese melts. Add the Worcestershire sauce, salt, and hot-pepper sauce.

4 Place the spinach and half of the cheese sauce in the prepared dish and mix with a fork. Place the deviled egg halves on top of the spinach and cover with the remaining cheese sauce. Sprinkle the reserved cheese over all.

5 Bake at 375°F for 20 to 25 minutes, or until bubbly and lightly browned. (Can be reheated at 325°F in a covered dish.)

Fennel Salad with Olives, Eggs, and Tuna

prep time 12 minutes ▪ **total time** 12 minutes ▪ **makes** 4 servings

Dressing

1 teaspoon lemon zest
1 tablespoon fresh lemon juice
4 tablespoons olive oil
¼ teaspoon salt
   Freshly ground black pepper
1 teaspoon chopped fennel greens

Salad

1 small red onion, peeled and thinly sliced in rounds
   White or rice wine vinegar, as needed
1 yellow bell pepper, seeded, veined, and thinly sliced
2 small fennel bulbs (about ½ pound total, trimmed), thinly sliced lengthwise
8 French Breakfast radishes
12 olives, green and black, mixed
2 hard-boiled eggs, quartered
1 small can tuna, drained
1 tablespoon capers

1 To make the dressing: Combine the lemon zest, juice, oil, salt, and pepper to taste in a small bowl. Whisk vigorously until smooth and well blended. Stir in the greens.

2 To make the salad: Toss the onion in a few tablespoons of vinegar and set aside to marinate, turning occasionally so they color brightly, while you assemble the salad. Arrange the bell pepper on a large plate and top with the fennel. Intersperse the radishes (scarlet ends facing outward) with the olives around the edge. Arrange the eggs attractively in clusters of 2 or 3 and mound the tuna in the center. Scatter the capers over the tuna. Drain the onions and set them around or over the salad. Spoon the dressing over all. Add another pinch or two of salt and black pepper and serve.

Garlic-Soy Spinach

prep time 3 minutes ▪ **total time** 14 minutes ▪ **makes** 2 servings

1½ teaspoons sesame or peanut oil
2 garlic cloves, minced
1 bunch spinach, washed and stems removed
1½ teaspoons soy sauce
   Pinch of sugar
1 tablespoon sesame seeds

1 Heat the oil in a wok or sauté pan over medium heat. Add the garlic and cook for 1 to 2 minutes, or until lightly browned.

2 Add the spinach and cook, stirring frequently, for 3 minutes, or until the spinach is fully wilted. (It will look like too much spinach in the beginning, but it will cook down quickly.) Add the soy sauce and sugar and cook another minute. Serve with the sesame seeds sprinkled on top.

Get Up and Go Veggie Omelet

prep time 5 minutes ■ **total time** 10 minutes ■ **makes** 1 serving

2 teaspoons canola, peanut, or olive oil

¼ cup egg substitute (or 1 egg white)

½ cup chopped spinach

½ cup chopped mushrooms

¼ cup chopped onion

½ teaspoon minced garlic

Mixed herbs to taste

¼ cup shredded reduced-fat cheese

Heat the oil in a small pan over medium-high heat. Add the egg substitute, spinach, mushrooms, onion, garlic, and chopped herbs and cook until set. Top with the cheese.

Grilled Chicken Burgers with Vegetable Salsa

prep time 15 minutes ■ **total time** 35 minutes ■ **makes** 4 servings

Burgers

1¼ pounds ground chicken

½ cup (2 ounces) shredded mozzarella or Monterey Jack cheese

2 garlic cloves, minced

½ teaspoon salt

¼ teaspoon freshly ground black pepper

Salsa

1 tablespoon olive oil

1 tablespoon balsamic vinegar

¼ teaspoon salt

½ tomato, seeded and chopped

½ small cucumber, peeled, seeded, and chopped

½ small red onion, finely chopped

½ yellow bell pepper, chopped

1 To make the burgers: Combine the chicken, cheese, garlic, salt, and black pepper in a medium bowl just until blended. Shape into 4 patties.

2 To make the salsa: Whisk the oil, vinegar, and salt in a large bowl. Add the tomato, cucumber, onion, and bell pepper and toss to coat well. Set aside.

3 Coat an unheated grill rack with cooking spray. Preheat the grill.

4 Place the burgers on the rack and grill for 20 minutes, or until a thermometer inserted in the center registers 165°F and the meat is no longer pink.

5 Serve the burgers with the salsa.

Grilled Eggplant

prep time 15 minutes ■ **total time** 1 hour 5 minutes ■ **makes** 8 servings

4 eggplant (1 pound each) with peel, cut lengthwise into 1" thick slices

2 teaspoons kosher salt

4 tablespoons olive oil

½ teaspoon freshly ground black pepper

1 Layer several paper towels on a baking sheet. Place half of the eggplant on top in a single layer. Sprinkle with 1 teaspoon of the salt and cover with paper towels. Arrange a second layer of eggplant, sprinkle with the remaining salt, and cover with paper towels.

2 Let the eggplant stand for 30 minutes, then rinse each piece and blot dry. (This helps extract excess water, reducing bitterness and preventing the eggplant from absorbing excess oil during cooking.)

3 Brush both sides of the eggplant slices with oil to coat and transfer to a large bowl. Season with the pepper.

4 Heat the grill to medium. Grill the eggplant, with the cover closed, for 16 to 20 minutes, or until browned and tender, turning once. Refrigerate leftovers in airtight container for a day or two.

Grilled Jerk Chicken with Pineapple and Red Pepper

prep time 10 minutes ■ **total time** 20 minutes ■ **makes** 4 servings

1 red bell pepper, quartered

4 thick, fresh pineapple slices

1½ tablespoons canola oil + more for coating

Salt

1½ tablespoons jerk seasoning

4 boneless, skinless chicken thighs (about 1½ pounds)

1 Coat a grill rack with cooking spray. Preheat the grill to medium-high. Toss the pepper and pineapple in a medium bowl with oil to coat. Remove and sprinkle with salt to taste.

2 Combine the jerk seasoning and 1½ tablespoons of the oil in the same bowl. Add the chicken and toss to coat. Grill the chicken, pepper, and pineapple about 10 minutes, turning once.

Grilled Shrimp with Mango-Lime Salsa

prep time 15 minutes ▪ **total time** 21 minutes ▪ **makes** 4 servings

¼ cup olive oil

½ teaspoon chopped garlic (from a jar)

2 cups diced mango (about 2 fresh mangoes; if using frozen, thaw in microwave)

¼ cup diced red onion

½ fresh jalapeño pepper, finely diced

Juice of 1 lime

2 teaspoons ground cumin

¼ teaspoon salt

1 pound frozen large shrimp, thawed

1 Coat a grill rack with cooking spray. Preheat the grill.

2 Mix the oil and garlic in a small bowl and set aside.

3 Combine the mango, onion, pepper, lime juice, cumin, and salt in a medium bowl. Set aside.

4 Place the shrimp on the hot grill and brush with the reserved garlic-oil mixture. Cook for 2 to 3 minutes per side, or until they turn pink.

5 Place the grilled shrimp on a platter and top with the reserved salsa.

Hawaiian Chicken Salad

prep time 5 minutes ▪ **total time** 5 minutes ▪ **makes** 2 servings

6 romaine leaves

8 ounces grilled chicken breast, cut into strips

1½ cups canned or fresh pineapple chunks

2 tablespoons flaked coconut

2 tablespoons raisins

2 tablespoons poppy seed salad dressing

1 Arrange 3 romaine leaves on each of 2 plates, then place the chicken on top.

2 Toss the pineapple, coconut, raisins, and dressing in a small bowl. Pour over the chicken and serve.

Honey-Pecan Smoothie

prep time 5 minutes ▪ **total time** 6 minutes ▪ **makes** 2 servings

½ cup 1% milk

½ cup low-fat vanilla yogurt

¼ cup chopped pecans

2 teaspoons whey protein powder

1 teaspoon honey

2 teaspoons ground flaxseed

6 ice cubes

Combine the milk and yogurt, pecans, protein powder, honey, and flaxseed in a blender and process until evenly mixed. Add the ice and pulse to blend until smooth. (For a thicker shake, you can toss in more ice cubes; you'll add volume without the calories.)

Kiwifruit Shakes

prep time 5 minutes ▪ **total time** 5 minutes ▪ **makes** 4 servings

2 kiwifruit, sliced

4 cups nonfat vanilla frozen yogurt

Combine the kiwifruit and yogurt in a blender and process until smooth. Serve in tall glasses.

Mocha Tofu Pudding

prep time 10 minutes ▪ **total time** 40 minutes ▪ **makes** 6 servings

2 packages (10½ ounces each) silken tofu

⅔ cup packed light brown sugar

5 tablespoons unsweetened cocoa powder

1¼ teaspoons vanilla extract

⅛ teaspoon ground cinnamon

2 teaspoons instant coffee powder

2 teaspoons boiling water

1 Rinse and drain the tofu and pat dry with paper towels. Place the tofu in a food processor. Add the brown sugar, cocoa, vanilla extract, and cinnamon.

2 Mix the coffee powder and water in a cup, stirring to dissolve. Add to the food processor. Process until smooth, stopping occasionally to scrape down the sides of the container.

3 Spoon the pudding into small dessert dishes. Cover and refrigerate for at least 30 minutes, or until firm.

Mushrooms and Broccoli

prep time 10 minutes ▪ **total time** 19 minutes ▪ **makes** 4 servings

2 tablespoons olive oil

1 garlic clove, minced

2 cups broccoli florets

1 cup sliced mushrooms

1 carrot, thinly sliced

Heat the oil in a large skillet over medium-high heat. Add the garlic and cook, stirring occasionally, for 1 minute, or until fragrant. Add the broccoli, mushrooms, and carrot and cook, stirring frequently, for 8 minutes, or until the vegetables are crisp-tender.

Okra with Tomatoes, Ginger, and Basil

prep time 10 minutes ▪ **total time** 22 minutes ▪ **makes** 6 servings

2 tablespoons vegetable oil
2 garlic cloves, chopped
1 tablespoon chopped fresh ginger
1 shallot, chopped
¼ teaspoon dried red-pepper flakes
1 pound fresh okra, untrimmed
1½ cups yellow grape tomatoes, halved
½ cup loosely packed basil leaves
Kosher salt and freshly ground black
pepper

1 Place the oil, garlic, ginger, shallot, and pepper flakes in a heavy skillet and cook over medium heat, stirring, for 1 minute.

2 Add the okra and cook, covered, about 10 minutes, or until just tender. Add the tomatoes and cook for 1 minute. Remove from the heat and stir in the basil. Season to taste with salt and pepper.

Organic Green Omelet

prep time 5 minutes ▪ **total time** 12 minutes ▪ **makes** 1 serving

5 large organic eggs
1 teaspoon soy sauce
1 teaspoon olive oil
2 tablespoons broccoli florets
5 asparagus spears, chopped
¼ cup halved string beans
½ cup fresh spinach
1 garlic clove, chopped
1 teaspoon freshly ground black pepper
¼ cup fresh parsley, chopped

1 Mix the eggs and soy sauce in a bowl. Heat the oil in a pan over medium-high heat. Add the broccoli, asparagus, beans, spinach, garlic, and pepper and cook, stirring frequently, for just 5 minutes to preserve vitamins and minerals.

2 Add the parsley to the egg-soy mixture and pour over the vegetables. Stir about 30 seconds, let it sit for a minute, and then stir it again until the eggs firm up. Let it sit for 1 minute, then flip it and remove it from the pan.

Pan-Fried Chicken with Tarragon

prep time 15 minutes ■ **total time** 35 minutes ■ **makes** 4 servings

2 tablespoons lemon juice

2 tablespoons olive oil

½ teaspoon Dijon mustard

⅛ teaspoon salt + more to taste (optional)

1 pound chicken breast tenders (12 to 16 tenders)

2 tablespoons poultry seasoning

1 tablespoon dried tarragon, crumbled

1 tablespoon dried garlic

8 cups (5 ounces) loosely packed baby salad greens

1 In a large bowl, whisk together the lemon juice, oil, mustard, and salt to taste. Set aside.

2 Place the chicken between 2 sheets of plastic wrap. With a kitchen mallet (or the bottom of a small heavy saucepan), pound the tenders 2 or 3 times until they are ¼" thick.

3 In a medium bowl, mix the poultry seasoning, tarragon, garlic, and ⅛ teaspoon salt. Coat the chicken with the mixture.

4 Coat a large nonstick skillet with cooking spray and place over high heat. When the skillet is hot, add 4 or 5 chicken tenders and cook over medium-high heat for 1 to 2 minutes per side, or until golden and firm. Wipe out the skillet with a paper towel to remove any burned crumbs, and repeat the process until all the tenders are cooked.

5 Add the greens to the large bowl and toss with the reserved dressing.

6 To serve, place 2 cups of the greens on dinner plates and top with 3 or 4 chicken tenders.

Peaches and Pork Chops

prep time 7 minutes ■ **total time** 17 minutes ■ **makes** 2 servings

2 bone-in pork chops (8 ounces each), 1" thick

1 teaspoon olive oil

Salt and freshly ground black pepper

2 firm peaches or nectarines, halved and pitted

2 tablespoons pine nuts, toasted

1 small red onion, thinly sliced

½ cup crumbled blue cheese

1 tablespoon balsamic vinegar

1 Preheat the grill on high heat. Brush the pork with some of the oil and season with salt and pepper. Grill for 4 to 5 minutes on each side.

2 Meanwhile, brush the peaches or nectarines with the remaining oil and place cut side down on the grill. Grill for 5 minutes, or until soft. Remove, slice, and toss with the nuts, onion, cheese, and vinegar. Add salt and pepper to taste. Top each chop with half of the peach mixture and serve.

Peachy Frozen Yogurt

prep time 8 minutes ▪ **total time** 10 hours 8 minutes ▪ **makes** 12 servings

3 cups frozen peaches or nectarines, partially thawed

2 cartons (16 ounces each) low-fat vanilla yogurt

¼ cup honey

1 Place 1½ cups of the peaches in a food processor with the yogurt and honey. Process until smooth. Finely chop the remaining peaches and stir into the yogurt mixture. Pour into a 2-quart pan. Cover and freeze for 4 hours, or until firm.

2 Break the frozen mixture into small pieces and place in the food processor. Pulse until fluffy. Return the mixture to the pan and freeze, covered, for 6 hours, or until firm.

3 Let the frozen yogurt stand at room temperature for 15 minutes before serving.

Peanut Butter Breakfast Shake

Prep time 5 minutes ▪ **Total time** 5 minutes ▪ **makes** 1 serving

1 cup fat-free milk

1 ripe banana, sliced

2 tablespoons creamy peanut butter

Combine the milk, banana, and peanut butter in a blender. Blend until smooth.

Pineapple Smoothie

prep time 5 minutes ▪ **total time** 5 minutes ▪ **makes** 1 serving

1 cup low-fat or light vanilla yogurt

6 ice cubes

1 cup pineapple chunks

Place the yogurt and ice cubes in a blender. Blend, pulsing as needed, until the ice is in large chunks. Add the pineapple and blend at "whip" speed until smooth.

Pork Loin with Apple Cider Glaze

prep time 10 minutes ▪ **total time** 5 hours 25 minutes ▪ **makes** 4 servings

1 small pork loin (1¾ pounds)
2 cloves garlic, finely chopped
Salt and freshly ground black pepper
3 cups apple cider
2 apples, chopped
1 bunch parsley, finely chopped
(optional)

1 Rub the pork with the garlic and salt and pepper to taste and place it in an 8½" x 11" pan or resealable plastic bag. Pour the apple cider around the pork, then add enough water to cover the pork. Let the pork marinate for 4 to 6 hours, or overnight.

2 Preheat the oven to 350°F. Coat a 9" x 13" baking dish with cooking spray.

3 Place the pork in the prepared baking dish. Reserve the marinade. Bake for approximately 1 hour, or until a thermometer inserted in the center registers 150°F.

4 Meanwhile, bring the marinade to a boil in a saucepan over high heat. Reduce the heat to medium-low and cook about 20 minutes, or until the sauce is reduced by half to make a glaze. Add the apples and cook for 15 minutes.

5 Remove the pork from the oven and let it stand for 15 minutes before carving. Cut it into slices and serve with the apple cider glaze. Sprinkle with the parsley, if using.

Potato Pancakes with Eggs

prep time 2 minutes ▪ **total time** 7 minutes ▪ **makes** 1 serving

2 Dr. Praeger's frozen home-style
potato pancakes
1 tablespoon safflower oil
½ cup liquid Organic Valley 100% egg
whites
¼ cup sliced red onion
½ fresh plum tomato, chopped

Brown the potato pancakes in a pan with half of the oil. In another pan, use the remaining oil and scramble the egg whites with the onion and tomato.

Pumpkin-Ginger Soup

prep time 10 minutes ■ **total time** 25 minutes ■ **makes** 4 servings

½ teaspoon canola oil
3 tablespoons minced shallots
½ teaspoon minced fresh ginger
2 cups canned pumpkin
2 cups fat-free chicken broth
½ teaspoon pumpkin pie spice
½ cup fat-free evaporated milk
3 tablespoons fat-free sour cream

1 Place the oil, shallots, and ginger in a large saucepan. Cook over medium heat for 2 minutes.

2 Add the pumpkin, broth, and pumpkin pie spice. Bring to a boil. Reduce the heat to medium-low and cook for 10 minutes.

3 Whisk in the milk and sour cream. Warm through but do not boil.

Roasted Brussels Sprouts and Onions with Thyme

prep time 14 minutes ■ **total time** 39 minutes ■ **makes** 4 servings

1½ pounds fresh Brussels sprouts, trimmed and quartered
1 large sweet white onion, quartered and cut into ½"-thick slices
1 tablespoon olive oil
4 teaspoons fresh thyme leaves
¼ teaspoon salt
⅛ teaspoon freshly ground black pepper

1 Preheat the oven to 400°F. Set out a rimmed baking sheet.

2 Place the sprouts on the baking sheet and toss with the onion, oil, thyme, salt, and pepper.

3 Roast for 20 to 25 minutes, stirring 2 or 3 times, until the vegetables are tender and lightly browned.

Roasted Carrots and Parsnips

prep time 10 minutes ■ **total time** 55 minutes ■ **makes** 6 servings

1 pound carrots, cut in 1" chunks
1 pound parsnips, cut in 1" chunks
4 small red onions, cut into wedges
6 garlic cloves
½ tablespoon olive oil
½ teaspoon salt
½ teaspoon lemon zest

Preheat the oven to 375°F. Coat a medium baking dish with cooking spray. Add the carrots, parsnips, onions, garlic, oil, salt, and lemon zest. Toss to coat evenly. Bake for 40 to 45 minutes, stirring halfway through the cooking time, or until golden and tender.

Roasted Garlic Soup with Pork and Broccoli

prep time 20 minutes ▪ **total time** 1 hour 5 minutes ▪ **makes** 6 servings

4 garlic bulbs

3 tablespoons olive oil

4 cups chicken broth

1 pound pork tenderloin, cut into ¾" pieces

1 small onion, chopped

1 red bell pepper, chopped

4 ounces mushrooms, sliced (about 1 cup)

½ small bunch broccoli, cut into small florets (about 1 cup)

2 teaspoons teriyaki sauce

½ teaspoon freshly ground black pepper

1 Preheat the oven to 350°F. Slice ¼" off the top of each garlic bulb. Discard the tops. Lightly brush the bulbs with 1 tablespoon of the oil. Place in a shallow baking dish. Cover with foil.

2 Bake for 55 to 60 minutes. Remove the foil and bake for 10 minutes, or until the garlic skin is browned and the interior is very soft. Remove to a rack to cool.

3 When the garlic is cool enough to handle, squeeze the cloves into a food processor or blender. Discard the skin. Add 1 cup of the broth. Process until smooth.

4 Heat the remaining 2 tablespoons oil in a large saucepan over medium-high heat. Add the pork, onion, bell pepper, and mushrooms. Cook, stirring occasionally, for 15 minutes, or until the pork is lightly browned and the vegetables are tender.

5 Stir in the garlic-broth mixture, broccoli, teriyaki sauce, black pepper, and the remaining 3 cups broth. Bring to a boil. Reduce the heat to low, cover, and simmer for 15 minutes, or until the pork is tender.

Romaine and Watercress Salad with Anchovy Vinaigrette

prep time 10 minutes ▪ **total time** 10 minutes ▪ **makes** 6 servings

½ teaspoon anchovy paste

½ teaspoon Dijon mustard

Salt (optional)

1 tablespoon balsamic vinegar

1 tablespoon red wine vinegar

Freshly ground black pepper

6 tablespoons olive oil

1 small head romaine

2 bunches watercress, large stems discarded

1 Combine the anchovy paste, mustard, and salt (if using) in a salad bowl. Add the vinegars and mix with a fork. Add the oil slowly while whisking constantly. Taste for seasoning, adding pepper and more salt, vinegar, and oil to taste.

2 When ready to serve, add the romaine and watercress and toss to coat.

Salmon with Ginger-Soy Butter

prep time 6 minutes ▪ **total time** 13 minutes ▪ **makes** 4 servings

2 tablespoons unsalted butter, softened at room temperature

½ tablespoons minced fresh chives

½ tablespoon grated or minced fresh ginger

Juice of 1 lemon

½ tablespoon low-sodium soy sauce

1 tablespoon olive or canola oil

4 salmon fillets (4 to 6 ounces each)

Salt and freshly ground black pepper

1 Combine the butter, chives, ginger, lemon juice, and soy sauce in a bowl and stir vigorously with a wooden spoon until the ingredients are incorporated. Set aside.

2 Heat the oil in a large stainless-steel sauté pan over medium-high heat. Season the salmon with salt and pepper. When the oil is lightly smoking, place the salmon flesh side down in the pan. Cook for 4 to 5 minutes, or until the skin is lightly charred and crisp. Flip the fish and cook for 2 to 3 minutes more, or until the flesh flakes with gentle pressure from your finger but is still slightly translucent in the middle. (Salmon is best served medium, but if you want yours completely cooked, sauté for another 2 to 3 minutes.)

3 Serve the salmon with a generous spoonful of the reserved flavored butter, which should melt on contact with the fish.

Sautéed Yellow Squash, Zucchini, and Onions

prep time 5 minutes ▪ **total time** 18 minutes ▪ **makes** 4 servings

2 tablespoons olive oil

2 onions, cut into ¼" slices

2 zucchini, cut in half lengthwise, then cut into ¼" slices

2 yellow squash, cut in half lengthwise, then cut into ¼" slices

3 garlic cloves, finely chopped

½ cup white wine

¼ teaspoon Italian seasoning

Salt and freshly ground black pepper

Place the oil in a large saucepan over medium-high heat. Add the onions and cook for 3 to 5 minutes, or until translucent. Add the zucchini and squash and cook for 4 to 5 minutes, stirring occasionally. Add the garlic and cook for 30 seconds. Add the wine, Italian seasoning, and salt and pepper to taste. Cook for 2 to 3 minutes, or until the liquid has reduced by half.

Seared Scallops with Pumpkin Soup

prep time 15 minutes ▪ **total time** 1 hour ▪ **makes** 2 servings

2 tablespoons roughly chopped hazelnuts

1 can (15 ounces) unflavored pumpkin puree

1 tablespoon honey

1 tablespoon unsalted butter

1 cup chicken broth

Salt and freshly ground black pepper to taste

12 ounces fresh sea scallops

½ tablespoon extra virgin olive oil

10 chives, chopped

1 Toast the hazelnuts, either in the oven (10 minutes at 400°F) or on the stove in a stainless-steel sauté pan (5 to 7 minutes over medium heat). Set aside.

2 Combine the pumpkin, honey, butter, and broth in a medium saucepan over low heat until completely warmed. Season with salt and pepper. Keep warm.

3 Preheat a cast-iron skillet or sauté pan over medium-high heat. Pat the scallops dry with a paper towel and season with salt and pepper. Add the oil to the pan, and then add the scallops. Cook for 2 to 3 minutes per side, or until the scallops are firm and completely browned and caramelized.

4 Pour the soup into a wide-rimmed bowl. Add the scallops and hazelnuts and garnish with the chives.

Seasoned Pepper Turkey with Portuguese Tomatoes

prep time 10 minutes ▪ **total time** 1 hour ▪ **makes** 6 servings

3 pints grape tomatoes (6 cups)

¼ cup olive oil (preferably extra virgin)

1½ tablespoons minced oil-packed garlic

½ cup chopped fresh parsley or cilantro

½ teaspoon red-pepper flakes

¼ teaspoon salt

1¾ pounds premarinated seasoned pepper turkey tenderloins

1 Coat a grill rack with cooking spray. Preheat the grill.

2 Combine the tomatoes, oil, garlic, parsley or cilantro, pepper flakes, and salt in a 13" x 9" grillproof pan. Toss until well mixed. Place on the grill over direct heat. Cook, stirring occasionally, about 10 minutes, or until sizzling. Move the pan away from direct heat.

3 Place the turkey on the rack or pan. Grill, turning once, for 5 minutes per side, or until browned. Move away from direct heat on the grill rack. Cook for 10 minutes per side, or until a thermometer inserted into the thickest portion registers 165°F or the juices run clear. Let stand for 10 minutes. Slice and serve with the tomatoes.

Shrimp Lettuce Wraps

prep time 10 minutes ▪ **total time** 15 minutes ▪ **makes** 1 serving

3 ounces medium shrimp

1 tablespoon prepared scallion-ginger glaze

¼ cup chopped celery

2 tablespoons minced red onion

¼ cup chopped red bell pepper

2 tablespoons cashews

4 large romaine leaves

Coat the shrimp with the ginger glaze and broil, then chill. Once cool, toss with the celery, onion, pepper, and cashews and roll in romaine leaves used as wraps.

Soy Hot Chocolate

prep time 1 minute ▪ **total time** 3 minutes ▪ **makes** 1 serving

1 cup vanilla-flavored soy milk

2 teaspoons maple syrup

2 teaspoons unsweetened cocoa powder

Miniature marshmallows (optional)

Heat the soy milk in the microwave about 2 minutes. Before it begins to boil, add the syrup and cocoa. Mix until frothy. Add marshmallows, if desired.

Soy Milk Berry Smoothie

prep time 5 minutes ▪ **total time** 5 minutes ▪ **makes** 2 servings

½ cup frozen unsweetened raspberries

½ cup frozen unsweetened strawberries

¼ cup unsweetened pineapple juice

1 cup soy milk or 1% milk

Combine the raspberries, strawberries, and juice in a blender. Add the milk and blend until smooth.

Spiced Butternut Soup with Crab

prep time 8 minutes ■ **total time** 15 minutes ■ **makes** 4 servings

4 cups roasted butternut squash
3 cups low-sodium chicken broth
¼ cup whole milk
½ teaspoon ground cumin
Pinch of freshly ground nutmeg
Dash of hot-pepper sauce
¼ teaspoon kosher salt
⅛ teaspoon freshly ground black pepper
6 ounces cooked lump crabmeat

1 Combine the squash, broth, milk, cumin, nutmeg, and hot-pepper sauce in a blender (or use an immersion blender) and puree until smooth.

2 Transfer the mixture to a medium saucepan. Heat over medium heat for 7 minutes, then season with the salt and pepper. Divide among 4 bowls and top each with 1½ ounces of the crabmeat.

Spinach and Goat Cheese Salad

prep time 10 minutes ■ **total time** 10 minutes ■ **makes** 2 servings

4 cups baby spinach
2 tablespoons crumbled fresh goat cheese (about 1 ounce)
1 cup red grapes, halved
2 tablespoons sliced almonds
1½ tablespoons olive oil
1½ tablespoons balsamic vinegar
Salt and freshly ground black pepper to taste

Combine the spinach, cheese, grapes, and almonds in a large mixing bowl. Drizzle with the oil and vinegar and mix thoroughly. Season with salt and pepper.

Steak and 'Shrooms

prep time 5 minutes ■ **total time** 15 minutes ■ **makes** 2 servings

2 sirloin steaks (6 ounces each)
Salt and freshly ground black pepper
1 teaspoon olive oil
¼ teaspoon dried thyme
1 garlic clove, crushed
¼ cup chicken broth
½ cup cremini mushrooms

1 Heat a skillet over medium-high heat. Add the steaks and sear them for 2 to 3 minutes per side, seasoning each side with a pinch of salt and pepper.

2 Remove the steaks from the pan and lower the heat to medium. Add the oil, thyme, and garlic and stir with a spoon about 30 seconds.

3 Add the broth and mushrooms and stir for 3 minutes, or until the mushrooms soften. Spoon the mushrooms and their liquid over the steaks.

Steamed Spinach

prep time 3 minutes ▪ **total time** 6 minutes ▪ **makes** 1 serving

10 ounces fresh spinach (about 1¾ cup)
Salt and freshly ground black pepper

Place the spinach in a steamer and cook for 3 minutes, or until wilted. Season with salt and pepper to taste.

Stir-Fried Kale with Almonds

prep time 10 minutes ▪ **total time** 17 minutes ▪ **makes** 6 servings

2 tablespoons olive oil
1 large garlic clove, finely chopped
1 teaspoon grated fresh ginger
¼ cup slivered almonds
1½ pounds kale, stems removed, chopped into 1" pieces
1 tablespoon tamari
2 tablespoons low-sodium vegetable broth

1 Heat the oil in a large nonstick skillet over medium-high heat. Add the garlic and ginger and cook for 30 seconds.

2 Reduce the heat to medium. Add the almonds and cook for 1 minute. Add the kale, tamari, and broth. Cook about 5 minutes, or until the kale is wilted but not soggy.

Stir-Fry of Asparagus and Bell Pepper with Ginger and Sesame

prep time 5 minutes ▪ **total time** 17 minutes ▪ **makes** 4 servings

1½ pounds asparagus, trimmed and cut into 2" pieces
¼ cup canola oil
½ large red bell pepper, seeded and cut into strips
1 tablespoon chopped fresh ginger
1 tablespoon reduced-sodium soy sauce
⅛ teaspoon red-pepper flakes
2 teaspoons toasted sesame oil
1 teaspoon sesame seeds

1 Bring ¼" water to a boil in a large nonstick skillet over high heat. Add the asparagus and return to a boil. Reduce the heat to low, cover, and simmer for 5 minutes, or until crisp-tender. Drain in a colander and cool briefly under cold running water. Wipe the skillet dry with a paper towel.

2 Heat the canola oil in the same skillet over high heat. Add the bell pepper and cook, stirring constantly, for 3 minutes, or until crisp-tender. Add the asparagus, ginger, soy sauce, and pepper flakes and cook for 2 minutes, or until heated through. Remove from the heat and stir in the sesame oil and sesame seeds.

Summer Salad with Green Goddess Dressing

prep time 15 minutes ▪ **total time** 15 minutes ▪ **makes** 4 servings

½ cup low-fat plain yogurt
¼ cup canola mayonnaise
¼ cup fresh Italian parsley, chopped
2 scallions, coarsely chopped
1 garlic clove
1 tablespoon white wine vinegar
1 tablespoon chopped fresh tarragon
⅛ teaspoon salt
1 package (7 ounces) mixed salad greens
1 cup grape tomatoes, halved
1 cucumber, peeled, halved, seeded, and sliced

1 Combine the yogurt, mayonnaise, parsley, scallions, garlic, vinegar, tarragon, and salt in a blender or a food processor fitted with a metal blade. Process until smooth.

2 Combine the greens, tomatoes, and cucumber in a large bowl. Toss with the dressing.

Summer Tomato and Arugula Salad

prep time 10 minutes ▪ **total time** 10 minutes ▪ **makes** 4 servings

2 large beefsteak tomatoes, sliced
2 tablespoons red wine, balsamic, or sherry vinegar
⅛ teaspoon Dijon mustard (optional)
¼ cup + 2 tablespoons extra virgin olive oil
Salt and freshly ground black pepper
2 cups baby arugula or other baby greens
½ pint yellow and/or red cherry tomatoes, halved
1 cup torn basil leaves or other fresh herb (optional)

1 Arrange the tomato slices on a large platter.

2 Whisk the vinegar and mustard, if using, in a large bowl. Add the oil in a stream while whisking. Season with salt and pepper to taste.

3 Add the arugula and cherry tomatoes to the bowl and toss with the vinaigrette to coat. Spread over the tomato slices. Sprinkle with the basil, if using.

Tossed Romaine and Radish Salad

prep time 5 minutes ■ total time 5 minutes ■ makes 4 servings

1 cup torn romaine
1 cup shredded red cabbage
½ cup sliced radishes
2 tablespoons honey
4½ teaspoons olive oil
¼ cup lemon juice
½ cup honey mustard

Combine the romaine, cabbage, and radishes in a salad bowl. Shake the honey, oil, lemon juice, and mustard in a covered jar. Pour over the salad and toss well.

Tropical Smoothie

prep time 5 minutes ■ total time 5 minutes ■ makes 2 servings

½ cup 1% milk
2 tablespoons low-fat yogurt
¼ cup frozen orange juice concentrate
½ banana
¼ cup strawberries
½ cup cubed mango
2 teaspoons vanilla whey protein powder
3 ice cubes

Combine all of the ingredients in a blender and blend until smooth.

Tuna Salad

prep time 5 minutes ■ total time 5 minutes ■ makes 1 serving

1 can (6 ounces) water-packed chunk light tuna
1 tablespoon canola oil–based mayonnaise
1 teaspoon yellow mustard
2 grams glucomannan

Drain the tuna and place in a bowl. Add the mayonnaise, mustard, and glucomannan, mixing to combine. Chill before serving, if desired.

Turkey-Avocado Cobb Salad

prep time 8 minutes ■ **total time** 15 minutes ■ **makes** 4 servings

1 pound turkey breast cutlets
3 teaspoons olive oil
2 tablespoons cider vinegar
1 tablespoon water
1 teaspoon Dijon mustard
8 cups baby spinach
4 slices cooked turkey bacon, chopped
1 cup diced avocado
4 cherry tomatoes, halved
1 ounce blue cheese, crumbled
Freshly ground black pepper

1 Preheat a grill pan on medium-high heat for 2 minutes. Brush the turkey with 1 teaspoon of the oil. Grill the cutlets for 4 minutes, flip, and continue cooking about 3 minutes longer, or until the centers are opaque. Cut into chunks.

2 Combine the vinegar, water, mustard, and the remaining 2 teaspoons oil in a glass jar. Cover and shake well.

3 In a large bowl, combine the spinach with 2 tablespoons of the dressing. Toss to coat the leaves. Arrange the turkey, bacon, avocado, tomatoes, and cheese over the spinach. Drizzle with the remaining dressing and season with pepper to taste.

Watercress and Radicchio Salad with Honey-Mustard Vinaigrette

prep time 15 minutes ■ **total time** 15 minutes ■ **makes** 6 servings

2 tablespoons red or white wine vinegar
1 tablespoon honey
1 tablespoon Dijon mustard
½ teaspoon minced garlic
¼ cup + 2 tablespoons olive oil
Salt and freshly ground black pepper
6 cups lightly packed watercress, tough stems removed
3 cups lightly packed radicchio, torn into leaves
¼ cup sliced almonds, toasted

1 Whisk the vinegar, honey, mustard, and garlic in a large bowl. Add the oil in a stream, whisking. Season with salt and pepper to taste.

2 Add the watercress and radicchio and toss to coat. Divide the greens among 6 salad plates and top each with 2 teaspoons of the almonds.

Watermelon Salad

prep time 10 minutes ▪ **total time** 10 minutes ▪ **makes** 4 servings

1 bag (4 ounces) arugula, stems removed and roughly torn

2 cups cubed fresh watermelon

1 package (3 ounces) feta cheese, crumbled

2 tablespoons olive oil

Freshly ground black pepper

Combine the arugula, watermelon, and feta in a large bowl. Gently mix in the oil and pepper to taste.

Zucchini and Carrots with Walnuts

prep time 20 minutes ▪ **total time** 35 minutes ▪ **makes** 4 servings

½ cup chopped walnuts

2 zucchini

2 large carrots, peeled

1 tablespoon olive oil

⅛ teaspoon dried thyme

¼ teaspoon salt

⅛ teaspoon freshly ground black pepper

1 Toast the walnuts in a large nonstick skillet over medium heat, stirring often, for 3 to 4 minutes, or until lightly browned and fragrant. Tip onto a plate. Wipe out the skillet with a paper towel.

2 Halve the zucchini lengthwise and cut the halves crosswise in two. Cut each piece into thin strips lengthwise.

3 Use a vegetable peeler to cut long strips from the carrots, reserving the core for another meal.

4 Heat the oil in the same skillet over medium heat. Add the carrots and sprinkle with the thyme, salt, and pepper. Cook, tossing often, about 3 minutes, or until nearly tender. Add the zucchini and cook, tossing, for 3 to 4 minutes, or until tender. Sprinkle with the walnuts.

Zucchini with Garlic and Oregano

prep time 10 minutes ▪ **total time** 16 minutes ▪ **makes** 4 servings

1½ pounds zucchini

1½ teaspoons olive oil

4 garlic cloves, minced

1 large tomato, seeded and diced

¾ teaspoon dried oregano

¼ teaspoon salt

Pinch of freshly ground black pepper

1 Trim the zucchini and cut it into ¼"-thick slices.

2 Heat the oil in a large skillet over medium heat. Add the garlic and cook for 30 seconds, or just until fragrant. Add the zucchini and toss to mix. Add the tomato and oregano and toss well. Reduce the heat to medium-low, cover, and cook about 5 minutes, or until the zucchini softens. Add the salt and pepper and stir gently.

Zucchini and Red Pepper in Lemon-Herb Butter

prep time 12 minutes ▪ **total time** 25 minutes ▪ **makes** 4 servings

6 small zucchini (24 ounces), sliced ½" thick

½ red bell pepper, chopped

3 tablespoons butter

2 tablespoons chicken broth

¼ teaspoon salt

⅛ teaspoon freshly ground black pepper

2 teaspoons grated lemon zest

1 tablespoon lemon juice

2 tablespoons finely chopped fresh parsley

1 Combine the zucchini, bell pepper, butter, broth, salt, and black pepper in a large skillet. Cover and cook over medium heat for 3 minutes, or until steam comes from the skillet. Uncover and increase the heat to medium-high. Cook for 8 to 10 minutes, stirring occasionally, until the vegetables are tender but intact and practically no liquid remains in the pan.

2 Stir in the lemon zest and juice. Remove from the heat and stir in the parsley.

Resources

The following resources will help you find out more about resistant starch, seek out more recipes using RS, and even allow you to purchase resistant starch products directly.

For More Information and Recipes

American Association of Cereal Chemists International (AACCI)
www.aaccnet.org
AACCI is a nonprofit organization of specialists in the use of cereal grains in foods. Their Web site includes articles on resistant starch from the group's technical and trade publications.

Food Processing
www.foodprocessing.com
Food Processing magazine is the nation's largest trade journal covering food technology. Its Web site presents information on the technology behind food production in clear and easy-to-understand language, suitable for both those in the food industry and consumers. Here you'll find dozens of articles, news, studies, and white papers on resistant starch.

The Institute of Food Technologists (IFT)
www.ift.org
IFT is a global nonprofit organization devoted to the communication and advancement of food science and technology. On its Web site you'll find hundred of articles, studies, and news items about resistant starch.

National Starch Food Innovation
www.resistantstarch.com
National Starch Food Innovation spearheaded the majority of research and development of resistant starch and continues to be the go-to source for all things pertaining to health and science about resistant starch, especially that which is derived from corn. The group created this Web site devoted entirely to RS and includes research, news, recipes, and purchase information, along with a regularly updated, downloadable list of products in the marketplace that contain RS.
■ Recipes available

Oldways Preservation Trust
www.oldwayspt.org
Oldways was created by a small group of food enthusiasts to "combat the rising prevalence of 'pseudo foods' on the market and the threatening tsunami of chronic diseases propelled in part by our poor eating habits." In addition to studying the impact of "pseudo foods" on the increase of obesity and chronic disease in our society, Oldways promotes a return to focusing on the pleasure of good food as a better way to combat the epidemics of obesity and disease. As a creator of the

well-known Mediterranean Diet Pyramid, Oldways is a source for news, articles, books, and recipes featuring many of the foods that contain RS.
■ Recipes available

Wheat Foods Council
www.wheatfoods.org
The Wheat Foods Council was created through partnership of members of the wheat industries as a nonprofit promotion and education organization providing nutrition information, education, and research on grain technology. In addition to periodically updated charts of the RS content of wheat foods, you'll find resource lists and recipes, as well as fact sheets, posters, and cookbooks about whole grains and RS.
■ Recipes available

Whole Grains Council
www.wholegrainscouncil.org
The Whole Grains Council helps consumers find whole grain foods and understand their health benefits, providing short, easy-to-understand articles on ingredients such as resistant starch, as well as purchasing sources and recipes.
■ Recipes available

For Purchasing RS-Enriched Foods

Aunt Millie's Bakery (primarily in the Midwest)
www.auntmillies.com
—Healthy Goodness Fiber & Flavor Potato Bread
—Healthy Goodness Whole Grain White Bread
—Healthy Goodness Light Five Grain Bread
—Hearth 12 Grain Bread
—Whole Grain Muffins (available in blueberry, coffee cake, brownie, and chocolate chip flavors)

Bob's Red Mill
www.bobsredmill.com
—For corn, potato, barley, chickpea, bean, white whole wheat, and other RS-source flours and grains

Celiac Specialties (specializing in gluten-free foods)
www.celiacspecialties.com.
—National Starch Hi-maize Resistant Starch: Substitute Hi-maize RS for up to 20 to 25 percent of the flour in your favorite gluten-free recipes.

Ener-G Foods (specializing in gluten-free, dairy-free foods)
www.ener-g.com
—Corn Loaf
—Seattle Brown Loaf, Hamburger Buns, and Hot Dog Buns
—Wylde Pretzels
—Yeast-Free Brown Rice Loaf
—Brown Rice English Muffins (with Flax)

King Arthur Flour, Inc.
www.kingarthurflour.com
—Hi-maize Natural Fiber (Product number #1587): Substitute Hi-maize RS for up to 20 to 25 percent of the flour in your favorite recipes.
—Hi-maize High Fiber Flour (Product number #3511): Substitute High Fiber Flour with Hi-maize for 100 percent of the flour in your favorite recipes.

Racconto Imported Italian Food
www.racconto.com
—Racconto Essentials Glycemic Health pasta

Index

Underscored page references indicate boxed text. An asterisk (*) indicates the recipe photograph appears in the color photo insert.